THE *FATHER'S* EMERGENCY GUIDE TO DIVORCE-CUSTODY BATTLE

A tour through the predatory world of judges, lawyers, psychologists, and social workers in the subculture of divorce

BY

ROBERT SEIDENBERG

WITH THE LEGAL INSIGHTS
OF WILLIAM DAWES, ESQ.

JES
BOOKS

JES Books, Inc. • Takoma Park, Maryland

JES

BOOKS

Printed in the United States of America by Deadline Press, Inc., Washington D.C.

For my children,
Samuel and Jessica

DISCLAIMER

This publication is designed to provide accurate information in regard to the subject matter covered. It is sold with the understanding that the publisher is not engaged in rendering legal, accounting, or other professional service. If legal advice or other expert assistance is required, the services of a competent professional person should be sought. The opinions and conclusions expressed are solely those of the authors.

NOTES ON USAGE

To avoid the cumbersome clutter of writing "he or she" and "him or her" at every turn, I have used the traditional masculine form to denote both sexes except in instances where the distinction is important.

Because men and women have so many different levels of relations in the divorce-custody context, such as "ex-wife," "soon-to-be-ex-wife," "ex-girlfriend," or "mother-of-your-child," I often simply use the term "ex" to denote the other party in your children's lives.

Magistrate, master, and commissioner have different meanings in different jurisdictions but also have equivalent functions across jurisdictions. For example, a Virginia magistrate, a Maryland master, and a District of Columbia commissioner perform similar functions. For simplicity I have in some places used the term "magistrate" generically though that title would not be accurate for all jurisdictions.

Acknowledgments

First, I'd like to note the contributions of fellow fathers, journalist Kenneth Skilling, attorney William Dolan, and economist Don Bieniewicz. It was during our conversations on our early roadtrips to Richmond to meet our state delegates, that I first began to understand the deep-seated political and social causes of what initially appeared to be isolated incidents of judicial misconduct.

I'd also like to acknowledge author Warren Farrell, Ph.D. His works, particularly *The Myth of Male Power*, and *Why Men are the Way They Are*, have helped me and other activists to understand how the discrimination against men is pervasive, yet invisible to most people, because it is woven into our social fabric.

Other men's theorists whose writings have contributed to the development of the ideas in this book are Stuart Miller, Richard Doyle, Daniel Amneus, and Jack Kammer.

There are many fathers' and children's rights activists who contributed to my education in this subject, notably: David Levy, Murray Steinberg, Bill Harrington, Cindy and Michael Ewing, Cliff Clark, Paul Robinson, Steve Hoffman, Don Lewis, Tom Vail, and Lawrence Peckmezian.

My thanks to Neil Davison, Heather Dittbrenner, and John Young for their proofreading and editorial suggestions. And special thanks to Tony Spagnola for his efforts in bringing the book to publication.

On the personal side, I am fortunate that I had a strong family foundation to rely on when I was forced into the child-custody conflict. I am grateful to my parents, Jacob and Rosa Seidenberg, and to my life-long friend Greg Prakas; they provided me not only with emotional support, but with places to live when I was destitute after my initial custody battle. And I am always thankful to my sisters, Sheila Hutman and Lisa Bruner, who stood by me and my son throughout the ordeal.

Most of all, I owe an immeasurable debt to my wife, Ann. Though I was fully immersed in the custody conflict when I met her, she was willing to share this burden, and carry us through to a sunnier time.

CONTENTS

READ THIS NOW

Every day I talk to men whose lives have been propelled into frantic motion by the churnings of a vast bureaucratic monster—the American system for adjudicating divorce and child custody. The calls I get are filled with outraged stories and rushing torrents of questions. Dishonest courts, false abuse charges, parental kidnappings, unaffordable "child support" orders, legal fees that drive men bankrupt—these are the stories I hear on a daily basis. Above all, I hear how much fathers love their children, and the desperation they feel when faced with the realization that they may lose them.

This is a book for fathers involved in, or facing the prospect of, a child custody dispute. It is an effort to warn you of the catastrophes that can befall a man involved in such a conflict, to tell you what you can do to avert such misfortunes, and to explain the larger social and political context that may have a greater effect on the outcome of your personal crisis than will the factual merits of your case.

Before anything further can be said about a child custody battle, every father must know these three things:

(1) The *pendente lite* hearing could be the most important event in your life for the next twenty years. It is the single-most important event in a child custody dispute. This information alone may save you thousands of dollars and years of heartache.

Pendente lite—pronounced "pen • den • tee   lie • tee"—is Latin for "while the lawsuit is pending." Because a divorce-custody proceeding is expected to take the better part of one or several days, and because it may be months before you can get a court date, this short (30-minute to 3-hour) "temporary" hearing is scheduled as soon as possible so that interim arrangements can be made for custody, visitation, child support, alimony, and possession of the marital home.

The secret is: there is nothing temporary about this hearing. The agreement or ruling emanating from the *pendente lite* hearing is for all practical purposes set in stone. If you do go to the trouble of a full hearing—which will come three to twelve months down the road, during which time you could accrue costs ranging from $10,000 to $100,000 or more—it is unlikely that anything will change substantially from what was established at the temporary hearing. In this whole book, there is no single fact more important than this.

Strangely, it is rare that a lawyer will tell a client how important the *pendente lite* hearing is. In fact, lawyers commonly use the terms "*pendente lite* hearing" and "temporary hearing" synonymously, as in "Don't worry, it's only a temporary hearing." This second paradox leads immediately to the dark underside of divorce-custody: this is a multi-*billion* dollar[1] enterprise which every year siphons off the resources of nearly one million families caught in highly emotional personal conflicts. Some people who have been snared in this legal web believe that lawyers and judges actively promote and prolong conflict in order to make business for themselves. While at this point you may think such a statement sounds like an overreaction to the frustration and expense of litigation, you may come to share this belief if you end up spending $30,000 in court trying to resolve the simplest of issues. In any event, you should read this book before investing that kind of money.

(2) Don't sign anything until you have read this book and consulted at least one attorney. "Don't sign anything" is clichéd advice, yet surprisingly I have met many intelligent men who signed disastrous agreements without consulting a lawyer. These same people would have approached any other contractual agreement with the utmost care. But because they considered the arrangement for their children's upbringing to be a family issue rather than a business matter, they mistakenly presumed such agreements were flexible.

I have also met fathers who signed extremely disadvantageous agreements on the advice of "one of the best lawyers in town." It is a perplexing concept, but you need to be aware that your lawyer may put his own interests—that is, financial gain and a positive relationship with the judge and other attorneys—above yours, and knowingly cause you severe harm. This is why, if you are facing any kind of dispute that involves your children, it is just as important to read this book as it is to consult a lawyer.

Any notarized agreement you sign waiving custody is thoroughly binding (though a notarized agreement unfavorable to your child's mother may not be binding). Furthermore, if you make a verbal agreement in court and it is entered into the record by the verbatim court reporter, it is treated as if you had signed it. You may later refuse to sign it when it is drafted as an order, but if you do, the judge will more than likely enter it as an order anyway or make your life more miserable by entering a less favorable order.

The fact that so many men consent to unfavorable orders is a behavioral pattern I discuss in Chapter 3. You may be surprised how much the thought pattern described reflects your own.

(3) Don't move out of the house. Moving out invites your wife to initiate divorce and claim custody, or to claim you abandoned her. Whether you have amicably agreed to separate, or are furious because you have discovered your wife is having an affair, do not move out until you have read this book and consulted an attorney.

I put these comments at the front of the book in the hope that they will prevent one more father from making any of the most common fatal errors.

WHY THE "EMERGENCY" GUIDE?

I presume you picked up this book because you are a father currently caught in a divorce-custody conflict, a father in a marriage where divorce seems inevitable (whether it be six months or a year in the future), or a father who has a child out of wedlock and are on uncertain ground with the child's mother. If any of these is the case, then you might think of yourself as driving up a mountain road in a blinding snowstorm and this book as a warning "Danger: Bridge Out." Whether you are ardent in your pursuit of custody or simply seeking to assure regular visitation with your children, this conflict can plunge you into a nightmare of emotional turmoil and financial woe.

This is an emergency guide because the actions you take at the earliest stages of your case are of critical importance. This is an emergency guide because you are in a dangerous situation and probably unaware of it. The outcome of your divorce-custody battle can have damaging long-term repercussions on every aspect of your life. It can derail your career, ruin your prospects for remarriage, end any future education plans, and most certainly have a deleterious affect on your relationship with your children. Even lawyers not directly involved with domestic relations may be shocked at the level of inequity in this system.

In a hearing as brief as half an hour, you can have your children taken away from you and your finances crippled for years to come. A more common scenario is that in a series of hearings stretching out over several years, you will descend into an ever-deepening spiral of debt and alienation from your children.

At meetings of fathers'-rights groups, I have heard these stories over and over again. I have a story just like it myself. Men attending these meetings for the first time are frequently in a state of shock. "It was a kangaroo court!" is a phrase often exclaimed by new members who find their way to a support group a few weeks after the *pendente lite* ambush. Baffled by what has happened to them, each believes that his case is unique—the incompetent attorney, the indifferent or hostile judge. They are so amazed by their experience that they presume everyone else will be amazed as well. But, as anyone who has been involved in this business for any length of time is aware, the "kangaroo court" is the norm.

THIS IS MORE THAN A HOW-TO BOOK

If you are like most fathers, you will probably find this book is not what you expected it to be. At the outset of their custody fight, most fathers believe that the law is a precise instrument which, when properly applied, can be used to obtain the desired goal. What they are looking for when they come to a support-group legal clinic, and what I presume many people are looking for in this book, are precise legal maneuvers that can help them to win their cases. Such a book cannot exist. The realities of court in general, and divorce court in particular, are such that there can be no certainties.

Other how-to books on this subject tend to emphasize the legalistic aspects of divorce. This approach cannot be helpful, and I believe it is misleading. It perpetuates the myth that the law is objective and that cases are won or lost on their merits. For example, one book[2] spends 22 of its 133 pages describing the grounds for divorce in every U.S. jurisdiction. Reading that book may lead you to believe that the grounds for divorce will be a crucial part of your case. Yet, while burying you in a blizzard of laws, the author fails to state anything about the application of these laws. *The Father's Emergency Guide* spends only three pages discussing the grounds for divorce. Why? Because in the vast majority of cases the grounds for divorce are of no consequence, and it requires only a few paragraphs to identify the situations where grounds can be an important factor.

This book is different from any other in that it provides the reader with a comprehensive overview of the divorce-custody field. Several chapters are devoted to describing the patterns of events and behavior that recur in these conflicts. Women typically behave in one way, men in another. Lawyers usually take certain courses of actions, and tend to give different advice to women than they give to men. Judges, social workers, and the like also have characteristic behaviors and expectations. Being aware of these patterns can help you to anticipate your adversary's next move, and help you to avoid stereotypical behavior on your own part. In a way, this book is not so much an instruction manual as it is the map of a dangerous terrain, provided to you with the hope that it will help you avoid the mine fields along the way.

Nonetheless, there is plenty of how-to material in this book: how to pick a lawyer, how to deal with a lawyer, how to calculate child support, how to prepare an order or agreement, and a list of resources for special concerns. I describe the only strategy that consistently wins custody for fathers (on the rare occasions that they do win), and I describe how to end your battle quickly with a reasonable settlement. If you follow the recommendations made in this book, you will greatly increase your chances of obtaining your goals in a divorce-custody dispute. However—and this is what no other book will tell you—the hostility toward fathers in many courtrooms is so thorough that *no* legal maneuver can even ensure that you will continue to see your children, much less that you will win custody.

AN ABUSIVE LEGAL CULTURE

"Discrimination" or "gender bias" are not adequate terms to describe the phenomenon taking place in divorce-custody conflicts. An abusive culture has developed within our legal system, wherein it has become commonplace for judges and lawyers to brutalize men in domestic relations court. As one father put it: "It's a blood sport. You can't win, you can't split even, and you can't quit the game."

As detailed in this book, the successive outrages a father may be subjected to can be maddening. First he loses his wife (women initiate the great majority of divorces), then he loses his children. Next he starts into a spiral of debt from legal costs, psychologists' fees, and related expenses. Along the way he may very likely be falsely accused of domestic violence, and, in the worst instances, of child sexual abuse. Amidst this calamity, he may be ridiculed by judges, lawyers, and case workers. To crown these misfortunes a father may be saddled with a grossly unfavorable property settlement, and a combination of child support and alimony that he cannot afford. Yet, if he fails to meet these payments, he will go to jail.

It should hardly be surprising, then, that these conflicts sometimes culminate in violence.

> FORT WORTH, TX—Two attorneys were killed, and two judges were among three people wounded this morning when a gunman stood in a courtroom spectators gallery and opened fire with a handgun, authorities said. After eluding a daylong manhunt, a suspect

surrendered 30 miles away at a Dallas television station.

About 4:15 p.m. CDT, according to Byron Harris, a reporter at WFAA-TV in Dallas, a man walked into the station, signed the lobby register as George Lott, 45, of nearby Arlington and asked to speak with Tracy Rowlett, WFAA's veteran anchor.

"It's a horrible, horrible thing I did today," the man told WFAA in a taped interview. "I have sinned and am certainly wrong, but someone needs to look into what happened to me."

The man said he aimed at no particular judge but shot to draw attention to his divorce and custody dispute.[3]

"The Year of Litigating Dangerously," headlined an article in the October 12, 1992 *National Law Journal* which described seven fatal domestic relations confrontations in the first nine months of that year. It called 1992 "one of the bloodiest in divorce court history—a time when angry and bitter divorced litigants declared an open season on judges, lawyers, and the spouses who brought them to court."

Like George Lott, the people who commit these acts are aware only that their own lives have been ruined. What they do not recognize is that the problem is systemic and occurs on a national basis. It can happen to anyone. It could happen to you. *George Lott himself was a lawyer*, yet he was devoured by the system.

The increased violence at courthouses has become a cause of concern among lawmakers. But rather than examine how serious defects in judicial practice might be driving people to desperate acts, the official response has been to install metal detectors at more courthouses.[4] And, at least in one state, judges have taken to carrying concealed weapons to protect themselves *against fathers*.[5]

In other areas of public concern, editorialists frequently interpret blind violence as symptomatic of a system gone wrong. Such was the case with regard to the 1991 riot in the Adams Morgan section of Washington, D.C., and with the Los Angeles riot after the Rodney King verdict. Yet with regard to incidents of divorce and custody-related violence, no such conclusions are drawn. In these instances, the people involved are presumed simply to be "nuts." The media indifference to the case of George Lott is particularly ironic since Lott specifically stated that he sought to draw attention to his troubles. How many rioters acknowledge that they "have sinned," or ask the media to look into what has motivated them?

Contrary to some feminist characterizations of men as irresponsible, or dangerous and potentially violent beasts, the most distinctive characteristic I have observed among men in divorce is long-suffering endurance. When one considers that there are approximately one million divorces a year, and that the level of stress placed on men in divorce is immense, what is truly remarkable is that only a handful of these cases result in front-page news. If men were even one-tenth as barbarous as feminists make us out to be, there would be nationwide carnage.

The fact is that men are socialized from childhood to subordinate their own well-being to that of their wives and family, and to bear their burden without complaint. Consider for example that men fill 98 percent of the most dangerous occupations (e.g. fire fighting, logging, heavy trucking, construction, coal mining), suffer 94 percent of all workplace fatalities, and are more likely to die of overwork;[6] while women watch more television in every time category, control consumer spending in virtually every category (seven times as much shopping mall floor space is devoted to women's personal items as to men's), and live an average of seven years longer than men.[7] It took me a long time to comprehend the significance of male stoicism in divorce and custody disputes, but the reason that the widespread abuse of men in divorce has gone largely unreported is because men are disposed to suffer in silence.

WHERE THE PERSONAL AND THE POLITICAL COINCIDE

For this reason, this book is also a call to political awareness and political action. I know that fathers caught in the first throes of a divorce-custody battle are preoccupied with personal crises and, understandably, find it hard to be concerned about political issues or a "cause." However, as I will explain, you have reached a turn in life where your personal concerns and political interests coincide. Gender politics is not a side issue. It is integral to any practical discussion of divorce-custody litigation. In terms of commanding federal dollars, electing politicians, enacting legislation, controlling academic discourse, and influencing media to promote their cause, the feminist movement is one of the most powerful political forces in the United States today. Unfortunately, the public, including the middle-class professional men most affected by custody litigation, still tends to perceive feminists as the near-powerless victims they portray themselves to be. Judges, however, are astute political creatures; they understand the extent of feminist political power and act accordingly.

When you, a middle-class man, walk into a domestic relations courtroom, you have arrived at the confluence of many streams of social hysteria. The artificially inflated crises of child support collection, domestic violence, rape, child abuse, and child sexual abuse all come to a head in the domestic relations courtroom. And the villain is you.

WHAT EVERYONE KNOWS

While the politics is important, the primary purpose of this book is to deal with your immediate crisis. This book contains what "everyone knows"—that is, what everyone who becomes enmeshed in the subculture of divorce-custody takes for granted, but what you could not know unless you lived through it. This is the book I wish I had had when, in August 1990, I suddenly found myself caught in the turmoil of a custody dispute. I spent weeks of sleepless nights wondering when, if ever, I would see my son again. I spent thousands of dollars getting nowhere. My attorney, a former president of the local bar association and reputed to be "one of the best in the business," seemed unable to accomplish anything. His answers to my questions were evasive or ambiguous. The judge's observations and "suggestions" were baffling. Although my son was terrorized by his mother's behavior (she cut off all access between us for two months), it seemed that everyone involved in the case was acting as her advocate. Issues that in any other forum would be simple to resolve were magnified into problems of Byzantine complexity.

In the first six months of my case I incurred $17,000 in legal fees and $6,000 in child psychologist bills and miscellaneous expenses, merely to obtain a formal visitation schedule with my son. Subsequently I incurred thousands more in legal fees trying to get the court to enforce the visitation order. I have appeared in court about 30 times. The first four times I was represented by the above-mentioned attorney at the rate of $220-per-hour; another six times I was represented by a $120-per-hour lawyer; and many times thereafter I appeared as a *pro se* litigant (that is, representing myself). The $120-per-hour lawyer proved to be a much better practitioner than the $220-per-hour lawyer, and as a *pro se* litigant I have accomplished as much, or as little, as either of my attorneys. The good news is that because I have fought persistently, I continue to see my son every Wednesday night for dinner, every other weekend, and for a solid month in the summer. I am one of the lucky ones.

When I first began attending father support-group meetings, I learned that my situation was far from unique. Since that time I have become immersed in this subject. I have heard the stories of hundreds of fathers caught in similar nightmares. I have discussed cases with dozens of domestic-relations lawyers. As president of Fathers For Virginia and as a member of the Children's Rights Council, I have on many occasions testified before Virginia legislators, as well as before the Virginia Child Support Advisory Committee, the Federal Office of Child Support Enforcement, and the U.S. Commission on Child and Family Welfare.

William Dawes, the co-author of this book, is an attorney who specializes in divorce-custody litigation. In his fourteen years of practice in Maryland, Virginia, and Washington, D.C., he has handled well over 2,000 divorces. Because his experience, as well as mine, is primarily in this region, most of the examples in this book are drawn from these jurisdictions. However, the pattern of discrimination against fathers exists throughout the United States, as indicated by statistical data, and by reporting in fathers'-rights newsletters and Internet newsgroups around the country.

I met Mr. Dawes when I was well into my case, and was surprised by his frankness and cynicism. I was also surprised to learn that he won custody for fathers four or five times a year, and regularly obtained decent visitation-support settlements for fathers in short order and without exorbitant expense. Few lawyers can make such claims. Consequently I asked Mr. Dawes to co-author this book.

• • •

Your case does not have to be as catastrophic as those I have mentioned. Already you have an advantage in knowing that you must be prepared for the *pendente lite* hearing. It is the purpose of this book to inform you of the realities of the divorce-custody business so that you can traverse this treacherous terrain without ruining yourself financially, and emerge with a positive relationship with your children.

NOTES

[1] Levy, David L., ed. *The Best Parent is Both Parents. A Guide to Shared Parenting in the 21st Century.* Norfolk, Virginia: Hampton Roads Publishing Co., Inc. © by the Children's Rights Council.

The Children's Rights Council provides a conservative calculation for attorneys' fees as follows (end note 3, p. 111):

Attorneys' annual fees for divorces were estimated by multiplying the following three factors: 1,189,000 divorces per year (1980 data), 2 spouses represented assuming each requires 6 hours of attorneys' time, and an average attorney's billing rate of $70 per hour.

This gives a conservative lower limit estimate of $998,760,000 annually, or about one billion dollars in legal fees nationwide. The average cost is $840 per divorcing couple.

Attorney's fees were obtained from the ABA Journal, The Lawyer's Magazine, Volume 70, October 1984. Lauren Rubenstein Reskin reports in "Law Poll": that partner billing rates range from $90 to $134 per hour, while associate billing rates range from $59 to $87 per hour.

"What Fathers Tell Us," The Squire, Kansas City, June 14, 1984. This article reports statistics from a survey of 168 divorced fathers gathered by Divorced Dads, Inc., 9229 Ward Parkway, Kansas City, MO 64114. The average legal fees for all fathers was $5,545, with 53 percent of the fathers paying for their ex-spouses as well. For those fathers who sought sole custody, their average legal costs were $17,323. Using $5,545 per divorce multiplied by 1,189,000 divorces per year gives an upper limit of $6,595,005,000 annual legal fees, for divorce and custody nationwide.

2 Sandra Kalenik, *How to Get a Divorce*. Arlington, VA: The Washington Book Trading Company. 1984.

3 Elizabeth Hudson, Bruce Selcraig, "Gunman Kills 2 in Texas Courthouse," *Washington Post* July 2, 1992: A1+.

4 J.R. Malloy, "Murder and Suicide Result from Custody and Divorce Disputes," *The Liberator* June 1993: 12-13.

5 Brian McGrory, "Fear Invades the Courts, Ways to Protect Judges Studied as Threats Rise," *Boston Globe* October 16, 1994: 33. The article is particularly interesting in its quotes from the judges' spokesman. Note that he unashamedly alludes to the fact that only men (i.e., husbands) are getting "whacked," and that taking away someone's children and home might send them over the deep end, but it never occurs to him that judges ought to be making more equitable decisions:

> [O]ne ranking jurist said enough [judges] have been issued gun permits that officials are contemplating a ban on judges carrying firearms under their robes in court. Judges intended to use the guns for protection outside court, but the thought of them carrying firearms in the courtroom is worrisome, officials said....
>
> Yet the potential for violence grows, according to judges, much of it not in criminal sessions, but in Probate and Family Court, where shocked husbands angered over unfavorable divorce and child custody settlements take their wrath out on those who decided their fates.
>
> "The decisions they make in probate court strike much more toward ego—taking away children, taking homes away," said Joe McDonough, executive director of the Massachusetts Judges Conference, a judges' lobbying group.
>
> "When someone goes into court for the first time, they are taken by surprise when they are whacked by the judge, and that's when they might react violently. And in many times, their attorney hasn't prepare them. When they are hit, they are in such shock and react violently and go off the deep end."

6 Warren Farrell. *The Myth of Male Power*. New York: Simon & Schuster. 1993, p.106 and note 11, p.382; p.106 and note 5, p.382; p.183-84 and p.203.

7 Ibid., p.33 and note 18, p.374; p.33 and note 17, p.374; p.30 and note 6, p.373. Also, see pages 48-51 and 180-198.

CHAPTER 1

OVERT DISCRIMINATION

The most *overt* discrimination in the United States is not against women, or blacks, or hispanics, but against men in a specific situation—divorce-custody proceedings. Other groups may suffer broader and deeper discrimination. The discrimination against blacks, to take an obvious example, affects more people in numerous areas of life. But the largest part of this discrimination is subtle or hidden because no one today would want to be labelled a racist. The discrimination against men in divorce-custody proceedings, on the other hand, is blatant and shameless. Protective orders, evicting men from their homes at a moment's notice, are issued without evidence; restraining orders are issued without testimony; at times custody is awarded without testimony; and false child abuse allegations against fathers are rampant.

The discrimination against men is so deep-seated and pervasive that, in the vast majority of cases, you do not need to know the circumstances of a divorce or the jurisdiction in which it takes place to know which parent will get custody of the children. Neither do you need to determine the relative parenting skills of father and mother, the extent of their emotional stability and responsibility, or which parent is more likely to interfere with the children's rights to see the other parent. All you need to know is the gender of the parent. When the divorce-custody case of Marcia Clark (the prosecutor in the O.J. Simpson murder trial) came to public attention, the mainstream media began purveying the myth that fathers who "fought" for custody of their children, were winning 50 percent of the time. There is no factual basis for such a claim (see the "Marcia Clark" box in Chapter 5).

There are no national, or even state, data specifically measuring court decisions in child custody cases. In some states, like Virginia, fathers' groups have tried to make the monitoring of these decisions mandatory. Legislators have resisted such proposals because judges oppose such monitoring. Therefore, estimates have to be drawn from other sources.

Among professionals in the field, it is generally accepted that, nationwide, mothers are awarded custody 90 percent of the time and fathers, 10 percent of the time.[1] But this estimate is derived principally from U.S.

Census reporting on single-parent households. In 1991, 88 percent of single-parent households were headed by mothers, 12 percent by fathers.[2] This data alone suggests widespread discrimination, but it does not fully reflect the extent of judicial prejudice. If you know a father who has custody of his children, it is most likely because the mother gave up custody, and not because a judge decided in favor of the father. If you know parents who have a shared custody arrangement, it is most likely because the mother agreed to it, and not because the judge made that decision. Common experience, as well as local studies, indicate that judges award physical custody to fathers in substantially less than 10 percent of cases. You will note that some of the following studies try to make a distinction between contested and uncontested cases, or cases in which fathers "fought for custody." This is very difficult to determine from court records, since fathers often have to spend so much in legal fees that they capitulate before a judge makes a final decision. It is not unusual for a father to spend $30,000 or $40,000 merely to obtain a visitation schedule with his children. Yet, if such a case concluded with a *consent* order (i.e., the parties agreed) giving custody to the mother and visitation to the father, then it would be classified by some researchers as "non-contested," and it would be erroneously presumed that the father did not "fight for custody." Such an interpretation masks the extreme level of discrimination. Nontheless, the pattern of discrimination against fathers is so clear, that it is apparent regardless of the methodology used in a study.

A thorough study of all divorce-custody decrees made in the Circuit Court of Arlington County, Virginia over the 18-month period of July 1, 1989 to December 31, 1990, showed that:

> **No father** was given **any physical custody** of **any** of his child(ren), unless the mother agreed to it.

> Only 19 fathers out of 232 (8.2%) were permitted **any** amount of explicit **physical custody** (excluding mere visits/visitation) of their children, and then **only** with the **full consent of the mother.**[3] [Emphasis in original.]

In other words, the judges in this study *awarded* custody to fathers *zero percent of the time*.

A similar result was found in a Court Audit of the Superior Court of DeKalb County, Georgia for the Commission on Gender Bias in the Court System. The audit examined cases for the period January 1, 1991 to Sep-

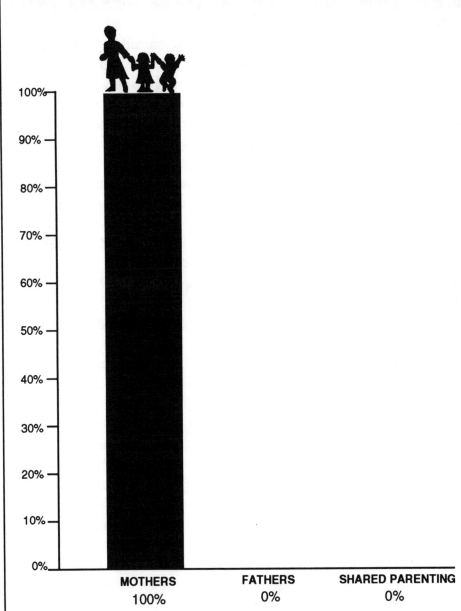

**WHO GETS CUSTODY WHEN
JUDGES DECIDE?**
*Summary of judicial decisions in Arlington, Virginia
July 1, 1989 – December 31, 1990 (18 months)*

MOTHERS	FATHERS	SHARED PARENTING
100%	0%	0%

Sample Size: 232 Divorce Decrees

Source: *Empirical Study of Child Custody in Divorce Decrees in Arlington County, Virginia
7/1/89 – 12/31/90,* © 1991 by William Dolan, Esq.

tember 9, 1991. It found that mothers obtained sole physical custody in 70 cases (86 percent); fathers obtained sole custody in 7 cases (9 percent); and the remaining 4 cases (4.9 percent) resulted in joint or split physical custody. But, of the 15 cases identified as "contested," *mothers were awarded sole physical custody 100 percent of the time.* All cases resulting in joint legal or joint physical custody were the result of an agreement between the parents.

A study of 238 randomly selected cases in one urban county in Ohio, with judgments entered in 1987 and 1988, shows a better judicial record, but still with substantially less than 10 percent of custody awards going to fathers. In the 157 (66 percent) of these cases which were decided by the court (rather than by agreement), judges awarded sole custody to fathers in only 5.7 percent of them. Joint custody was awarded in 5 percent of cases, while the mother was awarded sole custody 89.3 percent of the time.[4]

A 1990 audit of the domestic court system in Charleston, South Carolina performed by the *Post-Courier* newspapers, found that out of 512 cases, mother-only custody was granted 82 percent of the time. Of the 78 cases identified as "contested," mothers won sole custody 68 percent of the time (53 cases), fathers won sole custody 20 percent of the time (16 cases), with 12 percent resulting in joint or split custody (9 cases). Overall then, dads were awarded some measure of physical custody by judicial decision 5 percent of the time (i.e, 16+9 ÷ 512=.05), and sole custody 3 percent of the time.

A study of 1,087 cases randomly drawn from Utah's second, third, and fourth districts between the years 1970 and 1993 shows that when fathers "fought for custody," they won 21 percent of the time.[5] Sample sizes were about 220 for each time period, 1970-74, 1975-79, 1980-84, 1985-89, 1990-93. This study is significant in that it attempts to measure whether gender bias in court decisions has persisted since gender-biased laws (maternal preference) were removed. It shows that fathers have no better chance of winning custody today than they did when maternal preference was the law. As much as this study reveals discrimination (mothers win 4 out of 5 times when dads "fight for custody"), dropping the "fight for custody" criteria reveals much larger discrimination. For example, for the 1990-93 period, this study reports that 13 percent of fathers (about 29 out of 220) "fought for custody." Of these, 21 percent (or 6 out of 29) won custody. Overall, though, only 6 fathers out of 220 (less than 3 percent) won custody.

Studies of child support orders are another good indicator of custody awards.[6] In 1992, Frank Bishop, then Director of the Virginia Division of Child Support Enforcement, stated that almost 95 percent of custody cases in Virginia were won by mothers.[7] A study of child support orders in the District of Columbia showed that in 97 percent of cases, fathers were ordered to pay child support, contrasted with only about three percent of mothers.[8] A 1987 study of the Wisconsin Court Record Database, which derived "a sample of divorce, separation, and paternity cases from the family court records of 21 Wisconsin counties in which at least one child [was] potentially eligible for child support," produced a sample of 407 custodial fathers (7 percent) and 5,328 custodial mothers (93 percent).[9]

On a national basis, the Census Bureau's 1992 *Statistical Abstract of the United States* tells the story. While reporting in copious detail on the amount of child support owed and paid to women—providing breakdowns in terms of race, age, and number of children—the *Abstract* provides **no** data on child support owed or paid to men. This absence of data is some indication of the infrequency with which custody awards go to fathers.

As a practical estimate, fathers are awarded custody in only three to five percent of contested pleadings. However, if you are thinking in terms or your own case, even this figure may be optimistic when you consider two other factors: 1) the cases in which fathers prevail are almost always very expensive; 2) in the rare instances where a father is awarded custody, it is usually because the mother was shown to be extremely unfit (e.g. having a history of prostitution, drug abuse, child abuse, or mental illness.) Realistically then, in a contested pleading where the father and mother are equally decent parents, a father's chance of winning custody is somewhere between zero and three percent.

• • •

As the support figures indicate, money is involved here. While defenders of the current system, mostly feminists, argue that fathers only seek custody to avoid paying child support, the opposite appears to be the case. The support levels are so high, and women are so consistently awarded custody, that a woman has a positive monetary incentive to seek a divorce. On the rare occasion where a father gets custody, either by court decision or consent, the chances that a mother will actually *pay* child support are small. Judgments requiring a mother to pay child support to a father are much lower to begin with, usually in the realm of $50 to $200 per child, compared with $200 to $750 per child for a father.[10] Second, as a percentage, nearly twice as many women fail to pay child support as men. Third, enforcement of a child support order against a non-paying mother is virtually non-existent. In my own experience, I know of ten fathers who have custody of their children. Four have no support order at all. The rest were awarded token amounts (approximately $50/month), and these are rarely paid. As noted above, while the 1992 Census report provides detailed information on how much child support is owed to and paid to women, it provides no information on child support owed to or paid to fathers.[11] This absence of data tends to confirm common experience. "Child support" is a one way street where *men pay women* between $11 billion and $14 billion annually.[12] Financial gain obviously is not a motive for fathers seeking custody.

The discrimination against fathers in child support cases is so flagrant that it often produces absurd results. A series of Maryland appeals cases in 1994-95 affords a good example. The October 11, 1994 Maryland *Daily Record,* carried the following headline:

Truth No Defense to Paternity Judgment, High Court Rules

CA Reinstates Pair of Paternity Decrees Despite Conclusive Evidence Of Nonpaternity, Reasoning Their Finality Precluded Reconsideration

> A court's decision is final even when science later proves it wrong, Maryland's highest court ruled Friday, reinstating two paternity judgments that called the wrong men "father."[12]

The story reports on two cases where the putative father was proven not to be the father, but the Maryland Court of Appeals (the supreme court in Maryland) nonetheless upheld the paternity judgments. Thus the court required the men to pay child support for children who were not theirs, until the children reach the age of majority.

In the first case, *Tandra S. v. Tyrone W.,* blood tests ordered by a lower court proved that Tyrone W. could not be the child's father.

In the second case, *Baltimore City Office of Child Support Enforcement of the State of Maryland, Department of Human Resources v. John S. Jr.,* the mother, Vandella H., admitted that she had perjured herself in 1990 when she said that John S. Jr. was the father of her child. She subsequently changed the child's name from John S. III to a name that "reflect[ed] his true lineage and parentage." The real father, Randy S., consented to the name change on the child's birth certificate to show that he was the "true and legal father." Vandella H. and John S. Jr. then jointly attempted to get the Department of Social Services (DSS) to end the administrative order requiring him to pay child support. When the DSS refused to do so, John S. Jr. went to court to end the support order. (Note that in this case, the mother, the real father, and the falsely-alleged father are all in agreement about the child's true paternity, and all three want the government out of their lives. Yet the government insists on staying involved.)

In both of the above cases, the court rationalized its decision to continue the child support order by applying Maryland Rule 2-535, which provides that, if more than 30 days have passed since entry of a judgment, it can only be revised on a clear and convincing showing of fraud, mistake, or irregularity. To a normal person both these cases would constitute a clear showing of fraud, mistake, or irregularity. But the court tortuously reasoned that fraud, mistake, and irregularity are to be "narrowly defined and strictly applied," and that the circumstances found in these two cases failed to meet those narrow definitions.

When people who are not familiar with judicial practices hear about a judicial decision that defies common sense, they tend to think that there is some kind of rational explanation, but only an expert can understand it. Thus arises the myth of the "legal technicality." An alternative perspective is that judicial decisions are political, that courts make their decisions first, then find the rationalization. "Technicalities" are applied so that judges can determine any outcome they want. When we consider political motivations in the above instances: in the first case, the woman benefits; in the second case, the bureaucracy (Child Support Enforcement) benefits.

As if to flaunt its capriciousness, the same court decided a similar case a few months later, and handed down an opposite decision. In this case, though, the gender roles were reversed; the finality of judgment favored the man. The *Daily Record* again reported it:

> A 9-year-old girl won the right to sue a man that blood tests say is probably her father, even though her mother lost a paternity case against the same man, the state's highest court ruled yesterday....
>
> The case is an interesting counterpoint to the recent high court decision *Tandra S. v. Tyrone W.* 336 Md. 303 (1994) which held that a paternity judgment, once entered, could not be overturned— even when the adjudged father is later conclusively excluded as the biological father.[13]

The high court offered two rationalizations for allowing this case to be re-opened—one, they ruled that a mistake *that fit their definition of "mistake"* had been made in this case. The second, perhaps more astonishing reason, was the "lack of privity between mother and child." The idea that there is a lack of privity between mother and child is astonishing because:

> Privity signifies that [the] relationship between two or more persons is such that a judgment involving one of them may justly be conclusive upon [the] other, although [the] other was not party to [the] lawsuit. (*Black's Law Dictionary*, Sixth Edition, p.1199)

Since a paternity suit must of necessity be brought on behalf of a child, it is impossible to imagine how a "lack of privity" could exist in such a case.

• • •

These cases are not isolated instances. If you review domestic-relations case law in any state, a similar pattern emerges. Regardless of the issue, the court will produce some convoluted reasoning to effect a consistent result: women win, or the bureaucracy wins. Men lose.

Imagine any other civil litigation where you only had to know a single physical attribute of the parties in order to determine the outcome. Imagine if that attribute was skin color instead of gender. Many parallels might be elaborated, but I will simply say that a father in a divorce-custody case today has as much chance of getting a fair hearing as a black person going to court against a white person in the Deep South in the decades before civil rights.

NOTES

[1] John P. McCahey, J.D., LL.M, et al., *Child Custody and Visitation Law and Practice*. Mathew Bender, New York. Volume 3, 1983, Section 13.01 states: "Currently, in 90 percent of all disputed custody proceedings the mother is awarded sole custody of the children." (From Bratt, Joint Custody, 67 Ky. L.J. 271, 275, 1978)

[2] *Table No. 69. Children Under 18 Years Old, by Presence of Parents: 1970 to 1991.* Statistical Abstract of the United States, 1992. United States Department of Commerce, Economics and Statistics Administration, Bureau of the Census. 112th Edition. Bernan Press, Lanham, MD.

[3] William T. K. Dolan, Esq., *Empirical Study of Child Custody in Divorce Decrees in Arlington County, Virginia: July 1, 1989 – December 30, 1990.* © 1991.

[4] Wendy Reiboldt and Sharon Seiling, "Factors Related to Men's Award of Custody," *Family Advocate,* Winter 1993, p.42-44. Published by the Section of Family Law of the American Bar Association.

[5] Stephen J. Bahr, J.D. Howe, M. Morrill Mann, "Trends in Custody Awards: Has the Removal of Maternal Preference Made a Difference?" Family Law Quarterly. Vol. 28, 247-267, summer 1994.

[6] Child support orders can be made either administratively or judicially; the available studies do not make a distinction. Nonetheless, these statistics include all court-ordered support and custody orders. Child support orders and custody orders are not 100 percent congruent though, because, as discussed, when men are awarded custody they are not always awarded support.

[7] Rich Blake, "Father Says System is Unfair to Men in Custody Battles," *Alexandria (VA) Gazette Packet* , October 22, 1992 (1+).

[8] John Siegmund, *Analysis of the Child Support Data Base of the District of Columbia.* © 1993. Available through the Children's Rights Council.

[9] Daniel R. Meyers and Steven Garasky, Technical Analysis Paper No. 42, "Custodial Fathers: Myths, Realities and Child Support Policy" July, 1991, p.7-8. Published by the Office of Human Services Policy, Office of the Assistant Secretary for Planning and Evaluation, U.S. Department of Health and Human Services.

[10] Reiboldt and Seiling, op. cit. The authors report, "A court order for child support is largely dependent on the sex of the payor. When fathers received sole custody, the mother was not ordered to pay support 54 percent of the time. ... In cases in which the men got custody, the average child support payment per week per child was $18.31, compared to $54.61 in cases in which the mother received custody." ($73/month compared to $218/month).

   Child support data collected by the Vermont Agency of Human Services in 1988, and compiled in the 1989 study "In Support of our Children," showed that women pay 30% less of their gross income than men, and 56 percent of women pay under $40 per week. "Support Discrimination in Vermont," *The Liberator*, December 1991 (4).

[11] Statistical Abstract of the United States. *op cit.* This "National Data Book" summarizes information from the U.S. Bureau of the Census Current Population Reports. It includes two tables on child support recipiency: *Table No. 596. Child Support—Award and Recipiency Status of Women: 1981 to 1989* and *Table No. 597. Child Support and Alimony—Selected Characteristics of Women: 1989.* As the titles indicate, neither table provides information on how much child support is paid to fathers.

[12] Levy, p.21 and end note 26, p.116.

[13] Jane Bowling, "Truth No Defense to Paternity Judgment, High Court Rules: CA [Court of Appeals] Reinstates Pair of Paternity Decrees Despite Conclusive Evidence of Nonpaternity, Reasoning Their Finality Precluded Reconsideration." *The [Maryland] Daily Record*, October 11, 1994, (1A+).

[14] Jane Bowling, "State Error Opens the Door To Paternity Claim Rehearing: No General or Implied Authority to Dismiss a Case with Prejudice, If State First Fails to Obtain Client's Approval, Court of Appeal Rules." *The [Maryland] Daily Record*, January 10, 1995, (1A+).

CHAPTER 2

STORIES

Throughout this book I draw conclusions from my and Mr. Dawes' experience with thousands of divorce cases, as well as from statistical studies. But the human dimension is not quantifiable. In this chapter I have assembled a handful of first person accounts to give you some impression of the horror and absurdity of the divorce-custody culture. Although all of these accounts come from public forums, I have deleted the names, or changed them, to avoid causing any further difficulties for these individuals with ex-spouses, lawyers, or judges.

* * *

The first three accounts are from testimonies given at public meetings, regarding presumptive joint custody legislation. Fathers' and children's rights groups advocate a legal presumption of joint custody as a means to reduce litigation and encourage mediation in separation and divorce.

PHILIP C.
Statement made at the Public Meeting of Legislators from Alexandria, Virginia, December 20, 1995

Good evening. My name is Philip C, and I am a 24-year resident of the Commonwealth, currently residing in Springfield, Virginia. I have always had faith in the wisdom of America's experiment with democratic government. It is in this spirit of faith that I come before you to share my concerns about the way our government has dealt with my family.

My exposure to our justice system commenced two and one-half years ago when I arrived home one evening to find that my wife had vacated the premises and kidnapped my daughter. A long period of terror then ensued, during which I lost 35 pounds, endured countless abusive threats from my wife and her attorney, and lost hour after hour of sleep worrying about my daughter's welfare. I have used four attorneys during this time, including one recognized as one of the best lawyers in America. All have advised me not to seek joint custody, as the system is geared to award sole custody to mothers in knee-jerk fashion, absent compelling evidence dem-onstrating a lack of maternal parental fitness. My *pendente lite* hearing seemed to me to confirm this, as the two key pieces of evidence were my wife's identity as my daughter's mother, along with the fact that my wife was currently in possession of the child. In other words, rather than hold my wife accountable for kidnapping my daughter, the system was eager to reward her for it. In the subsequent J&DR *[Juvenile and Domestic Relations court]* hearing, I learned that my wife's perjury was of negligible concern to the justice system. I since discovered that those entrusted with prosecuting perjury simply assume that perjury occurs in all domestic cases, so no effort is made to prosecute people for commission of these felonies. I was further disappointed to find that the judge saw fit to allow my wife's attorney to write the court order, so the judge's input, for which I had paid a substantial sum of money, was effectively denied. Small wonder that my daughter does not even have access rights to me on Father's Day. I use the term "access rights," rather than the cruelly insen-sitive term employed by the State *[i.e., "visitation"]*, since I clearly do not visit my daughter: She lives with me part time.

My quest for acknowledgement of my parental rights continues. The process is now two-and-a-half years old, my wife and I are still married, and we have incurred legal and psychological fees of $70,000 to date with no end in sight. All this expense and emotional stress has been incurred to debate the obvious: that my daughter deserves to have her childhood development nurtured and guided by both her parents instead of a single parent selected arbitrarily on the basis of outdated sexual stereotypes. Of course, our society would not be any better off if the justice system merely commenced awarding more custody "victories" to male parents. The key to progress is to preserve the child's access to both parents. The system needs to devote its energy to positive, conciliatory, child-focused pro-cesses instead of adversarial turmoil which injures the very children it is supposed to protect.

No court in any civilized society should ever be permitted to sever a parent-child relationship absent compelling cause. The children of Vir-ginia desperately need your protection. They did not ask for divorce and the State need not punish them or their fathers for it.

• • •

MICHAEL V.

*Statement made at the Public Meeting of Legislators from
Fairfax County, Virginia, January 7, 1995.*

1. My name is Michael V. On the evening of 19 October 1994, my wife Karen and two friends helped me to check into the psychiatric ward at Holy Cross Hospital in Wheaton, Maryland. I refused to take my daily immunosuppressants which are required to keep me from rejecting a transplanted kidney. I was, in essence, holding myself hostage—demanding that my ex-wife and her attorneys stop their "madness." I remained in the hospital for five days under constant physical and psychiatric care. I was under the care of a psychiatrist until 31 December, when my health insurance again required deductible amounts which I currently cannot afford.

2. I was divorced in Fairfax County on 21 December 1992 after a year long custody deliberation. During that year, my ex-wife, Bridget L, lived in Denver, Colorado with her lover, Ross K. I lived alone in Alexandria, Virginia with my three children—Heather, David, and Richie (then 9, 7, and 3 years old, respectively). Bridget had met her boyfriend, Ross (a police detective), when he was attempting to bring my son's rapist to justice. (David was assaulted in the summer of 1991 while under Bridget's care.) In spite of the fact that Bridget abandoned the family for one year, destroyed the marriage with an adulterous affair, and placed our son with such incompetent child care that he was raped, the court-appointed psychiatrist recommended she have sole custody of the children. The children left with Bridget in July 1992 and have resided in Colorado since. I call and talk on the phone to my children about 5 times a week. I miss them.

3. In the course of the custody "battle," I lost my house, my automobile, and all savings to attorneys' fees and went heavily into debt. I also lost all interest in a business that Bridget and I jointly created and financed. I managed not to go into bankruptcy and to keep my job that I have had for 20 years with the government. After my children left, I shared an apartment with a friend in Washington, D.C. Bridget's state of affairs, on the other hand, was a bit different. Enclosure (1) provides her status. *[Enclosure (1) was comprised of copies of pages from a Colorado real estate magazine, which contained a story and photographs of Mr. V's ex-wife. The magazine reported that Bridget L was one of two partners in a $350,000,000 real estate business.]*

4. Besides losing my children and all my financial resources, begin-

ning January 1992 I was assessed a $1,400 per month child support obligation. After a child custody battle totaling $80,000, there was no way to meet that obligation. I had borrowed all that I could, including loans from friends and relatives, to care for my three young children and pay attorneys and psychiatrists. I was immediately in contempt of court *[for failure to pay the full child support amount]* and have remained so. It's either pay her the total amount and never see the children, or remain in contempt of court so that I have enough money for my children to see me when their mother permits. Even though I financially support my current wife, Karen, and our daughter Jane; even though I monthly send a $700 check to a woman who is the CEO and major owner of two corporations, who drives a J-30 Infiniti and lives on a ranch in Parker, Colorado, a woman who is a self-professed millionaire (refer to enclosure 1); your system calls me "Deadbeat."

5. I married my current wife Karen in November 1993. My ex-wife had "directed" me not to re-marry. She said that we might get back together one day. I disobeyed her order and received enclosure (2) as punishment. Please note her congratulatory remark in paragraph (1) of enclosure (2). That's the way it's gone, ladies and gentlemen, over the past year. I won't go into explicit detail on enclosures (3) through (6) other than to ask you to take a few minutes at a convenient time to thumb through them. *[Enclosures (2) through (6) are harassing letters from lawyers threatening to garnishee his wages and seize his retirement benefits in order to pay child support arrearages.]* They are examples of how a vindictive human being with money uses your legal system to hurt innocent people. I pray to God that none of you are asking yourself why I don't challenge her in court again. That would truly be disheartening!

6. I received the judgment letter (enclosure (5)) while at work the day after Ross K. *[the man Bridget left Michael for]* committed suicide. Ross had been living with Bridget and the children since they arrived out in Colorado. She had apparently "dumped" him for another man, and he put his police revolver to his head. I'm sorry to say that I had only fleeting feelings of sorrow for this policeman, but my concern for my children overwhelmed me. I kept thinking about David being raped, being separated from his father and relatives, and then finally having the surrogate father kill himself. And I was powerless to do anything. That was when I "snapped." Every conceivable negative emotion washed over me—I started crying, I screamed. I ended up walking into my supervisor's office and resigning. I somehow drove home (by the grace of

God), and announced to Karen that I would never be a free man, never have control over my life, never be able to protect my children. I then flushed my immunosuppressants down the toilet and stated that I would not take them again unless I could be a part of my children's lives. A few hours later I was admitted to the hospital.

I urge you to support presumptive joint custody legislation, as a first step to putting an end to adversarial litigation, and ending the madness that goes on in our courts.

• • •

JOHN W.

Statement made at the Public Meeting of Legislators from Arlington County, Virginia, January 4, 1995; and again at the Public Meeting of Legislators from Fairfax County, Virginia, January 7, 1995.

My name is John W. Twelve years ago I was afforded the privilege of becoming a resident of the Commonwealth. After eight years in the military, I chose to remain in Virginia because I believed I had found an area that provided a wealth of opportunities—in education, employment, and culture—and I still believe that.

Then, five and one half years ago, my nightmare started—my ex-wife left taking our two children and 95% of our belongings with her. The first four years of this nightmare were fairly benign. She remained in the Northern Virginia area, and our children had the benefit of both parents' love, attention, and guidance, albeit separate from each other. The children spent the weekends with their mother, Mondays and Tuesdays with me, and half a day with each of us for the remainder of the week. One and a half years ago, the real terror began. My ex-wife decided to move to her native state of Ohio—"to pursue her nursing degree."

After several months (and approximately $13,000 in legal fees), a Prince William County judge allowed her to remove my children from the only home they had ever known to accompany her to Ohio. This same judge graciously allowed me to have my children for one week a month. This entailed a sixteen hour round-trip to Ohio, and re-registering my children in school each and every month, only to endure another sixteen hour round-trip, often amid my children's tears and cries of "I don't want to go back" and "But I just got here!"

After six months of this torture, I approached the judge and expressed my displeasure over the detrimental effects of the arrangement on my children. The judge agreed and "rewarded" my concern with allowing me to "visit" my children two weekends a month—IN OHIO! This means, to remain a part of my children's growth and development, I must drive to Ohio, spend two days providing food, shelter, and entertainment for myself and two children, only to drive back to Virginia alone. I managed to do this for several months before I was financially unable to continue. Now, I'm lucky if I get to see my children for a week at Christmas, a week for spring break (if they get one), and a couple of weeks in the summer.

This places me in the position of choosing between a) my children by my first marriage, and b) my present wife and our new baby girl. It also places the stress of choosing on my two older children—between their mother, or their father and their new sister. This is an undeserved burden for two young children and has effectively destroyed two families. *The family unit, being the cornerstone of a strong and moral society, deserves to be better protected—even in non-intact families.* Please remember this as you enter this, and future, legislative sessions. Consider supporting presumptive joint custody and other legislation designed to support rather than separate our families. Thank you for your valuable time and attention.

• • •

The following two accounts are affidavits given in support of a federal case brought by Charles M. against a Virginia circuit judge for denying civil rights via gender discrimination in a divorce-custody dispute.

AFFIDAVIT OF DR. LAWRENCE B.

1. I, Lawrence B, am a resident of Alexandria, Virginia, and am self-employed as a surgeon.

2. I have observed that Circuit Judge Frederick H, and other Circuit Judges in Northern Virginia, have little respect for the federal Constitutional rights of men in the adjudication of domestic relations cases.

3. Out of what I have seen, the super-majority of contested child-physical custody adjudications in Virginia (including those in Arlington County), have been to divorced mothers, rather than to divorced fathers (or to both of them in some sort of parental-sharing arrangement), except

in the most extreme circumstances.

4. According to my observations, Virginia state court orders usually prevent the ordinary father from the regular opportunity to share in the everyday upbringing of his children after a parental divorce.

5. In a substantial number of Virginia cases of which I am aware, divorced fathers, who contest their presumptive non-custodial status and/ or who use federal Constitutional arguments, have been discouraged or penalized by Virginia Circuit Court judges via such methods as denial of ordinary legal discovery, punitively large child support orders, "abusive litigation" judgments, non-enforcement of visitation rights, sanctions, unduly large attorney-fee awards, summary contempt judgments and/or jail time.

6. In my experience, the typical, court-ordered removal of one parent, usually the father, from a young child's life, in a Virginia child-physical-custody order, has thereafter had a harmful effect on the child's development.

7. In my own divorce case, Judge H. was so incensed about my requesting the joint custody of my three children, that he made my attorney either force me to drop my request for joint custody or else resign from being my legal counsel in mid-trial. My office manager was present with me when this occurred and witnessed this event.

8. Judge H. distributed marital property in such a way that each spouse received half of the marital assets, but only I was held responsible for all of the marital liabilities, and attorney's costs for both sides (total $250,000). My "half" was reduced to 25 percent.

9. Judge H. awarded my former wife a lifetime alimony of $30,000 per year, despite her good health, young age, and two careers. In September 1991, I requested in court a decrease in alimony due to decreased income *[In addition to the $30,000/year alimony, Dr. B. was ordered to pay $24,000 per year in child support, for a total of $54,000 per year or $4,500 per month.]* This was rejected by Judge H.

10. After my income dropped substantially because of the huge debt and because of a change in business conditions, Judge H. refused, in about September 1991, to modify commensurately my $2,500 alimony, ruling, in so many words, that my role was to work harder to earn more money.

11. In February 1992, I appeared before Judge H. at a show-cause hearing to explain why I was one week in arrears in support payments. My liquid assets had been frozen because of an IRS seizure. *[In addition to the $250,000 in legal fees and the support/alimony of $54,000 a year,*

Dr. B. endured a severe decline in income, largely due to the turmoil caused by the litigation.] I presented documentary evidence of the same to Judge H. Lacking liquidity, I offered to transfer non-liquid real property in satisfaction of my arrearage. Judge H., nevertheless, summarily ordered me to be jailed immediately for contempt of court. He violated a basic point of law in doing this.

12. From the pattern of Judge H.'s behavior, I have observed that Judge H. unfairly prevented me, a man, from seeking joint custody and from expressing federal Constitutional rights to my children and to my property, and from objecting to their removal from my life without due process.

13. The Virginia Court of Appeals upheld Judge H.'s orders in all substantial respects.

14. Via the aforesaid acts, Judge H. has unlawfully been biased, prejudiced and punitive, contrary to federal law, and violated my Constitutional rights and freedoms.

I declare, under penalty of perjury, that the foregoing is true and correct, to the best of my knowledge.

> February 17, 1994
> (signature)
> Lawrence B.

• • •

AFFIDAVIT OF JAMES G.

1. I, James G., am employed as a Criminal Investigator by the Police Department of _____, Virginia. I have spent about two decades in law enforcement, including the enforcement of Constitutional law.

2. I have testified before the Virginia General Assembly on matters of domestic disputes, healthful juvenile development, and Virginia's need for more two-parent involvement in child-rearing.

3. In my professional capacity, I have seen that Virginia court orders which essentially prevent one parent, usually the father, from participating substantially in the parenting of minor children are highly correlated with incidents of juvenile delinquency in Northern Virginia.

4 After personal research and interviews concerning a large number of custody disputes in Northern Virginia, I have found that the great majority of child physical custody is "adjudicated" to mothers, merely be-

cause they are mothers, regardless of the evidence.

5. In my personal capacity I witnessed, during my own divorce and custody proceeding, extreme gender-bias on the part of a Circuit Court Judge in Northern Virginia concerning partial-physical-custody of my children. The Circuit Judge consistently refused to enforce my relevant legal discovery requests, refused to enforce my visitation rights to my children, and refused before Final Judgment to enforce my motion to compel the production to me of the medical and psychological records of my children (forbidden under Va. Code § 20-107.2). Over my objection, the Circuit Court Judge ordered a mediator to testify, in violation of the confidentiality provisions of the Virginia Code. The Circuit Judge thereafter unlawfully refused to allow me to use written documents and tape recordings to impeach the mediator at trial.

6. After I refused to voluntarily waive my parental rights to joint legal and physical custody of my children, the Circuit Judge held me in contempt of court for writing letters which requested federal intervention, after he had agreed to issue a Letter Rogatory to a state court in San Antonio, Texas, which was designed to produce evidence of perjury by the children's mother. The Circuit Judge refused to reverse his decision.

7. As in the custody case of Charles M., the Circuit Judge charged me substantial attorneys' fees and sanctions, as a penalty for the expression of my Constitutional rights and for the expression of my interest in participating actively in my children's development. The Circuit Judge abruptly and summarily issued a judgment against me when I subpoenaed the financial records of my former wife in connection with a child support hearing/motion.

8. In my experience, it is a widespread practice in Northern Virginia for state Judges to issue child custody orders which essentially remove equally fit and caring fathers, who were primary caretakers of their children, from the lives of their children, regardless of the evidence, except in the most extreme cases of maternal unfitness. This demonstrates a system of gender bias and sex discrimination.

I declare, under penalty of perjury, that the foregoing is true and correct, to the best of my knowledge.

February 13, 1994
(signature)
James G.

Should Scheming Mother Have Custody?

Reprinted with permission, from "Flying Solo," syndicated column by J.L. Warner & J.C. Stucker, April 11, 1995. Knight Ridder Newspapers

Q: As an unmarried airline pilot, I am away from home several times each month. I met a woman on one of my trips whom I continued to see for a number of months. She told me she was divorced, living with her two young children, and receiving alimony from her wealthy ex-husband. We took trips all over the world. She told me her ex was looking after the children. Then she became pregnant with what she said was my child. We talked about getting married, and I paid for her prenatal care and the expenses of birth and began giving her money to support our child. Then she broke things off and the situation got nasty. She told me what I was giving her was not enough and filed a support petition. I hired a lawyer and, in the course of discovery, I learned that she had never been married, was not receiving alimony, and her two other children were the results of out-of-wedlock unions with two other single airline pilots. She is receiving guideline child support from both other fathers to the tune of nearly $50,000 a year tax-free! My lawyer tells me that with my contribution according to the child support guidelines, this woman will have spendable cash flow of nearly $72,000 annually—Tax-Free! In addition, she gets health insurance for each of the children through three different employers. My lawyer says there is nothing I can do but pay according to the guidelines. I feel like there must be something else that can be done. Who will be next?

A: Who will be next? is right. Although your lawyer has certainly told you the law, we believe the focus of the inquiry should be more toward this woman's fitness to have custody of your child—and at the same time, the children of the other pilots. As the father, you have a duty to make sure your child is being taken care of in an appropriate environment. Here is a woman with two young children who travels all over creation with you, leaving behind her children by two other men with an ex-husband whom you now know does not exist. The logical question is who really looked after the children while she was gone? And while she's gone with the next pilot, who will take care of your child? Does she work outside the home? What does she do all day? Are the children placed in day care? What does she do with the money she receives? What are the conditions of the children's health? What is her background? Has she had any psychiatric counseling? We believe that the first step might be a private investigator to detail her comings and goings.

Under these circumstances, it would appear that a court should consider requiring her to undergo a mental evaluation. You have the right to inspect and copy her banking records. After your investigation, a strong case may be made that your child could be better off with you—or maybe with your parents. You may want to contact the other two fathers to see what information they have. It appears to us that this enterprising young woman may just be starting a whole new cottage industry from her home: having children by different fathers with money to live off the child support. If so, this is a dangerous precedent that should not be allowed to continue.

• • •

The following three accounts were posted on fathers' rights newsgroups on the Internet.

Date: Tue, 28 Mar 1995 11:02:26 -0800
From: John D— <d—@----.COM>
To: < ------- >
Subject: Arrested for calling my children

Hello,

This is my first message to the list, having just joined. I'd like to share a recent experience. Last September, my ex and her divorce lawyer-boyfriend (yes—she is living with him, and he has a "front" lawyer now representing them) got a restraining order against me. It prohibits me from calling or writing either of them except in extreme emergencies regarding my two children (ages 6 and 3).

As part of my visitation orders for my kids, I can call them 3 times a week for 10 minutes a call. Last January, I called for my son, and her boyfriend answered. He told me I was violating the restraining order and would call the cops. I told him I could call my kids per the visitation order, whereupon he refused to let me talk to them, hung up, and called the county sheriff.

Sure enough, I got arrested, booked, fingerprinted, the whole nine yards.

I went to court, pled not guilty, and represented myself. I went to trial and was found not guilty because I had a very clear paper trail showing I had the right to talk to my kids, a right I fought for 3 years to get, and a right that was reaffirmed in the very restraining order they used against me.

Why was I arrested? Because the cop who took the complaint did not care that I had these rights. He was only interested in the fact that it appeared I violated the restraining order. His report was 2-1/2 pages on what her boyfriend told him, and only 1/2 page on my statements, with no mention of my visitation rights, which I quite clearly told him. Her boyfriend, being a divorce lawyer and knowing everyone in the system, clearly steered this his way.

So, I've filed a four-page complaint with the California State Bar Association, plus I'm now filing for increased visitation and joint custody of my kids. One cannot allow others to interfere with their ability to parent.

My message to all: maintain your documentation, examine it for possible civil actions against you, and get it changed if you find something. I spent 15 months worried sick over the possibility of a year in jail because of this nonsense.

Thanks for reading, regards, john d—

• • •

Date: Wed, 12 Apr 1995 18:31:28 -0400
From: David S— <D....s@----.COM>
To: < ------- >
Subject: My children are being violated!

HELP!

My soon to be ex-wife is putting a terrible strain on my kids.

I just got out of the Child Protective Services (CPS) building where a social worker there has strip-searched my kids for about the fourth time in two months. The Army hospital doctors have looked at them three times, and I know others I don't know have done sex assault exams on them.

The social worker doesn't believe that I am abusing either of my daughters. She also says that these repeated exams can really screw a kid up.

She also says that there is absolutely NOTHING I can do about it either! She can have them examined like that anytime she wants.

I am temporary managing conservator of my daughters. (I have custody.) That's why she is being so cruel. After she gives birth to another man's baby, we'll have the divorce and custody ar-rangement. She doesn't understand that she isn't hurting me nearly as much as she is hurting my children.

What scares me is each time she makes an allegation, she gets better at running the system around in circles. She plays one agency against another. (I'm in the Army so the military has it's own investigation as well.)

What do you think?

Sincerely, David S— (Dave)

• • •

Date: Thu, 07 Mar 1996 23:52:24 -0800
From: RM <r—@----.com>
To: < ------- >
Subject: I CAN'T BELIEVE THIS

In the middle of 1995 I received a summons from the District Attorney of _____ stating Welfare wants to sue me to establish parentage and child support for a child that was born in 1985 (10 YEARS AGO!).   According to the summons, they started paying this woman welfare in 1991. It took them FOUR YEARS to serve me? All they had to do was make a call to the local DMV, and you can find anybody if you know their name. It just takes a phone call.

Well I have to say this was a surprise to me. Now no woman ever told me that I was a father, but after further investigation (on my own with no help from Welfare!), I found out that this woman received welfare for less than one year and was not interested in help from the father of her child. I also found out that this woman had three men listed as the father of her child in her meeting with welfare. She is not interested in receiving child support, and wants nothing to do with the father of the child. But welfare wants to pursue this even though it is costing them much more to do so than they will ever get.   They are launching this lawsuit to collect back child support and current monthly payments, even though they only paid her welfare for 4 months, 5 years ago. And she will receive nothing.

Even though Welfare does not know who the father is yet, they want all the men named to pay for their paper work, even though at least two of them can't possibly be the father. Now to top this off, the woman is now married and her husband wants to adopt the child. How can he adopt this child without the father's signature and if the father was never found and he was allowed to adopt the child, what happens with the case if the father is found after the adoption is complete? So let's sum up this letter and number the damages.

    1) The alleged father is being sued for something he had no knowledge of, and because the welfare department took its time in locating the alleged father they want him to pay for back-support which would not have been necessary if they located him by making a phone call. So they want him to pay for THEIR laziness. (P.S. How can the system get back-support when a support order was never filed?)

    2) The father never got to meet or see the child.

3) The father was never able to bond with his child.

4) The father did not get to see this child grow up.

5) The child does not have the father's name.

6) The father must pay back child support even though he knew nothing of this child's existence.

7) The father must pay monthly child support, even though the woman is married and her husband is adopting the child and they want nothing to do with the father.

8) The welfare department is paying out all this money in an effort to try to collect its payments of four months, when just starting this investigation will cost them more than they will receive.

9) The welfare department is not trying to help. They're hurting everyone in this lawsuit, even themselves. This is so typical of governmental red tape. They think this is in the best interest of the child but what it really is, is what will keep this cash cow going.

This is so unbelievable it's giving me an ulcer.

RM.

• • •

CHAPTER 3

PERCEPTIONS AND BEHAVIOR

The primary reason that men have their lives undone in divorce-custody proceedings is because the system is thoroughly biased. But there are certain perceptions and patterns of behavior that make men readily susceptible to the depredations of the system. If your behavior fits the standard male pattern, you fit right into the system and you can be crushed. If right now you are thinking "My case is not typical," then very likely your behavior fits the standard male pattern. There are four principal players in a custody dispute—the mother, the father, the lawyers, and the court.[1] To a large degree, these cases have similar outcomes because of the lawyers and the courts. But in most cases, the die is cast from the beginning by the simple fact that women seek legal counsel first.

The generalizations I make here arose first from hearing so many similar stories in fathers' support groups, and later from discussing these patterns with numerous domestic-relations attorneys, and numerous men and women involved in divorce-custody disputes. Ultimately, they can only be validated by your own experience. Think about the divorces of friends and relatives. Do they conform with the patterns described in this book? Above all, examine your own thoughts and actions. If these generalizations don't fit you, disregard them. But if they do closely follow your thoughts, you should give due consideration.

MEN ARE REACTIVE RATHER THAN PRO-ACTIVE
In the literature of divorce, it is consistently reported that women initiate court action the great majority of the time, with studies giving figures ranging from 67 to 87 percent for wife-initiated divorces.[2] These figures square pretty well with what I have learned from lawyers as well as from men and women who have been through divorce. Particularly pertinent to this discussion: all the domestic relations lawyers I spoke with concurred that *in disputes involving child custody*, women initiate divorce *"almost all the time!"* Furthermore, in cases where men do initiate the proceedings, their behavior is still usually reactive; that is, typically, a man will only initiate a divorce-custody suit after his wife has in some manner cut him off from his children.

35

These are the most common scenarios which commence an adversarial divorce-custody proceeding:

(1) A man comes home one day to find that his wife has moved out and taken the children. It may be weeks before he finds out where his children are. When he does, it is usually because he has just been notified that his wife is suing him for divorce, custody, and support.

(2) The woman goes to the magistrate and says that her husband is dangerous, is threatening her, or has actually hit her. The magistrate issues a protective order evicting the man from the house for 35–365 days (depending on jurisdiction). Then the wife sues for divorce, custody, and support.

(3) The husband and wife have an amicable separation, with the husband agreeing to move out of the house. For a long time (months, frequently a year or two), the husband continues to be active in caring for his children, and sees them without interference. Out of the blue, the wife sequesters the child and refuses to let the father have any further contact. Then she sues for divorce, custody, and support.

A man faced with any of these actions usually thinks his wife has gone crazy. But to understand what is going on here, we have to look back long before the moment of crisis. For most couples divorce is a long drawn out affair marked by guilt and acrimony, bitter fights, brief reconciliations, trial separations, and perfunctory sessions with a marriage counselor. Both parties should be able to see the end coming from a long way off. Yet when the crisis hits, men always seem to be taken by surprise.

Another way of regarding this phenomenon is that it is not so much that women act first, as that men procrastinate endlessly in this matter, and women finally act to get it over with. A woman does not suddenly wake up one morning and decide to move out. The moment of crisis is a culminating act that took months of planning. Typically, on the day of the crisis the husband will be running around in a panic trying to find a lawyer. Later he will learn that his wife began consulting a lawyer months before.[3] Women are also more likely to interview several lawyers before choosing one. Once the lawyer told her her options, she very likely may have procrastinated before committing to a plan. And then she had to make a plan. For example, if a woman decides to move out and take the children, she has to plan when to move, where to move, and what to take; she may have to hire a moving van; she has to arrange to take the day off work; she has to know where her husband will be that day; and she has to make sure that the children are with her that day. She must also coordinate the plan with her attorney so the petition can be promptly filed. While she was doing all this planning, the husband was whistling in the dark, hoping that things would somehow work themselves out.

When I advise fathers who are in the midst of degenerating marriages that they should take first-strike legal action, I repeatedly encounter the same objections:

- "It will start a war. I don't want to do that to my wife and children."

- "We don't need to go to court, we can work it out ourselves."

- "The kids would hate me if I did that." (i.e., took them and left, and didn't let them see their mother until court.)

- "I can't afford a lawyer."

- "That's crazy."

- "I don't have to have sole custody. Why can't we have some kind of joint custody arrangement?"

- "We're getting along now. I would never betray her like that."

These are all good sensible responses. Taking the children and leaving is a terrible thing to do to the children as well as to the other parent. Going to court is a nightmare for the whole family. Children *are* angry with the parent who hides them from their other parent. It is absolutely the best thing for children if their parents can amicably work out a joint custody arrangement. Unfortunately, good sensible responses do not work in court.

I asked a number of domestic-relations lawyers why they think fathers rarely initiate custody disputes. Here is the gamut of explanations:

(1) Fathers do not really want custody. When the wife sues for custody and support, the father turns around as a revenge motive and sues for custody. *This is what most lawyers and judges believe, and they act accordingly.*

(2) Men have a primitive belief in their own machismo. Believing they are in control of the situation, they do not take any action until they suddenly find themselves out of control.

(3) Men tend to emphasize reason and suppress emotion, and believe they can win with reason.

The first explanation is blatantly discriminatory, and provides lawyers and judges the justification to continue with business as usual. The second and third explanations conform with what divorced fathers have told me about themselves. Overall, there are five main strains to the way men think and act in divorce-custody cases:

(1) It is typical for a man to believe that his case is exceptional. Like so many other people, he has assimilated the media myth of the Evil Male. While he knows that he is a great father himself, he thinks everyone else is a deadbeat dad. Consequently he ignores warnings from other fathers who have been to court. He thinks that things did not work out for them because of some failing on their part. He thinks the judge will pin a medal on him when he hears what an involved and generous father he is.

(2) Men expect to be able to work things out reasonably. The man believes that he is being so reasonable that it is only a matter of time before his wife, the attorneys, and the judge realize the soundness of his position and come around to his way of thinking.

(3) Fathers tend to favor a joint custody arrangement.

(4) Typically, a father believes that the judge will give him brownie points for not "snatching" the children (that is, doing what the wife did) when he had the opportunity to.

(5) Fathers retain affection for their wives, even during this conflict.

All these are self-defeating ways of thinking. The judge meets generous, devoted fathers every day and ruins their lives. Reason and moderation are out of place in this forum. Halfway measures and moderate
proposals are not viewed as prudent; they are interpreted as meaning you
do not really want custody. Lastly, joint custody is a fantasy. I have often
heard fathers lament, "All I want is joint custody," believing they are
asking for nothing more than the basic rights due to them and their children. Asking for joint custody is like asking for the sun and the moon.
Although an award of joint custody is provided for in the statutes of most
states, judges rarely award it. In the rare instances where it is awarded, the
court is unlikely to uphold it if the mother violates the order.

WHY FATHERS CONSENT TO UNFAVORABLE AGREEMENTS

Frequently, after a woman consults an attorney, she will not resort
immediately to one of the radical solutions described above. Her first
course of action may be to try to talk her husband into signing a consent
order. She will be friendly and cajoling, assuring him of an ongoing
relationship with his children. These are commonly the worst agreements,
drafted unilaterally by the wife's attorney, with the husband not even
consulting an attorney. They are generally blanket agreements ceding
custody to the mother. Visitation may not even be mentioned, and if it is,
it will not be specified as to days and times, making it impossible to
enforce. Child support may or may not be included in the agreement. It
does not matter. Child support cannot be waived. The mother can after-
wards go to court and have child support awarded. Or, if you agreed to
what you considered a reasonable child support, she can still go to court
and have it raised in accordance with the guidelines (see Chapters 10
and 11).

Men consent to these agreements to avoid a court battle and because
they fail to consider the long-term consequences. When a man signs such
an agreement, he and his ex are getting along well. But sooner or later the
ex-wife may want to move a thousand miles away, or, once she has established a new marital relationship, she may consider her ex-husband an
irrelevant encumbrance. Going to court to fight for visitation after you
have waived custody can be just as difficult as fighting a full-fledged
custody battle.

Fathers have also been known to agree to unfavorable orders when they have good (i.e., expensive) attorneys. Such an agreement may be made after the case has gone on for a prolonged period, or it may be made "on the courthouse steps" (that is, in the waiting room at the courthouse on the day of trial). When a lawyer realizes it will be hard to get any more money out of you, he may "hang you out to dry"—that is, he may attempt to browbeat you into agreeing to a miserly visitation schedule and an astronomical child support payment. Judges do not like to make decisions, and lawyers know that, so as the time when the judge has to make a decision draws closer, you (and your ex) will be under a lot of pressure to settle.

At this point you will be stressed by the spiralling costs, the anxiety of subpoenas and depositions, the workdays lost to court, and the torment your children have been going through. Under these pressures, you have to be wary of talking yourself into signing a bad agreement.

One frequent rationalization in accepting a paltry visitation schedule is: "After the fight is over, things will settle down, and she'll let me see the children as much as I used to." She might, but it's chancy. As months and years of not speaking to each other drag on, your ex is not likely to get more generous.

As regards child support, it is natural to presume that your own attorney and the judge know what they are doing and are concerned with obtaining a fair settlement. Consequently you might agree to a support payment you cannot afford, thinking there is something wrong with you when you are stunned to hear the amount they want you to pay. At that moment in court, with all these pressures swirling around, the child support issue strikes a blow to your masculinity and to your pride in parenting. The scorn with which the judge, your wife's attorney, and maybe even your own attorney, treat your protest, says "You think that's a lot?! What's wrong with you, you cheapskate. Don't you want to take care of your own children?" The truth is that most judges and attorneys have little or no idea of what constitutes reasonable child support, and they do not care whether it is fair or not. All they know is that women's groups are always hollering about child support, so they want to be sure you pay a lot. As a result, many child support awards are more than a normal father can afford.

Signing or not can be a hard decision. A bad agreement will make your life miserable, but continuing to litigate may make your life more miserable. Keep in mind that *if you sign a consent order, you cannot appeal it to a higher court.* If you don't like the visitation schedule or don't think you can afford the proposed level of child support, don't sign the consent order. This way the judge will have to order it himself and then you can appeal the decision.

MOTHERS' PERSPECTIVE

Much of this book makes generalizations about women which may be considered politically incorrect. First of all, it should be recognized that we are talking about a small subset of the population—people involved in custody disputes. Still, only a person blinded by politically correct dogma believes that men and women behave the same in all circumstances. In the question of custody there are distinct differences. Notably, women are fierce in their pursuit of sole custody. But this pattern, too, has obvious external causes.

It might be said that the courts discriminate against women, that they think that the only thing women are capable of is taking care of children. Because most courts are in the habit of awarding custody to the mother unless she is shown to be seriously unfit, losing custody is a terrifying prospect for many women. They regard it as a horrible stigma. If a father loses custody, however, nobody thinks any less of him. It is considered normal. Many men, tacitly understanding their wives' dilemma, take the joint custody approach, which, as I've explained, is untenable.

One rule of thumb is that your case will be as difficult as your ex wants to make it. If your ex was normally a reasonable and fair person, then you should be able to resolve this conflict without too much difficulty, though she will be surprisingly less reasonable than she was before. If your ex was always emotionally high-strung, you are likely to have a difficult time. The judicial system will provoke women to their worst behavior. Lawyers do it by actively inciting women to belligerence. Judges do it by tolerating any offense committed by a woman, even contempt of court. Consider too, that these are emotionally charged situations to begin with, and that each party tends to feel that his or her own position is wholly justified. Under these circumstances many mothers tend to believe that they "own" their children. They forget that the children have their own lives, and that children need their fathers. When this attitude is reinforced by official authority, it is hard for a woman to recognize the harm she is doing to her children.

NOTES

[1] Although all of this is ostensibly being done in the interest of the children, children rarely have any say in a custody dispute. Judges, lawyers, guardians *ad litem*, and social workers pontificate about the best interest of the children, while they keep the conflict going, running up thousands of dollars in bills. Obviously the very best interest of the children would be served by ending the conflict between the parents.

[2] Daniel Amneus, Ph.D. *The Garbage Generation.* Note 62 on page 142 lists, in part, the following sources:

> Lenore Weitzman, *The Divorce Revolution: The Unexpected Social and Economic Consequences for Women and Children in America* (New York: The Free Press, 1985), p. 460: "These researchers (Robert Schoen, Harry N. Greenblatt,and Robert B Mielke) report that 78 percent of all divorce petitions in California were filed by wives..." P. 147 (quoting attorney Riane Eisler): "By social convention, the vast majority of divorces were filed by women." P. 174: "In California, in 1968, under the adversary system, over three-quarters of the plaintiffs—those who initiated the legal divorce proceedings—were wives filing charges against 'guilty' husbands." According to David Chambers, *Making Fathers Pay* (Chicago: University of Chicago Press, 1979), p.29, "the wife is the moving party in divorce actions seven times out of eight." According to the *Legal Beagle*, February, 1986, 72 percent of divorce filings are made by wives. According to Joan Kelly, author of *Surviving the Breakup*, "Divorce is sought about three to one by women" (cited in *Joint Custody Newsletter*, January, 1988). According to Christopher Lasch, *NYRB*, 17 February, 1966, three-quarters of divorces are granted to women. According to Elsie Clews Parsons' *The Family: An Ethnographical and Historical Outline* (New York: G.P. Putnam's Sons, 1906, p.331), "A large majority of divorces are obtained by women." According to a three-day survey by the County Clerk's Office in Orange County, California, two of every three divorce petitions listed the wife as the plaintiff (*Fathers' Forum*, August, 1987). According to court records in Marion, Howard, Hancock, Grant, and Ruch counties in Indiana in 1985, of 2,033 dissolutions granted, 1,599 (76%) were filed by wives, 474 (23.3%) were filed by husbands (National Congress for Men *Network*, Vol. 1, No. 3).

[3] A number of lawyers have told me that women "shop around" more for a divorce attorney. An article on the top divorce lawyers in Washington (Emily Couric, "The Terminators," *Washingtonian* July 1992: 78–84.), supports this observation. Attorney Robert Shoun is quoted: "Women are a lot more prone to do extensive research into divorce lawyers than are men. Probably one third of my women clients belong [to support groups or organizations] or seek out these services."

CHAPTER 4

PERCEPTIONS OF COURT

Q: *What do you call a lawyer with an IQ of 40?*

A: *Your Honor.*

A father caught in a custody dispute commonly goes through a phase in which he will recite his case in infinitesimal detail to anyone who will listen. This concern for the facts reflects an underlying perception of court as a truth-seeking forum. The purpose of this chapter is to dissuade you of any such notions.

For most of us, when we reflect on our perceptions of court, we *must* think of television dramas. Much as we would like to believe we are more sophisticated than this, television forms a major part of our perception of things we have not experienced personally. Obviously, any moderately intelligent person is aware that lawyers are not detectives like *Perry Mason* or *Matlock*, and that the legal profession is not as glamorous as *L.A. Law*. Yet if we look not at the assertions, but at the *presumptions* in television court dramas, we can readily recognize where our misconceptions are formed.

- In television court dramas, the judge is *interested*, paying keen attention to the smallest details of a case. He actively seeks *the truth*. And, though he may for a time be confused by contradictory evidence, in the end he is able to put together the pieces and recognize *the truth*.

In reality, many judges flaunt their indifference to the cases before them. A few actually sleep in court. As for *the truth*, well, consider this: perjury is commonplace in domestic-relations court, and it is *never* prosecuted. If you don't believe this, ask your attorney how often he's seen perjury in domestic-relations court. Then call your District Attorney's office, and ask how often they prosecute perjury. I have known several instances where fathers have taken documentation of perjury to the DA's office and been told flat out, "We don't prosecute perjury." Now consider this: Lawyers know that perjury is never prosecuted, and many advise their clients accordingly.

- In television court dramas, evidence is presented in a clear, orderly fashion.

In reality, it may prove impossible to get simple items entered into evidence (e.g., your child's report card showing that your wife never gets him to school on time, or cancelled checks showing that you paid the child support she says you owe). Or, evidence may be entered, but mislabeled and impossible to reference at a later time.

- In television court dramas, a trial is always represented as a *clarifying* experience. In the development of the drama, numerous facts are presented, many of which appear to be contradictory. But during the trial at the end of the show, all the facts fall in place, like a complex and beautiful jigsaw puzzle.

In a real courtroom, the simplest, most obvious facts can become hopelessly muddled. Everyone in your community may know that you're the Boy Scout troop leader and president of the PTA, and that your wife is an alcoholic barfly, but in court it could come out just the opposite.

- In television court dramas, the judge always rules on the merits of the case.

As discussed throughout this book, judges have many concerns other than the merits.

- In television court dramas, the case always has a final resolution.

This is perhaps the greatest misconception. People commonly expect that there will be one culminating "day in court," after which all issues will be resolved, and the case will be over. In reality, the case will never end, unless you and your ex decide never to return to court no matter what, or until your children reach the age of majority.

These same presumptions are reinforced by Judge Wapner on *People's Court*, what Hollywood writers call "reality-based programming." *People's Court* takes cases from California small claims courts, with the real litigants pleading their cases. Mixing common sense with sound jurisprudence, Judge Wapner time and again renders a verdict every viewer can appreciate. You can definitely feel good about the law after watching *People's Court*. But small claims court really is different from any other kind of court because generally lawyers are not involved. More importantly, Judge Wapner is performing for a television audience. It is literally his job, not to represent reality, but to fulfill your expectations.

There is one thing that Judge Wapner frequently does that creates a very misleading impression. He often quotes the law. Moreover, on many episodes, after a commercial break, he returns to the bench and says that he was just in his chambers consulting the law, then he proceeds to read it. In a regular civil proceeding it would be unusual for the judge to consult the law on his own initiative. In fact, many judges act as blank slates.

For example, child-care cost is always factored into child support. In Virginia, it "cannot not exceed the amount required to provide quality care from a licensed source." All the judges know this, and, because they've done hundreds of these cases, they also know that the county provides before- and after-school care for about $160 per month. But, if your ex claimed that child care costs her $500 a month, many judges would factor in $500, unless you cited the statute and showed the evidence proving that you don't have to pay more than $160.

You must never presume that the judge knows the law; or, if he knows it, that he cares to apply it. If your judge keeps ignoring the statute, your lawyer should vociferously remind him what the law is and to obey it.

In your lifetime you have seen hundreds, if not thousands, of television court dramas. It is virtually impossible that you have not in some measure assimilated the presumptions presented in them. You have to consciously counter these presumptions in order to respond appropriately to the realities of our court system.

Was the Judge Raised in a Cave?

It would be hard to grow up in America today and not hold egalitarianism as a central value. The virtues of equality are trumpeted from the transmission towers of every television and radio station and proclaimed in every major newspaper.

If you are like most men who become involved in custody disputes, you probably were raised in the mainstream middle class and have a deep-seated presumption that women are your equals. Common experience reinforces that presumption every day. While thirty years ago, a woman's employment would almost inevitably be at a low wage-earning level, today women have rough parity in job status and income.[1] While thirty years ago, women made up a small percentage of college enrollment, today *more* women than men attend and graduate college.[2] Everywhere in the United States it is easy and usual to find successful women in business, medicine, law, and other careers. In the workplace, it is not at all unusual for a man to have a woman supervisor. It is not at all unusual today to find marriages in which the wife earns more than her husband.

Conversely, it is also commonplace today to find men as active partners in child care. A generation ago, a father changing diapers or giving a baby a bottle would have been noteworthy. Father's ineptness with baby was a good setup for a comedy skit. Today, in airports and shopping malls, you find baby-changing tables in the men's rooms.

Consequently, when a father goes to court over divorce-custody, he is likely to be baffled by the judge's attitude: Every woman is treated as a delicate flower, and every man as a cossack.

A judge may be looking across the bench at a husband and wife with equal income; both parties may be represented by women attorneys earning $100,000 a year; the judge herself may be a woman, and thus her own evidence to social change; yet still the ruling handed down will be identical to any made in 1966.

In 1966, in a divorce-custody suit, the likely outcome would be that the mother would get sole custody of the children and the father would get "standard visitation." In 1996, in a divorce-custody suit, the likely outcome would be exactly the same.

In most cases the judge will show at least a pretense of objectivity. But it is not unusual for judges to treat fathers with open rudeness. Guilty until proven innocent is a rule that too often applies to fathers in the courtroom. And the father will not even know what he is supposed to be guilty of.

What happens in domestic-relations courts is completely at variance with what normal people expect of court. It is a highly politicized forum where fair play, equal justice, and common sense have no meaning.

• • •

NOTES

[1] Statistical information confirms common experience, as was copiously shown in an article by Sylvia Nasar, "Women Progress Stalled? Just Not So: Popular wisdom aside, women were big winners in the 80's, new data show, and gains should keep coming." (*New York Times*, 10/18/92, Section 3, p.1+). Nasar reports that in the 1979-90 period, women's median income increased by 10 percent, while men's median income declined by 8 percent. In 1979, the median female income was $18,663, rising to $20,656 by 1990. Men's median income in 1979 was $31,315, declining to $28,843 by 1990. In 1990, women earned 80 cents for every dollar earned by men. The remaining disparity can be almost entirely explained by factors other than discrimination.

The fact that higher-echelon jobs tend to be held by older men skews the male median income upward. These men began their careers decades ago when there were far fewer women entering the workforce and very few entering professions. As the older generation retires, the remaining disparity in male/female earnings will further dissipate. Also, gender realities, not gender discrimination will always be a factor. Male/female career choices are not identical; and because women still have babies, they are more likely to take a career hiatus. Direct comparison within a field shows virtually no discrepancy between male/female earnings. For example, women with doctorates in economics earned between 95 percent and 99 percent as much as male peers with the same experience. Even taking the 80 cents on the dollar comparison: if fathers won custody in the same ratio, it would be miraculous.

[2] Warren Farrell. *The Myth of Male Power.* New York: Simon & Schuster. 1993. P.39. Note, p 375: U.S. Department of Education, National Center for Education Statistics, Digest of Education Statistics 1991, p. 167, table 161, "Total Enrollment in Institutions of Higher Education" shows that women are 54 percent of those enrolled in college; p. 234, table 228, "Earned Degrees Conferred by Institutions of Higher Education," shows that women are 55 percent of those receiving bachelors' degrees from college.

CHAPTER 5

THE POLITICS OF DIVORCE-CUSTODY

"The one great principle of the...law is, to make business for itself. There is no other principle distinctly, certainly, and consistently maintained through all its narrow turnings. Viewed by this light it becomes a coherent scheme, and not the monstrous maze the laity are apt to think it. Let them but once clearly perceive that its grand principle is to make business for itself at their expense[.]"

— Charles Dickens, *Bleak House* [1]

What goes on in domestic-relations court is so much at variance with what the normal citizen expects from our legal system that it demands some explanation. While this chapter may not have direct application for your custody battle, it is important in that it might help you to keep your bearings if your case takes a turn for the surreal.

As a first response, most people find it hard to imagine how politics is involved in domestic relations. Specifically, a father might ask, "How on earth could politics affect my little case when my wife and I are political non-entities?" The answer is that the details of your individual case, while looming large in your own mind, constitute only a small component of the judge's view.

Whether obtained through appointment by the governor, election by the legislature, or popular election, judgeships are political positions, and judges are politically sensitive individuals. There are intrinsic and extrinsic political influences that come to bear on the judge's decision-making habits. By intrinsic politics I mean the judge's immediate constituents—those people and organizations the judge comes in contact with on a regular basis—the people who might have some say about his reappointment. Essentially this means the lawyers who appear before him, the local bar association, and the representatives of two large bureaucracies—the Child Support Enforcement Agency and Child Protective Services. Frequently, Child Support Enforcement and Child Protective Services are housed in the same building as the court.

The extrinsic politics involves the larger political picture: such as the electoral influences on the state legislators (some of whom may also be lawyers who appear before the judge) and the popular mood.

Frequently, judges make nonsensical rulings that are contrary to evidence and contrary to law. Once you understand the politics, however, you will find that such rulings not only have a logic of their own, they are largely predictable.

The Nature of the Fraud

In order to see how our courts are motivated, you first have to recognize that in domestic relations, judges tend to rule by rote. Whether you are the most involved father in the world or the most indifferent, whether your case costs $3,000 or $30,000, the almost certain outcome is that your wife will get sole custody, and you will get to see your children one night a week for dinner and every other weekend.

This custody-visitation arrangement is known as "standard visitation" because it is handed down so frequently. Moreover, because it is handed down so frequently, many people believe it is written in the law. It is not. A judge can award any custody-visitation arrangement he wants. In most states, the law also provides the possibility for the judge to award joint physical custody and/or joint legal custody instead of sole custody. This allows the courts enormous latitude. For example, a judge could make a 50/50 custody arrangement, or 60/40, or 45/55, or 65/35, and so forth. He could award sole physical or legal custody to one parent, and still give the other parent much more than standard visitation. Or he could award sole physical custody to one parent, while giving the parents joint legal custody with more or less than standard visitation for the noncustodial parent. In other words, there are countless rulings that could be made.

One might think that judges rule with so much conformity because there is a body of sociological and psychological literature that recommends the "standard" arrangement. But the opposite is true. All the major literature on the subject holds that children of divorce do best when they have full access to both their parents and their parents' extended families.[2] Then too, one has to wonder how a judge, or anyone, could discern that one parent rates 51 percent and the other 49 percent, and therefore one parent should have sole custody while the other is reduced to a visitor. In cases where both parents are good and caring parents (which is most cases), the testimonies of individual psychologists are not truly relevant. If there were money enough and time, each party could line up eight psychologists to testify that he or she was the better parent.

Obviously, if judges were making their decisions based on the merits of each case, there would be a wide variation in the rulings. Instead, the rulings come down with numbing consistency. The question that naturally springs to mind is: *If the ruling is a foregone conclusion, why do so many of these cases turn into protracted litigation costing tens of thousands of dollars?*

By way of analogy, imagine if it were discovered that an optometrist in your area had 200 patients a year—and gave them all the same prescription! Of course, everyone would think he was a crook. They would think he was all-the-more a crook if it turned out that he had terrorized his patients by telling them they might be going blind and had brought them in for numerous visits, running up thousands of dollars in bills. There would be a public outcry. The optometrist's license would be instantly revoked, and he would be prosecuted.

Some people feel that a fraud of this proportion is what is going on in our courts, on a nationwide basis, every day, as parents, terrified of losing their children and their livelihoods, are dragged through a court process that seems to be little more than a charade.

Another hypothetical situation further elucidates the chicanery of the courtroom. Imagine that every state legislature passed a statute such as this one:

> § 20-107.x In all custody disputes, the mother shall be awarded sole custody unless she is shown to be extremely unfit (e.g., having a history of prostitution, drug addiction, or mental illness). In cases where the mother is not automatically awarded custody, a heavy burden of proof rests upon the father to prove that the mother is extremely unfit.

Such a law would be unconstitutional, of course, because it is gender biased. But if such a law could be enacted, we would have in law what we already have in fact. And there would be no need to go to court! The legal profession would lose hundreds of millions of dollars a year. The divorce-custody industry would practically disappear overnight.

This is the key to understanding divorce-custody politics. It is an industry that depends on conflict for its livelihood. The judge is the central player. He is the ringmaster in the circus, the one who keeps all the craziness going.

Keeping the Conflict Going

Within the subculture of the divorce-custody industry—among members of fathers' rights, children's rights, and grandparents' rights groups—one increasingly hears the opinion that the judges and lawyers are engaged in racketeering.[3] By now, so many people have had negative experiences with the courts, that this view is edging toward the mainstream. Author Kitty Kelly puts it thus bluntly, "Divorce lawyers have a license to steal." [4] Other critics of our civil justice system have made general observations that apply well to the field of domestic-relations. A George Washington University professor writes:

> The modus operandi of lawyers [is to] seek minor adjustments rather than comprehensive solutions; delay as much as they can; and frequently lay the groundwork for future conflict (which ensures future business for themselves).[5]

Syndicated columnist Robert Samuelson, whose essays appear in the *Washington Post* and *Newsweek* magazine, comes closest to the mark:

> The real issue is that the legal system—and I'm talking mainly about the civil justice system, not criminal law—is increasingly run for the enrichment of lawyers and not for the public. Lawyers have fostered a system that works ponderously, intensifies conflict and creates uncertainty. It's good for business.
> Let's review some facts. In 1991, law firms collected an estimated $100 billion in revenues, up from $10.9 billion in 1972. That's double the growth rate of the total economy. And it only partially covers our total legal expenses, because one-third of lawyers work for companies, government, or nonprofit groups. ...
> Beyond soaring legal costs, *the result is rising fear among ordinary people that they will be entrapped by a legal system that bankrupts and terrorizes them.* Lawyers are giving law a bad name. ...
> Lawyers have an economic interest in generating and prolonging conflict.[6] *[Emphasis added].*

It is also worth noting that between 1960 and 1988 the number of lawyers in the United States increased by 153 percent, while the population increased by only 37 percent. Lawyers tend to have high expectations for the kind of living they should earn, and they cannot obtain that level of income without conflict. There is now one lawyer for every 340 people in the U.S.[7]

Judges are nothing more than lawyers with robes on. And the current culture of litigation would not be possible if *judges* did not make it possible. In domestic-relations, the role of the judge in prolonging litigation is eminent.

We hear constantly that our courts are over-burdened; that a judge's first concern is to clear his docket. But when one goes to court, the opposite appears to be true. The rule of thumb seems to be that *the court favors the belligerent party.* In doing so, it generates work for lawyers and perpetuates its own bureaucracy.

A patent example of this unspoken policy can be found in the way courts handle denial of access (when the mother will not let the father and children see each other). Denial of access is one of the most common reasons fathers come to court initially and the most common reason they return to court. Recall that most cases begin with the mother sequestering the children from the father in some manner (Chapter 3). This happens so frequently because lawyers tell women to do this to ensure that they will win custody. The courts condone this behavior, never holding it as a point against the mother in the ensuing custody litigation. If, instead, the courts considered denial of access as evidence of parental unfitness, then lawyers would be telling women not to hide their children, and a huge number of cases would settle without coming near a courthouse.

More remarkable, perhaps, the courts will seldom enforce their own orders. After a father spends a fortune in court, loses custody, is saddled with extortionary sums of alimony and/or "child support," he has obtained one small item of value—a court order for "standard visitation." But what is this court order worth if the mother violates it? Not much. A famous case is that of baseball player Steve Garvey. Over a ten-month period, he brought 43 contempt charges against his ex-wife, Cynthia Garvey, for denying visitation, before a judge finally imposed a sanction. She spent a night in jail. Thereafter she stopped denying access.[8]

Why did Steve Garvey and his children have to go ten months without seeing each other? How much did it cost the State of California to have all these hearings? How much did it cost Steve Garvey and his wife in lawyers' fees? If the judge had imposed a sanction against Cynthia Garvey at the first hearing, doesn't it seem likely that she would have ceased the hostile behavior immediately?

Prompt firm action would have saved the State of California, and both parents (and, hence, the children), thousands of dollars. The children would have been spared the emotional turmoil of parents at war, not to mention the distress of having their mother put in jail. It seems very likely that a severe reprimand at the first hearing would have prevented this financial and emotional waste.

Many judges who preside over domestic-relations cases were at one time practicing lawyers with domestic-relations as a substantial part of their business. The lawyers who appear before a judge are often his friends and peers. Before becoming a judge, he was probably a member of the same local bar association.[9] A judge thinks like a lawyer (perhaps even like a divorce lawyer). He knows how much a lawyer expects or needs to make on a case, and he is able to size up the litigants for what they are worth.

Because a judge has seen hundreds of divorce-custody cases, both as a lawyer and as a judge, he has the experience to readily determine which party is the "troublemaker." Judges have the knowledge and the ability to nip these conflicts in the bud. Instead, by putting off decisions, or by making decisions favoring the troublemaker, the judge keeps the litigation going.

While this may sound glib, you have to consider that lawyers are aware that judges are violating the law by ruling with gross gender bias.[10] Yet there is no outcry from the bar associations. You would think there would be some outrage—over the blatant display of gender bias, or over the failure of judges to uphold their own orders. But there is none. Instead the local bar associations routinely approve these judges for reappointment, giving them the highest ratings.

However, lawyers are not the only participants in this charade. None of the players in this drama—not the social workers, or the guardians *ad litem*, or the custody investigators, or the mediators—benefits from a case that is quickly resolved.

By prolonging litigation, the judge is simply serving his constituents.

WHY FAVOR MOTHERS?

The tender years presumption, dating to early 1900s, was a legal doctrine that held that the mother was presumed to be the natural custodian of a child of tender years. By the early 1980's, though, all states had discarded the tender years doctrine (the majority of states had done so by the mid-70's), replacing it with "best interest of the child" as the standard for custody decisions. Understandably, there is still a lingering cultural presumption in favor of the mother, and we might expect it to influence some judges in some measure. But it can hardly account for the pervasiveness and degree of bias manifested in courtrooms throughout the country. First of all, as a legal matter, most states include in their statutes a statement prohibiting gender discrimination in custody awards. So judges should be alert to guard against their own prejudices.

Second, at least as much as the average citizen, judges must be aware that the last three decades have wrought expansive changes in the American family profile.

Third, when we consider that a domestic-relations judge sees a great diversity of mothers and fathers, we would expect greater diversity in his decisions. And last, when we consider that fathers who are deeply involved in their children's lives are the ones more likely to seek custody, we should expect a certain tilt in favor of fathers in custody disputes. All things considered, the cultural presumption of mother-as-best-parent cannot account for judges ruling in favor of mothers 95–100 percent of the time.

THE POWER OF FEMINISM

There is a certain popular presumption that because most judges are men, they are more likely to favor men, and because there are more male politicians than female, men have all the political power.

When you reflect on this presumption for a moment, though, it is easy to see why politics does not work this way. For example, Bill Clinton is not gay, but he favors gay rights (in 1992, they gave $3 million to his campaign and provided a 4% voting block). Most politicians are not of retirement age, yet they are highly responsive to the concerns of the American Association of Retired People (AARP). Polls continuously show that most Americans favor gun control laws, yet it took years to pass the Brady bill. As governor of California, Ronald Reagan enacted the most progressive abortion rights laws in the country, and in subsequent years routinely increased spending for them. Yet as a presidential candidate and as president he became staunchly anti-abortion. Similarly, George Bush openly favored legalized abortion, then changed his mind about it.

What all these examples demonstrate is that as a politician you do not have to be something (e.g., gay or old), or even hold a strong personal opinion (e.g., abortion rights) to act that way politically. In America, there are two kinds of political power: organized money and organized people. Where a large, vociferous block of voters exists, politicians will respond. The group that can produce the most petitions, send the most telegrams and letters, organize demonstrations, and make funding contributions, is the group that will get its way.

It is true that most judges are men, as are most politicians. And men are prominent in hundreds of associations like the American Medical Association (AMA), the National Rifle Association (NRA), and the American Bar Association (ABA), to name a few. **But men have no political organization addressing their needs *as men*.** What men's groups there are, are rag-tag armies of fathers who have been driven to bankruptcy by litigation, who are working two jobs to keep up with their child support and alimony, and who face jail if they fall behind.

The women's movement, on the other hand, has been developing for a hundred years and today is a huge steamroller of a lobby with enormous financial resources. These resources are magnified by state and federal funding, and by foundation grants. Every year, women's groups push through new legislation that creates new jobs for women, as well as new commissions, studies, and programs on issues of special interest to women.

Every state has a women's commission, and within most states, nearly every county has such a commission. In the whole country there is only one government-funded men's commission. It opened in Washington, D.C. in 1993.

Currently 620 colleges and universities offer degree programs in women's studies, while over 2,000 of the slightly more than 3,000 accredited colleges and universities in the United States offer some women's studies courses.[11] The propaganda force is immeasurable. Men's studies courses, if there are such things, are rare, and there are certainly no degree programs in "men's studies."

To get an idea of how organized women are *as women*, simply open your local phone book. For example, in the business white pages of Montgomery County, Maryland there are 44 organizations listed that begin with "Woman/Women's"—organizations devoted to the special health, therapy, business, and educational needs of women. The same phone book lists only two such organizations beginning with "Man/Men's."

FORMIDABLE MEDIA PRESENCE

The media presence of the women's movement is formidable. To get an idea of this presence, think about some recent heroines of feminism— Elizabeth Morgan, Jean Harris, Lorena Bobbitt. Elizabeth Morgan brought false child abuse charges against her husband, and then had her parents spirit her daughter off to New Zealand. She was in jail on contempt for failing to produce the child until women's advocates had special legislation passed to get her released. A TV-movie was made about her that transformed her into a saint.

Private school headmistress Jean Harris murdered her ex-lover (the Scarsdale Diet doctor) in cold blood after he jilted her. She was found guilty and served time in prison but was released early when thousands of women wrote to Governor Mario Cuomo on her behalf because she had been "emotionally battered." The battered woman precedent had been set in 1990 by the governor of Ohio, who released from prison 25 women who had been convicted of killing or assaulting their husbands or companions. Each woman claimed that the man had abused her.[12]

Perhaps most astonishing, is the Lorena and John Wayne Bobbitt story. When Lorena Bobbitt cut off her husband's penis in Manassas, Virginia, she received letters of support; the Virginia chapter of NOW set up a support hot line; and women demonstrated on her behalf, claiming it was an important act that called attention to the problem of violence *against women*!

When John Wayne Bobbitt was put on trial for alleged spousal rape, middle-aged housewives stood outside the courthouse selling t-shirts and boxer shorts emblazoned with jokes in blood red ink: "Manassas Virginia, A Cut Above the Rest" and "Manassas Virginia, Don't Cut Us Short." [13]

The problem is not only that women are supporting women under inappropriate circumstances. The problem is also that there are no men supporting men. In addition to being mutilated, John Wayne Bobbitt was subject to national humiliation in jokes told by late night comedians, and repeated in major weekly magazines.

If, instead of Lorena Bobbitt cutting off her husband's penis, the story had been that John Wayne Bobbitt had cut off his wife's breast, does anyone imagine that men would have made a hero of him; or that Jay Leno and David Letterman would have made jokes about the severed breast; or that *Newsweek* and *People* magazines would have run whimsical, pun-filled features?

Remarkably, the above-mentioned women, who might objectively be considered psychopaths, are, under the dispensation of feminism, considered to be victims worthy of our deepest sympathy.

And that is a problem for men in divorce court. Because the media is saturated with the image of woman-as-victim, judges are incapable of viewing male/female relations in any other way. Like every politician in America, judges walk on egg shells to be sure they do not say or do anything "sexist" (that is, against women). A judge will never catch any flak for ruining a man's life, but he could quickly feel retribution if he offends a woman. What the courts are doing, of course, is extremely sexist; it's just that, since the discrimination is against men, no one cares.

One would think that the National Organization for Women (NOW) would be a leading advocate of custody reform. It stands to reason that the more often fathers have sole custody or a shared role in parenting, the more firmly the woman's role in the workplace is established, and the more gender-neutral our social outlook in general. But this is not the case. On every divorce-related issue—custody, child support, alimony, civil protective orders, false child abuse charges—NOW resolutely takes a one-sided position for more money and more control for women.

The women's movement for so long was a movement for equal rights, and so vociferously continues to promote itself that way, that it is difficult for most people to recognize that it is now an advocacy group—like the NRA, or the ABA, or the AARP—whose interests are not equality but a bigger share of the pie for its own constituents and more power for its political leaders.

When talking about feminism today, most people still think in terms of "equity feminism"—the movement of the sixties, seventies, and early eighties that sought equal opportunity in the university and the workplace, and equal pay for equal work. When these goals were largely obtained, the mainstream dropped out of the women's movement, leaving it to the radical element—what academics call "gender feminists,"[14] and what men's rights activists refer to as "misandrists."[15] This element dominates feminist politics today.

The original feminist position, given in Betty Friedan's *The Feminine Mystique*, urged women to stand on their own feet and face life's challenges "without sexual privilege or excuse." It discouraged women from accepting alimony. Today's feminist authors, like Lenore Weitzman, Terry Arendell, and Friedan herself, unblushingly seek to reduce men to alimony slaves. As in every other aspect of today's feminism, women in divorce are portrayed as victims, even though women initiate the great majority of divorces (see note 2, Chapter 3).

Ms. INFORMATION

In her book, *Who Stole Feminism?*, equity-feminist Christina Hoff Sommers reports on a remarkable phenomenon: feminist scholars commonly purvey false or grossly misleading information on gender-related issues, and the major media commonly accept the information without question! Ms. Sommers details numerous examples, three of which I provide below.

- In the early 1990's Gloria Steinem, Naomi Wolf, and Joan Brumberg published books in which they asserted that 150,000 females died every year of anorexia nervosa. That figure, though absurd on its face (it is three times the number of Americans who died in Vietnam in 10 years) was widely repeated in the major media and subsequently published in college text books. In reality, fewer than 100 people die of anorexia nervosa per year. In 1991, according to the National Center for Health Statistics, only 54 people died of anorexia nervosa.[16]

- From 1991 through 1993, newspapers, magazines, and television networks reported that "Domestic violence is the leading cause of birth defects, more than all other medical causes combined, according to a March of Dimes study."[17] Yet the assertion was totally false. The March of Dimes had not produced any study linking domestic violence to birth defects, nor had anyone else. The entire story had evolved out of "misunderstanding" on the part of a domestic-violence advocate, which turned into a rumor within feminist academia, and emerged in the mainstream media as a "fact." When *Time* magazine reported the "fact" in January 1993, the March of Dimes called for a retraction. *Time* printed the correction, but not until December 1993—almost a year later. Again, the assertion is absurd on its face. Ms. Sommers appropriately marvels:

  > Why was everybody so credulous? Battery responsible for more birth defects than all other causes combined? More than genetic disorders such as spina bifida, Down syndrome, Tay-Sachs, sickle-cell anemia? More than congenital heart disorders? More than alcohol, crack, or AIDS—more than all these things *combined*? Where were the fact-checkers, the editors, the skeptical journalists?[18]

- The third example is the one that has come to be known as the "Super-Bowl Hoax."

  > In January 1993, newspapers and television networks were reporting an alarming finding: incidence of domestic battery tended to rise by 40 percent on Super Bowl Sunday. NBC, which was broadcasting the game that year, made special pleas to men to stay calm. Feminists called for emergency preparations in anticipation of the expected increase in violence on January 31.[19]

But again, the story turned out to have no factual basis whatsoever.

I call these preposterous examples to your attention because feminist misinformation, or "Ms. Information" as Ms. Sommers has termed it, has enormous impact on fathers in divorce-custody conflicts. To begin with, the gross exaggeration of the domestic-violence problems has created an environment of extreme hostility toward fathers in court. As you will read later in this book, the false assault charge has become a standard tool for women to use in divorce-custody battles.

There are three other areas of feminist misinformation that directly affect you. One, as we saw in Chapter 1, is the erroneous assertion that men are not discriminated against in court. The purpose of this lie is to diffuse public sympathy for men whose lives are terrorized by the courts. The feminists perfectly well understand the power and control that women are given by the courts. By asserting that there is no discrimination, they help to ensure that legislators make no attempt to correct the problem.

A second area of feminist misinformation is the gross exaggeration of the child-support-collection problem. In 1995, with the onset of the 104th Congress, child support enforcement became a major issue as a key to welfare reform. President Clinton, Secretary of Health and Human Services Donna Shalala, and Attorney General Janet Reno, along with a host of senators and representatives, proclaimed there was a "$34 billion child-support gap"[20] and claimed that stronger child support enforcement measures could remove 800,000 mothers and children from the welfare roles. But the "$34 billion gap" is a fiction. It has its roots in a *hypothetical* model that occurs in a single paper[21] created by a single individual— Elaine Sorensen of the Urban Institute, a liberal think-tank in Washington, D.C. According to the statistics of the Census Bureau and the Federal Office of Child Support Enforcement, the "collection gap" for the period Ms. Sorensen examined was not $34 billion, but somewhere between $3 and $5 billion.[22] Child support enforcement has been ineffective in bridging even this gap, as the Government Accounting Office (GAO) has reported, because 66 percent of unpaid child support is due to the obligor's inability to pay. Further, 73 percent of all child support collections comes from non-welfare cases.[24] Collecting more money from these fathers has no effect on the welfare roles. Nonetheless, based on "Ms. Information," the 104th Congress passed draconian bills to revoke driver's and professional licenses from fathers who fall behind in child support.

The third, and most long-standing influence of feminist misinformation, occurs in discussions about the comparative financial well-being of

WHY MARCIA CLARK AND OTHER PROFESSIONAL WOMEN...

When the divorce-custody case of Marcia Clark (the prosecutor in the O.J. Simpson murder trial) came to public attention, the mainstream media began purveying the myth that fathers who "fought" for custody of their children got *at least* a fair shake in court, maybe better. For example, without citing any source, the March 15, 1995 NBC Nightly News reported that overall "women still get custody 90 percent of the time. But when fathers fight for custody they are winning more than 50 percent of the time."

In Chapter 1 of this book, I amassed a collection of clinical studies which confirm common experience—that fathers are discriminated against in court. In fact, I am not aware of any study that contradicts this assertion. Why then do major media report to the contrary? Where do they get their facts?

The answer is, they don't. This is an ideal example of how "Ms. Information"—the unchecked reporting of false feminist "facts," described elsewhere in this chapter—directly affects men in divorce. In this case, I believe I know the origin of the false fact.

A few months before the Marcia Clark story broke, the *Washington Post* ran a front-page article with a large headline proclaiming, "As Custody Laws Level the Field, Father Often Does Better."[30] It was one of a series of articles that the Post ran about working mothers and custody decisions after a D.C. Superior Court awarded custody to the father in the case of Prost v. Green.

I call attention to this article because at the time it appeared, it was constantly thrown up to father advocates as "proof" that men are not discriminated against in court. The story was picked up by the *International Herald Tribune* and thus circulated around the world. Among men's-rights advocates, the *Washington Post* is notorious for its biased coverage of gender issues Below, I provide an analysis of the above-named article to show how a "respected" newspaper engages in what might be called active propaganda.

Birth of a Feminist "Fact"

As the headline indicates "...Father Often Does Better," the gist of the article is that there is little if any discrimination against men in court. The second and third paragraphs of the article reinforce that assertion:

> Once it was virtually unheard of for a mother to lose custody of her children, and children still end up in their mother's homes without a court fight in most divorces. But when custody disagreements come before a judge, *studies suggest* that fathers are winning at least half the battles.
>
> *That has been true* in a series of recent court rulings.... [Emphasis added.]

The language here suggests that the authors will now reference a series of cases to prove that fathers are winning custody half the time. Instead, they go on to cite three isolated cases in which women lost custody—Sharon Prost from D.C., Jennifer Ireland from Michigan, and Elizabeth Rood of Maryland. Three cases from three separate jurisdictions do not a trend make, much less prove that fathers are winning half the time. Moreover, all of the cited cases had received *national media coverage,* a fact that itself throws the authors' "50-percent" premise into question. Thousands of fathers lose custody every week, and nobody writes about it. But when a mother loses custody, it is, literally, headline news. The media is its own best evidence that a father winning custody is still a "man-bites-dog" story.

...STILL HAVE A 90% CHANCE OF WINNING CUSTODY

The article is not only disingenuous, it is openly deceptive. On the front page, the authors boldly assert that "studies suggest" fathers are winning custody "at least" half the time. Yet, twenty-eight paragraphs later, on an inside page, they acknowledge, "There is very little research on what happens when custody cases end up in court." They then go on to cite not many studies, but *one*. Here, in its entirety, is what the *Washington Post* tells us about this 380-page study:

A California study by psychologist Eleanor Maccoby and law professor Robert Mnookin in the late 1980s found that out of 930 families, only 14 ended up before a judge. In those cases fathers won half.

This is dishonest reporting, with the clear intent of misleading the reader to believe that only 14 out of 930 fathers cared enough to "fight" for their children, and that, for those few, the courts were fair.

Quite to the contrary, the findings of the Maccoby-Mnookin study[31] are consistent with other studies reported in this book. Nowhere does the study say that "only 14 families ended up before a judge." While it does have the remakable figure of only 14 cases (1.5 percent) being *finally* resolved by judicial decision (most studies show 15 to 20 percent).[32] it identifies 50 percent of cases as contested (i.e., having court-related activity), and specifically calls attention to the fact that more than 50 percent were probably contested but could not be identified as such from court records. From their own survey, Maccoby-Mnookin report that, "Nearly 70 percent of responding fathers expressed a desire for a form of residential custody other than mother custody."[33] Further, they report ample evidence of discrimination against fathers:

Our analysis of the cases in which the parents made conflicting physical custody requests shows that the mothers' requests were granted about twice as often as the fathers' requests. ... The most common form of conflict arose when the mother requested sole physical custody and the father requested joint physical custody.

The second most common form of conflict involved each parent requesting sole physical custody. ... [T]he outcome in these cases was *sole mother custody* (45 percent) *four times as often as sole father custody* (11 percent).[34] (*Emphasis added*).

In fact, father sole-custody outcomes were so rare, that in the 50-50 figure described for the 14 cases concluded by judicial ruling, "joint custody" and "sole custody" are lumped together as "father wins," while only sole custody is considered a "mother win."

One further indication of prejudice at the *Washington Post*, is that despite the fact that they have no evidence to prove that fathers are winning half the time, they push the envelope further, asserting that fathers are winning more than half (i.e., "at least half") of custody conflicts. A later *Washington Post* article entitled, "Trials of a Female Lawyer: Should Marcia Clark Be In Court or in the Kitchen?"[35] repeated the assertion:

Actually fathers are winning custody battles at least half the time, according to several studies.

Yet this article cited no study whatsoever.

The reader should consider: If NBC News, the *Washington Post*, and the *International Herald Tribune*, with all their resources, cannot produce a single study to support the assertion that fathers are treated fairly in court, why are they telling us that it's true?

men and women after divorce. The assertion that women are victims in divorce is grounded largely in the feminist myth that the divorced man's standard of living rises by 42 percent in the first year after divorce, while the divorced woman's standard of living falls by 73 percent; a myth that has been repeated so often that it has attained the status of "fact."

However, this "fact" stems entirely from one book—*The Divorce Revolution* by Lenore Weitzman[25]—and is based entirely on one study conducted by Ms. Weitzman. The study was conducted with a highly-selective (i.e., non-random) sample group and is riddled with omissions of essential factors, such as the relative earnings of the parties before marriage, the property settlement in the divorce, and whether or not alimony and child support are being taken into account. Her conclusion, that men should pay women more alimony and child support, is arrived at through fantastic leaps of logic.[26] Eleven years later, Ms. Weitzman acknowledged that her figures were wrong, but by that time they had been reported in, at least, 175 newspaper and magazine stories, 348 social-science articles, 250 law-review articles, and 24 appeals and Supreme Court cases.[27]

Putting methodological error aside, it is amazing that so many people readily accept a statistic that defies common sense and common experience. Daniel Amneus, a professor at California State University at Los Angeles, approaches this feminist myth from another perspective:

> Dr. Weitzman's statistics concerning the ex-husbands' improved and the ex-wife's deteriorated standard of living are spurious. *But suppose they were valid.* What then?
>
> First, it follows that there are excellent economic reasons for placing children of divorce in the custody of fathers rather than mothers.
>
> Second, it follows that during the marriage the husband performed extremely valuable services for the wife, so valuable that when they are withdrawn, her standard of living falls by 73 percent.
>
> (The wife's "unpaid" services to the husband during marriage are frequently referred to in feminist literature as something justifying compensation. How can a woman's standard of living be lowered by 73 percent by divorce if all she is losing is the nonpayment of *nothing*?).
>
> Third, it follows that the husband performed these services at great sacrifice to himself, so great that even with his continued sub-sidization of her by alimony and child support payments, and despite the ex-wife's withdrawal of her "unpaid services" worth $25,000 a year (Gloria Steinem's estimate), his own standard of living, once he is partially emancipated from her, skyrockets by 42 percent.[28]

In brief, if Ms. Weitzman's statistics were accurate, then women contribute *nothing* positive to marriage, and therefore there can be no justification for paying them alimony or giving them custody of the children. In reality, of course, a man derives many benefits from having a wife and children; namely, the joy, love, and emotional security that give his life purpose and is the motivation for the work he does. Contrary to Ms. Weitzman's assertions, the dissolution of a marriage—with the loss of wife and children, and in many cases the loss of the complementary benefits of a second income, plus the turmoil of litigation—rarely, if ever, improves a man's situation. Frequently, it plunges a man into economic and emotional ruin. Nonetheless, the feminist influence on media with regard to divorce, custody, and child support, is so overwhelming that many people are not even aware that there is another side to these issues.

WINNING ISN'T EVERYTHING

In taking this divisive stance, today's feminists have polarized men and women, and made it impossible for them, as parents, to stand up against the predations of divorce judges and lawyers.

Although women almost always win in court, it is often at a devastating financial and emotional cost. Judges are less likely to award attorney's fees to women than they once were, because in many cases they realize that the only person in the relationship left with money is the woman, and the only way the attorney will get paid is if the woman pays. Even feminist Terry Arendell, reporting an interview with a divorced mother, has noted:

> [T]he parents are paying attorneys a fantastic sum for this kind of work. The money should be going to the children's welfare. *This whole business should be taken away from the courts.* The sad thing is that the lawyers are eating up the money that rightfully should be used to raise these children. [Emphasis added].[29]

Not only in monetary terms, but also in terms of the damage they do to their own children—through on-going litigation, through false assault or child abuse charges, and by denying the children their father's love and guidance—women lose enormously in divorce-custody litigation.

• • •

In sum, in forming decisions in custody cases, judges are responding first to the needs of local attorneys to generate fees and the needs of the local bureaucracy (Child Support Enforcement and Child Protective Services) for new "victims." Secondly, judges intuitively recognize that they can only maintain this game (and hence their own jobs), if they do not offend any political power. Because fathers have minimal political power in this realm, and because women have quite a lot, the courts can continue to play their game by rewarding women.

With all these political and bureaucratic forces focussed in one direction, the particular merits of your case appear of small consequence to the judge. But the merits of your case are *a* factor. If your case unfolds with the routine the judge is so used to seeing, you are going to get a routine ruling. If you can make the judge sit up and take notice, then you might be able to prevail.

NOTES

[1] Charles Dickens, *Bleak House* (1853). Published by Penguin Books Ltd. (London, New York, etc.), Penguin Classics 1985 (pp. 603-4).

[2] Levy, op cit. *The Best Parent is Both Parents, A Guide to Shared Parenting in the 21st Century.* This volume provides an excellent introduction to literature on shared parenting. The Children's Rights Council also offers a Catalog of Resources (see Chapter 17 for further information).

[3] My co-author, Mr. Dawes, takes exception to this opinion. Like other lawyers I've spoken with, he believes that the reason judges so often make bizarre decisions is because too many of the people appointed to judgeships are not qualified.

[4] Couric, op cit., p.78.

[5] Levy, op cit., p.15.

[6] Robert J. Samuelson, "Hustling the System," *Washington Post*, December 23, 1992, page A17.

[7] Sources: *Table No. 314. Lawyers—Selected Characteristics: 1960 to 1988* and *Table No. 315. Lawyers, by State: 1970 to 1988.* Statistical Abstract of the United States, 1992, op. cit. For 1960 U.S. population: *The Encyclopedia Britannica,* © 1964.

[8] John Kendall, "Cynthia Garvey Freed After 1 Day Pending Contempt Case Hearing," the *Los Angeles Times,* October 4, 1989, Part 2, p.3.

[9] A local bar association is something like a chamber of commerce. It is not the official organization with power to admit people to the bar or to disbar them. Upon becoming a judge, an attorney must resign from the local bar association.

[10] The Maryland Special Joint Committee on Gender Bias in the Courts (1989 Report) found that 70 percent of female lawyers and 95 percent of male lawyers believed that it is always, often, or sometimes true that custody awards are tilted towards mothers.

Most states have specific statutes prohibiting gender bias in custody awards, and most states have Equal Rights Amendments which also makes this bias illegal.

[11] K. L. Billingsley, "Women's Studies Imperialists," *Heterodoxy*, November 1992, p.1.

[12] Farrell, op. cit., p.261.

[13] Elizabeth Gleick, Rochelle Jones, Mary Huzinec and Jane Sugden, "Severance Pay," *People*, December 13, 1993, pp 92-96.

[14] Christina Hoff Sommers, *Who Stole Feminism? How Women Have Betrayed Women* (New York: Simon & Schuster, 1994). p.16 etc. I do not know if Ms. Sommers coined this phrase, but here she defines the distinction between equity and gender feminists. I had seen the terms used before her book was published.

[15] "Misandry," meaning hatred of males, is a term coming into increasingly common use in men's rights newsletters. It is the inverse of "misogyny"; hence, also, misandric, misandrist.

[16] Sommers, op. cit., p.12.

[17] Ibid., p.13.

[18] Ibid., p.14.

[19] Ibid., p.15.

[20] Stuart Miller, "Times lets Clinton Overstate the Scale of Our Child Support Problem," *The Washington Times,* April 9, 1995 (B2). See also: U.S. Department of Justice, Press Release, December 22, 1994, "Attorney General Reno Announces Plan to Crack Down on Dead-Beat Parents Who Fail to Pay Child Support;" and the Congressional Record for February 1, 1995, "Special Order On Cost-Effectiveness in Welfare Reform: The Issue of Child Support."

[21] Elaine Sorensen, *Noncustodial Fathers: Can They Afford to Pay More Child Support?* Project report, January 1994, produced at The Urban Institute, 2100 M Street, NW, Washington DC 20037, (202) 833-7200.

[22] Department of Health and Human Services, Office of Child Support Enforcement *Seventeenth Annual Report To Congress, For the period ending September 30, 1992.* See also: Stuart Miller, "The Myth of Deadbeat Dads," *The Wall Street Journal*, March 2, 1995 (A14); and Levy, op. cit., p.21 and end note 26, p.116.

[23] Ibid. Miller, *The Wall Street Journal.*

[24] Department of Health and Human Services, Office of Child Support Enforcement, op. cit., p. 52.

[25] Lenore Weitzman, *The Divorce Revolution: The Unexpected Social and Economic Consequences for Women and Children in America* (New York: The Free Press, 1985).

[26] For a full rebuttal, see Jed H. Abraham, "The Divorce Revolution Revisited: A Counter-Revolutionary Critique," *Northern Illinois University Law Review*, Vol. 9, No. 2, 1989, pp. 251-298.

[27] Associated Press, "New study discredits size of 'hit' in women's income after divorce," Washington Times, May 18, 1996 (A5).

[28] Amneus, op. cit., pp. 167-168.

[29] Terry Arendell, *Mothers and Divorce*, Berkeley and Los Angeles (University of California Press, 1986).

[30] Barbara Vobejda, D'Vera Cohn, "As Custody Laws Level the Field, Father Often Does Better," *Washington Post*, November 14, 1994 (A1+).

[31] Eleanor E. Maccoby, Robert H. Mnookin. *Dividing the Child: Social and Legal Dilemmas of Custody*. Cambridge, Massachusetts: Harvard University Press, 1992.

[32] As noted elsewhere in this book, it is true that in a great many cases a judge does not make a *final* ruling because the parties, exhausted by litigation, come to agreement. But judicial prejudice is usually made evident to a father long before a final hearing—for example, at the *pendente lite* hearing, where women virtually always get custody. Nonetheless, the Maccoby-Mnookin report of only 1.5 percent being decided by a judge is so inconsistent with other studies, and common sense that it calls out for explanation, but the authors provide none.

[33] Maccoby-Mnookin, op. cit., p. 99.

[34] Ibid. pp. 103-104.

[35] Marc Fisher, "Trials of a Female Lawyer: Should Marcia Clark Be In Court or in the Kitchen?" *Washington Post*, March 3, 1995 (B2).

CHAPTER 6

BEHAVIOR AND THE SYSTEM

The purpose of this chapter is to explain how the system interacts with the distinct behavioral trends of men and women to produce intensely belligerent custody litigation. By "the system," I mean: the laws, the advice lawyers typically give to women, the advice lawyers typically give to men, and the nearly standard responses one can expect from magistrates and judges.

As noted earlier, the most common scenarios which trigger custody litigation are:

(1) A man comes home one day to find that his wife has moved out and taken the children.

(2) The woman goes to the magistrate and obtains a civil protective order evicting her husband from the house.

(3) The husband and wife have an amicable separation that seems to be working when, out of the blue, the wife sequesters the children from their father.

That custody litigation so often begins with one of these actions is due to the volatile combination of the factors enumerated as parts of the system.

WOMEN AND THE SYSTEM

As discussed in Chapter 3, women tend to seek legal counsel first and tend to vehemently desire sole custody. Hence, the battle usually begins when the woman goes to see a lawyer. It would not have to be a battle, however, except for the advice that lawyers typically give to women.

The first thing a lawyer will tell a client (any client) is that to file for an *absolute* divorce the parties have to be separated for a certain period of time[1] (a year in most states, though only six months in the District of Columbia). These are not really bad laws; they take marriage seriously and presume people need time to give serious consideration before divorcing. However, practically speaking, by the time a party seeks out a divorce lawyer, he or she has already given the matter ample consideration.

By the time anyone goes to see a lawyer about anything, they are usually fed up with their situation. This is especially true in divorce. Other means of resolution have already been tried and failed. Most people have to build up a certain amount of desperation and courage, not to mention a willingness to pay legal fees, before they seek an attorney. Not surprisingly, then, when a woman goes to see a lawyer about divorce she is seeking a prompt resolution. (Her husband may be ready for a prompt resolution as well, but hasn't mustered the courage to pursue it.)

Thus, for the woman still living under the same roof with her husband (as in the first two scenarios described above), the idea of waiting a whole year to file for a divorce is extremely frustrating. Moreover, she may feel that it will be difficult to talk her husband into moving out, which means it could be longer than a year. A woman who does not want to wait a year to obtain the benefits of divorce will want to hear alternatives. A lawyer will then tell her the following.

While waiting for the required period of time to pass, she can obtain a *limited* divorce. A limited divorce is akin to a court-ordered legal separation. People file for a limited divorce when they have not been separated long enough to obtain an absolute divorce but desire immediate relief in the nature of support, custody, injunctions, and so forth. In other words, as far as all the important issues are concerned, a limited divorce *is* a divorce, except that you are still legally married![2]

In order to file for limited divorce, the husband and wife must be living apart. The lawyer will further advise the woman that to ensure she is awarded sole custody of the children, she must already have sole physical custody when she files for divorce.

Practically speaking, this means that the woman must either get her husband to move out, leaving her with the children; or move out herself and take the children. Unless the woman believes that she can talk her husband into leaving, she is stuck with moving out herself, an alternative that is extremely inconvenient. At this juncture, some women express frustration, wondering why the court won't just make the husband move out. Here the lawyer will tell her: "Well, the only way the court will make your husband move out is if he has actually assaulted you, or ... if you *feel* threatened by him. In that case, you could seek a protective order."

By obtaining a protective order the woman can have her husband evicted from the home immediately, the same day the order is issued, within hours. It is a trump card, because in one stroke the woman has created the separation leading to divorce, has effectively won custody, and has obtained possession of the marital home. This is why the protective order is sought so often under false pretenses (see Chapter 14).

In the third scenario, "amicable separation," the couple is already living apart so there is no concern about who will have to move out. Under these circumstances, the wife usually goes to see an attorney because she is planning some major change in her life—like moving 1,000 miles away or re-marrying—and wants to obtain sole custody. Here, as in the other cases, the lawyer will advise the mother that at present she and her husband both have custody, and that to obtain sole custody she must sequester the child. The idea is to create a pattern to prove that she is the sole or "primary" caretaker of the child.

Thus, in all "common scenarios," lawyers advise women to commence divorce proceedings with intense belligerence. These are violent, aggressive acts. Imagine having your children suddenly disappear or to be cut off from them. Imagine being put out of your house at once with no place to live, with little or no time to gather even basic possessions. At this point, the man may also discover that his wife has cleaned out their joint bank accounts.

No matter who you are, your children, your home, and your livelihood are vital interests. Terrorized by the assault on these interests, a father who had previously tried conciliation will now respond with anger. Thus, where a fire of emotions is smoldering, the lawyers pour gasoline, creating a violent conflagration in their first moments on the job. Any hope for a cooperative mediated settlement (as opposed to an adversarial litigated settlement) has now vanished, as all trust between the parties has been destroyed.

The fault here does not rest exclusively with lawyers. None of this would be possible except for the fact that the courts are known to rule with extreme bias in favor of women. Through long experience, lawyers know that few judges will look adversely on a mother's hiding the children from their father. Through long experience, lawyers know that magistrates will issue protective orders to women without evidence. Through long experience, lawyers know that judges will usually uphold a protective order without evidence, and that even if a judge overturns a protective order, no punishment will be imposed on the woman for bringing false charges. Thus, in motivating a woman to hide her children or to file a false assault charge, a lawyer is only acting in conformance with the system.

FATHERS AND THE SYSTEM

As noted, a father usually starts looking for a lawyer after his wife has instigated some action against him. Because of this characteristic reluctance to seek counsel, the prospect of winning custody is frequently already foreclosed to a father by the time he obtains a lawyer.

A few lawyers will give fathers the big picture right away, but far too many create unrealistic expectations. By simply discussing a father's alternatives (e.g., cross-petitioning for sole or joint custody) without apprising him of the statistical improbability of winning, a lawyer creates the misleading impression that winning is a reasonable possibility.

Fathers tend to seek a moderate solution, favoring joint custody. Lawyers tend to respond to a man's moderate attitude with a moderate approach. If the mother has sequestered the children but has not yet petitioned for custody, the father still has the legal alternative of "counter-snatching" the children and suing for custody. Most lawyers will not apprise a father of this alternative, and, in fact, will counsel against doing anything rash. A lawyer may even lead a father to believe that the judge will be angry with the mother for sequestering the children. One phrase you frequently hear is, "Somebody's got to act like an adult in this." All of these things are just what most fathers want to hear because they don't want to fight and they have every faith that justice will prevail in the end.

NOTES

[1] There are grounds that allow one to file for divorce immediately (see Appendix B). Here I am assuming that these grounds do not apply. Adultery is the most common ground used to seek an absolute divorce when the parties have not been separated the required period of time. However, it is difficult to prove, and by the time the parties get to court it is often irrelevant. Consequently, it is used infrequently.

[2] At the end of the required waiting period, your limited divorce does not automatically convert into an absolute divorce. You have to return to court to get the absolute divorce. This is important to know. Some couples, having been to court on one or more occasions, having divided up the property, established custody, alimony, and child support, presume logically enough that they are divorced. But if this was done short of the required waiting period you have only a *limited* divorce. You are still legally married. This can prove troublesome for men ten or twenty or thirty years later, because if you are still married, your wife may be able to make a claim on your income or your pension.

CHAPTER 7

YOUR LAWYER, YOUR ENEMY

Q: *You're locked in a room with Adolph Hitler, Jeffrey Dahmer, and a lawyer. You have a gun but only two bullets. What do you do?*

A: *Just to be safe, you shoot the lawyer twice.*

Q: *What's the difference between a rooster and a lawyer?*

A: *The rooster clucks defiant.*

It is, of course, unfair to disparage an entire profession. Lawyers are as varied as humanity. Some are the proverbial "shysters." Others are people of integrity. Many men and women enter the legal profession specifically for idealistic reasons. In fact, a number of lawyers have provided assistance to me at low cost and free of charge, both in the preparation of this book and in giving advice when I was conducting my own case as a *pro se* litigant.

Nonetheless, there is substantial justification for the popular disdain for the legal profession, and the divorce-custody industry affords abundant examples. The nature of the system is such that it virtually compels attorneys to be deceptive in order to make their living. Young idealistic lawyers are often outraged when they enter the system, but in time they become inured to the absurdities and injustice.

Most of the fathers I have counseled have dealt with several domestic relations attorneys. It is unusual for a father to be pleased with his lawyer in a divorce-custody dispute, especially his first lawyer.[1]

INTERVIEW NOW

If a custody dispute is even a distant possibility for you, you should be interviewing lawyers *now*. As noted elsewhere, most fathers coming into a custody conflict need to find an attorney in a hurry. It may have occurred to them weeks or months before that they should probably talk to a

71

lawyer, but because of the expense and bother they put it off. Finding a good lawyer under any circumstances is difficult. Finding one in an emergency is more difficult because you have to settle on someone quickly. The more lawyers you talk to, the better you will be able to make a choice.

AVOID THIS TRAP

Many fathers hire the first divorce lawyer they talk to. Then, having given the lawyer a retainer, they feel bound to him. There are several practical reasons why it is hard to move on to a new lawyer. One, it may be hard to get the retainer back. Two, once you have paid a lawyer some money, he will probably give you a certain amount of credit; that is, he will work more hours than can be covered by your retainer and then begin billing you monthly. If you move on to a new lawyer, you have to come up with a retainer again, and again you will have the initial expenditure for the time it takes the lawyer to become familiar with your case.

The mystery of the law, and the tendency toward denial, are two other factors here. Since the typical father has no idea what the lawyer is doing, and since he doesn't want to believe he threw money down the drain, he convinces himself that the lawyer is doing a good job. For these reasons, many fathers tend to stay with unproductive lawyers for far too long.

To avoid this trap, avoid paying a large retainer. Some lawyers will ask for a retainer of $3,000 or $5,000. $1,500 is as high as you should go. Never be afraid to bargain. If the attorney asks for $2,000, tell him you will give him a $1,000 retainer and see how things go. Many lawyers are hungry for business and they want to get you hooked in, so chances are good that they will accept your counter-offer. Some lower-priced attorneys will not insist on a retainer, and it is not unusual to start with a retainer of $500.

HOW MOST FATHERS FIND AN ATTORNEY

There are two ways most people find a lawyer: 1) look in the yellow pages, or 2) get a recommendation from a friend. Unless you are talking to a father who has been through divorce-custody litigation, any recommendation is unreliable. For instance, suppose your college roommate is corporate counsel for Exxon. While you know he can't help you himself, you figure he should know someone who's good in the field, so you give him a call. He comes back with the name of the Edward Bennett Williams of custody cases. Yes, EBW costs $250/hour but he's worth it. Your roommate had lunch with him just three months ago. He's a nice guy, you'll like him. Moreover, *Washingtonian Magazine* named him #24 in the top 50 divorce lawyers.

The problem with such a recommendation is that attorneys who are not in domestic relations don't know what makes a good divorce lawyer. The famous ones are not the ones you want. The lawyer who makes the most money is not necessarily the best practitioner—he's the best at making money. Lawyers who frequently appear in local publications are usually people who are good at self-promotion. As with any business, they may send out their own press releases.

Other people who appear in court, such as custody workers, court clerks, psychologists, and paralegals, are also unlikely to provide good recommendations (though an informed paralegal would have the best knowledge). These people have a limited view. They may see an attorney loudly advocate a mother's cause in court and therefore believe the attorney is a vociferous advocate. What they don't realize is that some attorneys, knowing they are likely to win a woman's case regardless of the merits, make a big show to impress anyone in the courtroom. Conversely, knowing that they are unlikely to win a father's case even when the facts are in his favor, they tend to be very tame in court when representing men.

Your attorney may seem like a lion when, in the privacy of his office, he tells you how he's going to advocate your cause. But in front of the judge, he may suddenly turn into a lamb.

How to Find a Decent Attorney

The best way to find a good lawyer is to attend the meetings of a fathers' group. Most metropolitan areas have one or two. Many groups have a different guest lawyer at every meeting. Over time, you will get to meet a number of divorce lawyers, see how they handle questions, and get a feel for their style. Ask the fathers there what lawyers they have used, whether they were pleased with them or not, what results they got, how much they cost, and so forth. If someone has already recommended a lawyer to you, ask the fathers' group if anyone there has ever hired this lawyer or if they know someone who has.

The most important factors in hiring a lawyer, are 1) you have an easy rapport with your lawyer, and 2) your lawyer has a plan. *The plan is the most important thing*, and many lawyers don't have one. After you have described your case and defined your goals, your lawyer should be able to outline a plan of action according to a timetable and be able to give you an estimate of the cost. The plan should be a step by step process like the ones described in Chapter 9.

Some attorneys, especially the big name ones, are so busy that they don't return your phone calls. Some clients, both men and women, believe that this "busy-ness" is a sign that the attorney is truly excellent. So they stick with the busy attorney, only to discover on the day of court that he has no idea what their case is about.

Usually, your attorney should be able to return your phone call the same day. Allow for some leeway; sometimes your attorney will be in court all day or have other obligations. Nonetheless, if your attorney regularly fails to return your phone calls within 24 hours, get a new attorney.

HIRE A LOCAL ATTORNEY

One of the main reasons you want to hire an attorney (instead of representing yourself) is because he's a member of the club. If your attorney appears regularly in the courthouse where your case will be heard, he has probably appeared before most of the judges, and may know one or two quite well. This gives you immediate credibility. It also means that your attorney may know the judge's quirks and prejudices, and he may know how to play off them. Equally important, a judge is not likely to do anything rash when a local attorney is involved.

SHOULD I HIRE A WOMAN ATTORNEY?

There appear to be as many women practicing domestic relations law as men. And, from the number I've met, there appear to be just as many good, bad, and mediocre women attorneys in domestic relations as men.

Some fathers think that it is advantageous to hire a woman attorney because it sends some kind of softening message to the judge (as if to say, "See, I'm part mother too. I have a *woman* attorney.") Perhaps there is some merit in this, but as far as I can tell, the courts rule with such numbing consistency that it is impossible to perceive a difference.

You are doing well if you find one divorce lawyer you really like. If you actually find two who seem equally good, one a man and one a woman, it might give you a slight edge to hire the woman. Still, the most important criteria in choosing an attorney are the ones described above.

DO I NEED TO HIRE AN EXPENSIVE LAWYER?

Here is one question that can be answered unequivocally: **No.** While a high priced attorney may be a competent practitioner, there is absolutely no correlation between success and cost. In fact, the inverse is probably true. I have known far more fathers to be displeased with expensive attorneys than with moderately priced ones. Of the attorneys most often recommended at our support group meetings, only one is priced at $200/hour. The others are in the $100 – $150/hour range. In the Washington area, the top domestic relations lawyers charge $250 – $300/hour. All the attorneys written up in *Washingtonian* magazine have this kind of hourly rate. There is absolutely no reason you should pay more than $150/hour for excellent representation, and it is reasonably possible to pay less.

Some lawyers will tell you that their usual rate is $200/hour, but that they will make an exception in your case and only charge $120. What they mean is they can't really fill their schedule with $200/hour clients, so they'll take you. Again, don't be afraid to bargain. If the lawyer doesn't offer, you can ask for a lower rate than the one he says he usually gets.

There are two outstanding reasons why there is no correlation between cost and success. First, as noted repeatedly in these pages, because the courts rule by rote. You are likely to come out with the same ruling no matter how much money you spend. Second, cost is unlikely to make a difference because most of your lawyer's work is procedural.

Expensive lawyers seek to maintain an aura of mystery. They want to leave you with the impression that the law is so arcane you could not possibly understand what they are doing. But it is not arcane. Your lawyer has to file a petition for divorce, and/or custody, visitation, and support. Whether you pay $250/hour to file this petition or $100/hour makes no difference. The petition will look the same and have the same effect. Your lawyer will have to file subpoenas for documents to get your spouse to produce income information, subpoenas for witnesses, and some motions.

Domestic relations attorneys produce documents like these every day. They usually have templates set up in their word processors so that all they have to do is change a few words and press the button. But with a $250/hour lawyer, it will cost you more than with a $100/hour lawyer.

LAWYER GAMES
The divorce-custody dispute is a shark feed, and your income and assets are what your lawyer is going to be feeding on. That may be how he regards you—as lunch. One of the first things your lawyer will ask you for is an income statement. He needs this to determine property settlement and support payments. But it also helps him to evaluate your income and

assets, as well your ability and willingness to make extended monthly payments after the case is over.

Lawyers tend to prolong cases by counselling moderation and attempting to negotiate between you and your wife. If you and your wife were unable to negotiate a settlement yourselves, you are certainly not going to succeed with two lawyers in between. Lawyers love to get involved in a "correspondence war," writing letters back and forth to argue your respective positions. There is no point in this. Unless the argument is made in front of the judge, it is useless. The correspondence war is simply a means for the lawyers to generate fees. Lawyers may also advise the two of you to seek mediation.[2] It seems like admirable advice, and I hate to tell people that mediation is worthless. But with the playing field slanted overwhelmingly in favor of the mother, mediation is not a likely solution. Mr. Dawes emphatically insists that mediation is a waste of time and money. And from what I have seen, it is hard to disagree with him.

One major problem is that if you and your wife come close to reaching a fair mediated settlement, your wife's attorney may tell her he can win a much better settlement in court. You will not be willing to accept an unfair settlement, so you'll end up back at square one. Another problem is that while mediation is going on, conflict continues to go on (for example, your wife might deny access), and this will engender more costly letters between your attorneys.

As the conflict escalates, lawyers may seek to involve child psychologists, a custody investigator, and a guardian *ad litem*. (A guardian *ad litem* is a court-appointed attorney who, supposedly, has no vested interest and is solely representing the interests of your children.) These players usually situate themselves firmly in the middle, prolonging the litigation while making no contribution to progress. The lawyers, meanwhile, will have to have periodic telephone conversations with all of these people, which means they make more money.

Most lawyers bill by the eighth or tenth of the hour. But a few lawyers bill a minimum of twenty minutes each consultation, so if you have a five minute phone call they will bill you for twenty minutes. If your lawyer does this, get a new lawyer right away.

Lawyers tend to create incomplete agreements which end up bringing you back to court to settle further disputes. Make sure your agreement is as comprehensive as possible (see Chapter 12).

Lastly, most lawyers will not tell their male clients how important the *pendente lite* hearing is. Failing to accomplish your goals at this hearing condemns you to the expensive uphill battle of a full hearing. If, in response to your questions about *pendente lite*, a lawyer tells you, "Oh, don't worry, it's just a temporary hearing," don't hire him. If you have already retained a lawyer who minimizes the importance of the *pendente lite* hearing, fire him and find someone else.

INTERVIEWING LAWYERS

Client: *Would you answer three questions for $500?*

Attorney: *Sure. What are your other two questions?*

These are the basic questions you will want to ask a lawyer:

- How long have you been practicing law?

- What percentage of your business is divorce-custody?

- How long have you been doing divorce-custody work in this jurisdiction?

- Are you regularly in litigation?

- Have you ever won custody for a father?

- If "Yes":
  - How many times?
  - How much did it cost (each case)?
  - Was the mother a fit mother (each case)?
  - Were there extenuating circumstances (each case)?

- How often do fathers win sole custody in this jurisdiction?
  - Could you name some cases?

- How often do fathers win joint custody in this jurisdiction?
  - Could you name some cases?

Regarding the previous two questions: At the very least, the lawyer should be able to provide you with the names of cases he has won for fathers. Any cases that were in Circuit Court will be part of the public record.

- What is your plan for helping me win sole or joint custody?

- If custody seems impossible because of jurisdiction: What is your plan for helping me achieve my limited goals and getting this case closed as quickly as possible?

- How much is your hourly rate?

- How much is your retainer?

- Is the retainer refundable?

SHOULD I HAVE TO PAY TO INTERVIEW?

The highest-priced lawyers usually charge their full hourly rate for the initial interview. Other lawyers will do something like give you the first 20 minutes or half hour free (it will usually take you at least an hour to sketch out your case); or they will charge you half rate for the first hour. You probably will have to pay some lawyers to interview. Father-support groups can be very helpful in this respect. Many hold regular meetings with a different lawyer to answers questions at each meeting. This is a good way to meet a number of lawyers for free.

NOTES

[1] This observation was echoed in an article on the top divorce lawyers in Washington, D.C. (Couric, op cit., p.81). Divorce-attorney Bruce Goldberg is quoted as saying, "It's rare for a lawyer's own client to say thank you."

[2] Some jurisdictions require a few mandatory mediation sessions before the parties can get a hearing date. Because of its official status, this mediation may be more effective. If your jurisdiction requires them, you should make your best effort at these sessions to reach a settlement.

CHAPTER 8

AN OVERVIEW OF DIVORCE-CUSTODY LITIGATION

With your children and livelihood at stake, custody litigation cannot help but be a horribly stressful experience. Part of this stress, though, stems from confusion. You find yourself suddenly thrust into a legal battle with legal jargon swirling around your head like so much mumbo-jumbo. What your lawyer is doing, why he isn't doing what you want him to, what is going to happen next, all blend into a murky fog.

It is not unusual for a father to be on the phone to his lawyer every day just trying to figure out what is going on. Some lawyers are not very good at explaining things to their clients. Others purposely seek to create an air of mystery about the law in order to justify their fees. Regardless, every telephone call to a lawyer costs you money.

This chapter provides a step-by-step overview of the divorce-custody conflict and definitions of the most commonly used legal terms in context. Knowing what your lawyer is talking about and what is supposed to happen next can relieve a large measure of anxiety.

PRE-LITIGATION

STAGE 1. MARITAL CONFLICT
Long before court, the custody battle begins to evolve in the day-to-day petty conflicts of your marriage. After months or years of hesitation and building animosity, one or both of you finally decides to see a lawyer. Chapters 3 and 6 describe typical male/female behavior in these early stages of the conflict; most importantly, that women tend to seek counsel first, and, in doing so, gain a distinct advantage in the ensuing litigation.

STAGE 2. LAWYERS BECOME INVOLVED
Many divorcing couples, initially seeking an uncontested divorce, expect that one attorney can divorce them much as one clergyman or one justice of the peace married them. But in its *essence,* our legal system is adversarial. A lawyer, by most state codes of ethics, is supposed to repre-

sent his clients *zealously*. If a lawyer is zealously representing a woman, he will be telling her to gouge her husband for all he's worth; while if he's zealously representing a man, he will be telling him not to pay a dime. (If the same requirements were applied to marriage—each party having their own attorney before a marriage contract could be signed—very few people would be getting married).

To represent two parties is a conflict of interest, leaving the lawyer open to malpractice claims. This is why, when one party goes to a lawyer and says, "My spouse and I want to get a divorce," the attorney will tell that party that the spouse must have his or her own attorney. Once two attorneys are involved, there is conflict.

There are a few attorneys who act more in the way of mediators. The bottom line, though, is that in divorces involving children, it is unusual to have an uncontested divorce unless the husband signs an unfavorable agreement. For the remainder of this discussion, I am presuming that this is a contested divorce.

Once both parties have lawyers, the first thing the lawyers usually do is exchange letters stating their clients' respective positions. The ostensible hope is to resolve the issue without going to court. On the face of it, this is commendable, as are the lawyers' suggestions that the two of you seek mediation.[1] The problem is that the playing field is not level, and, knowing this, your wife's attorney may provoke her to seek far more than is reasonable. Since you will not be willing to give her more than her fair share, and since you might imagine you can get an equitable settlement from a judge, no agreement will be reached.

The mediation period gives lawyers the chance to get involved in a "correspondence war"—writing letters back and forth to argue your and your wife's respective positions. These letters are pointless because neither one of you is going to change your mind because of a letter a lawyer wrote. But the lawyers make money each time they write, and each time they read, a letter.

A child psychologist may also be brought in during the mediation period. Frequently, the mother's attorney will advise her to unilaterally hire a psychologist to prove that the child is better off with her than with you. The psychologist may invite you to participate in the study. If not, you'll have to go to court to get a mutually agreed upon psychologist.

It is possible to spend a long time and a lot of money on mediation, only to have a lawyer (usually hers) undermine it just when you have reached a settlement. Then you have to go to court and replay the same story all over again. Consequently, there is a popular opinion that mediation and the "correspondence war" are just delaying tactics to generate fees for lawyers. As is evident in Chapter 9, I believe an aggressive strategy, skipping mediation, is the best way to gain quick closure to the custody fight.

However, if in the time you've known your wife she has generally been a reasonable person, and you think you can obtain a reasonable settlement, then mediation is the much preferred way to go—but only prior to retaining counsel.

LITIGATION

Step 1. Petition—How the Court Action Begins

A court action is initiated when one party **petitions** the court to hear its case. In a divorce-custody proceeding, the petition will be "a complaint for limited divorce" or "a complaint for absolute divorce" (see Chapter 6). Your lawyer must go to the courthouse to file the petition. The party who files the petition is called the **Petitioner or Plaintiff.** The party who must respond to the petition is called the **Respondent or Defendant.** If your wife files the petition, then she is the petitioner and you are the respondent. If you file the petition, then you are the petitioner and she is the respondent.

Step 2. Notice

When the petition is filed, a court date is set. This date may be two weeks to two months from the date of the filing. In any event, it must allow ample time for the court official (the Sheriff) or a private process server to **serve notice** on the opposing party. In Maryland and D.C. you must hire a private process server. **Serving notice** means that the respondent must receive official notification that a case is to be heard against him on a certain day, at a certain time, in a certain courtroom.

A respondent must be served notice a certain number of days in advance so that he has time to prepare for the hearing or respond to the notice. A witness subpoena and a subpoena *duces tecum* (subpoena for documents) must also be filed well enough in advance to allow the summoned parties to respond. In many jurisdictions there is a specific number of days within which each of these documents must be filed and served, but generally lawyers do it by feel. Usually filing anything three weeks in advance is sufficient.[2] If you are having an emergency hearing this is not a concern.

The process server serves notice on the party by handing the notification directly to him, or in some cases, by attaching the notice to the door post at the person's home or place of work. If this is done within the allowable jurisdiction within the required time frame, then it is called **good service.** The process server returns a receipt to the **case file** showing good service has been made. If good service has been made and the respondent does not show up on the court date, he can have a default judgment made against him.

STEP 3. THE *PENDENTE LITE* HEARING

The *pendente lite* hearing is the so-called "temporary hearing." It is a brief hearing before a judge where "temporary" decisions are made on custody, child support, and possession of the marital home. Presumably, when complete evidence is presented at the full hearing, the judge may change his mind on any of the issues decided at the *pendente lite* hearing. But this rarely happens, except perhaps to increase child support and alimony. *The pendente lite hearing is the only real hearing you will get.* It is the single-most important event in a custody dispute. See the Introduction and Chapter 9 for details.

STEP 4. DISCOVERY

Discovery is the process by which each party can obtain facts and information about the case from the other party in order to make proper preparation for trial. Discovery can take place before the *pendente lite* hearing, and if you have a good lawyer, he should subpoena all your wife's income information in time to use it at the *pendente lite* hearing.

If you are in Juvenile and Domestic Relations Court (J&DR),[3] discovery is limited. You can subpoena documents such as your wife's income tax statements, her pay stubs, and her bank records. But there is no formal discovery with interrogatories or deposition of witnesses unless both your lawyers agree to it. You may not want to agree to it because it opens a Pandora's box of expense. The disadvantage is that you will not know who her witnesses are until the day of trial.

If you are in Circuit Court, then formal discovery, including interrogatories and depositions of witnesses, is a part of the normal chain of events. **Interrogatories** are written questions which the principals in the case— that is, you and your wife—may be required to answer (if they send you the interrogatories, you are required to answer them). Your wife's lawyer will send you interrogatories which you must answer in writing, and attest by signing a sworn statement that they are true. Your lawyer will send them similar questions. The lawyers will also exchange a list of the witnesses they intend to call, and those will be the only witnesses they can call on the day of court, unless surprise or some other exigent circumstances are alleged. As a general rule, the court will not let "surprise" witnesses in, but the court can do what it wants to.

Prior to the court date, either party may **depose** any of the witnesses. This simply means that you arrange a date to hear a witness's testimony before you go to court. The deposition is usually held in one of the lawyer's offices. The lawyers for both parties must be present along with a court reporter. The lawyer who will be calling the witness asks questions first ("on direct"), then opposing counsel cross-examines the witness. The court reporter records the testimony, which is called the witness's **deposition**. This testimony now can be entered as evidence in court. If while under oath in court a witness gives testimony that is contradictory to his own deposition, it is a good way to discredit the witness.

Depositions are expensive. You are paying your lawyer's hourly rate plus the fee for the court reporter. You may then need a **transcript**, which is a typed version of the witness's deposition. Most court reporting services charge about $3.00 per double-spaced page for a transcript. Usually the parties split the cost. A two-hour deposition can turn into 80 pages of transcript. A few such depositions can become very costly.

Subpoena: a court order for a person to appear at a certain time and place to give testimony upon a certain matter.

Subpoena *Duces Tecum*: a court order compelling production of certain specific documents and other items, material and relevant to facts in issue in a pending judicial proceeding, which documents and items are in custody and control of person or entity served with process.

As with the petition, a subpoena or subpoena *duces tecum* must be filed a certain number of days in advance and must be served a certain number of days in advance in order to obtain good service. A person who fails to respond to a subpoena or subpoena *duces tecum* can be found in contempt of court.

Keeper of the Records: the person at any institution who is responsible for the records, and hence, responsible for vouching for the authenticity of the records. If you have to subpoena documents from your child's school or your wife's workplace, you will also have to subpoena the "Keeper of the Records" to appear in court to testify that these are the real records.

STEP 5. MOTIONS

A motion is a request by one of the parties for the judge to do something in their favor. It is called a motion because you **move the court** to do this or that. It is almost always a formal written request in advance of the court date, with proper notice being given to the other party. The notice for a motion is usually given by mail rather than delivered officially like the petition and the subpoena. But if you are having difficulty getting the party to respond, you can have the notice served officially. Occasionally, a judge will hear an oral motion made in court on the day of the hearing, without notice.

A petition (see item 3 above) is a form of motion; it is the motion that sets the case in action. A motion is usually made within the framework of an existing action or proceeding (the action created by the petition). Some common motions in divorce-custody cases include:

Motion for continuance: When one party or the other is unable to make a certain court date, or does not want to, they will ask the court to *continue* the case to a later date. The party must offer some good reason for why the case cannot be heard on the date that had already been set.

Motion to compel: When a party fails to respond to a subpoena or document request, the other party must file a motion to ask the court to compel compliance. The court may simply order them to comply or may impose a sanction. Frequently a motion to compel is combined with a **Request for Sanctions**, which means you are asking the court to punish the party for not responding to the subpoena in the first place. For example, you might ask the court to award you a default judgment and attorney's fees.

Motion to quash: If one party makes a motion which the other party thinks is inappropriate, or files a subpoena the other party thinks is inappropriate, the responding party can move the court to quash the motion or subpoena. "Quash" means to annul, set aside, or suppress.

Motion for examination by a mental health expert: In divorce-custody hearings, it is commonplace for one party to ask that the other parent, or the children, or both parents and the children be required to undergo examination. The results will be submitted as evidence for the court.

Motion for a paternity test: In order to collect child support, a mother may ask for a paternity test to prove that a certain man is the father of her child. In order to prove that he is not the father of a certain child and thereby not be required to pay child support, a man may seek a paternity test.

STEP 6. HEARING

A hearing is any appearance before a judge or a quasi-judicial officer where you present your case. In some jurisdictions, a quasi-judicial officer called, depending on jurisdiction, a hearing commissioner, a magistrate, or a master, will hear certain domestic relations matters before a judge does. This judicial officer will recommend that an order be signed with a specific result. If one or the other party does not like the recommendation, he may file an exception. If no exceptions are filed, a judge will sign an order reiterating the master's recommendations.

Let us presume that your case will be before a judge.

There can be several hearings on different subjects. For example, there may be separate hearings for custody, child support, property, and alimony. Often property and alimony are decided at one hearing, and custody and child support at another. Equally often, all the issues are decided together. In the course of a custody battle, it is also common to have a number of small hearings leading up to the main event. For example, you may have a hearing on a motion to have the child examined by a mental health expert.

The full scale divorce-custody hearing is the subject here. Such a hearing may last from one to five days or more. In extreme cases, these hearings can take weeks.

At the end of the hearing, you will either arrive at an agreement, which will be read into the record as a consent order; or, if you cannot reach settlement, the judge will decide and enter his ruling as an order.

STEP 7. COURT ORDER

Your case will be settled (or be as close to settled as it will ever be) when the judge signs a court order determining the disposition of all the issues in dispute. There may be several separate orders—one for custody, another for visitation and child support, and so forth—but for simplicity, we will presume here that there is only one order.

The order will be derived in one of two ways. It will be a **consent order** if you and your wife agree to the terms of settlement. If you do not, then the judge will make a **ruling** (that is, a decision), which he will direct one of the attorneys to draft as a written order.

A court order may be made after all or part of the evidence and testimony has been presented at a hearing. Often, after partial evidence and testimony have been presented, the judge will make a "suggestion" as to the custody/visitation arrangement and ask the parties to see if they can come to an agreement. If the parties come to an agreement at this point, then the order is entered as a **consent order.** If the parties do not come to an agreement in the course of the trial, then the full trial will be heard, after which the judge will make a decision and enter his **ruling** as an order.

In terms of effect, there is no difference between a consent order and a ruling. Both have the effect of law. Once the order is entered, if you do not obey its stipulations, you can be found in contempt of court and fined or jailed.

However, there is a large difference between these types of orders. If the order is a consent order, you cannot appeal it because *you agreed to it.* If instead, the judge creates the order by ruling, you can appeal it. There are two reasons why most judges prefer a consent order: 1) it minimizes their risk of being overturned on appeal, and 2) if you *agree* to the order, the judge cannot be held accountable for gender discrimination. The vast majority of orders in divorce-custody disputes are consent orders—but this does not mean that men willingly give up their children. By making "suggestions," the judge can let the litigants know his inclination (which is usually for sole custody for the mother, standard visitation for the father). By his demeanor, he can express his displeasure with the father. Then the father's lawyer, the mother's lawyer, and the guardian *ad litem* will join ranks to browbeat the father into signing an agreement. Your lawyer might tell you something like, "This is the best the judge is going to give you. If you go on with the trial, he's going to be mad. It will cost you more, and he will probably give you less."

It is a tough choice, especially since you may not be able to afford an appeal. But if you do not like a consent order, do not sign it.

If you come to an agreement "on the courthouse steps," then your lawyers will write down the terms of the agreement, court will be reconvened (the judge had been in chambers while you were working out the agreement), and the agreement will be read into the record. Although you haven't signed anything at this point, once it is read into the record it is as good as law. It is best to have your lawyer read the agreement into the record, because if her lawyer reads it, he might change things slightly in the reading which can have a big effect when you see it in writing. If your wife's attorney does read the order into the record, pay close attention to make sure no changes are slipped in. If they are, be sure to have your lawyer object.

If the judge makes a ruling then he will read his ruling into the record.

STEP 8. PRESENTATION OF THE ORDER

After the agreement or ruling is read into the record, one of the attorneys will be assigned to draft the order. Whichever party drafts it will send it to the other for approval. This usually takes place within a few weeks of the hearing. If your wife's attorney drafts it, you have to be sure to read it carefully, because it is possible that he will slip an unfavorable change into it. If you doubt that the written order is accurate, you should get a transcript of the order that was read into the court record.

After you, your wife, and your lawyers agree that the written order is correctly drafted, a court date will be set. You will appear in court again for the **presentation of the order**, at which time your attorneys and the judge will sign it.

It is not essential to have a presentation of the order. Your lawyers could endorse the order in triplicate and mail it to the judge, who could sign it and mail your copies back to you. This is often done.

The court appearance for the presentation of the order is really nothing more than a "billing event" for the attorneys.

STEP 9. RULE TO SHOW CAUSE

After your case is over, your now ex-wife may, contrary to the court order, continue to deny access between you and your children. If she does, you cannot, as many people believe, simply call the police to come enforce the order. What you have to do is go down to the courthouse and file a Rule to Show Cause. This is a standard motion. The clerk will provide you with a form to fill out and you will set a court date for a hearing.

At the hearing, you (and witnesses) will testify that your ex denied access. Your ex must "show cause," that is, give a satisfactory explanation of why she denied access. If her explanation is unsatisfactory, then she will (theoretically) be found in contempt of court, and the judge will impose a sanction. In reality, judges do little to enforce visitation, and you may have to come to court many times before you can get her to stop denying access.

NOTES

[1] A few jurisdictions (that is, a few counties or cities in certain states) have mandatory mediation. If that is true in your jurisdiction, then you and your wife will be required to have several meetings with a mediator (not a private mediator, but a social worker) before you can petition a court for a divorce-custody trial. Under these official auspices, you may have more success with mediation than you would otherwise.

[2] Ask your lawyer about the specific requirements for serving notice in your state. The following examples give you some idea of the variation and similarity from state to state:

In Virginia, 10 days notice must be given for a petition, a motion, or a witness subpoena. This means that the party must receive notice 10 days before the hearing, which usually means you have to file it a few days before that. A subpoena *duces tecum* must be filed 15 days before a hearing, and the respondent must receive 10 days notice.

In Maryland, a party must receive 15 days notice for a petition or motion, 10 days for a subpoena.

In Washington, D.C., because of the backlog of the court docket, it usually takes at least three weeks to get a hearing; service is on a case by case basis. Generally a party must receive 10 days notice on a motion.

[3] The trial forum varies from state to state, as does the succession of courts. In some states, such as Virginia, child custody cases are heard in the Juvenile and Domestic Relations (J&DR) District Court rather than in the Circuit Court. This is problematic for several reasons. In J&DR, custody must be decided separately from divorce, property, and alimony (which means you have to have two trials). Worse, J&DR is not a court of record. This means that if you do not like the outcome of the case, you can take it to the Circuit Court, but you cannot simply appeal the lower court decision. The case must be retried in its entirety. Presently, Virginia courts are being restructured to fold all custody cases into a new Family Court, which will be the equivalent in status to the Circuit Court.

CHAPTER 9

STRATEGIES

The preceding discussions of judges, lawyers, and the behavior of men and women in custody disputes should have, in some measure, prepared you for the following litigation strategies. Because fathers are inclined to moderation, and because lawyers tend to counsel fathers to take moderate action, few fathers coming into custody disputes are willing to accept "activist" advice like that given here, whether it comes from a lawyer or from fathers who have been through the courts.

Each father's situation is unique, of course, and yours will require specific judgments from you and your attorney. One crucial judgment *you* have to make is to evaluate how reasonable or unreasonable your wife is likely to be. If your lawyer knows the reputation of your wife's attorney, he can advise you as to what level of hostility you are likely to encounter. Your lawyer also has to judge the strength of your case and the impression you and other witnesses are going to make on the court. Nonetheless, despite the many unique features of each case, there are only a few broad courses of action available to you.

Earlier I identified the three most common scenarios that commence custody litigation (see Chapters 3 and 6). Accordingly, there are several basic strategies for obtaining your goals. I will discuss a number of basic initial situations, providing strategies for winning custody or obtaining limited objectives, as they apply.

In all cases, you have a twofold objective: to obtain an agreement you can live with, while avoiding a financially devastating protracted legal battle.

HOW TO WIN CUSTODY

As a caveat to this section, it bears repeating that in most states a father has only a remote chance of winning custody *no matter what the circumstances*. Generally speaking, the mother has to be either a drug addict or a prostitute or have a history of mental illness for the court to award custody to a father. And even when one of these circumstances holds true, a father stands only a 50/50 chance of winning custody. Consequently, the plan described here is *not* a guaranteed formula for winning custody. However, it is *the only plan* I am aware of that has, with some measure of consistency, won custody for fathers.

That said, let me add Mr. Dawes' view: A father who applies this strategy has an excellent chance of winning custody. Mr. Dawes has won custody for fathers four or five times a year for 8 years, and all but one of these cases cost under $10,000.

If you know the field, these are extraordinary results. Most divorce attorneys are lucky if they win custody for a father once in ten years, and when they do, it is usually a horrendous case that costs in the range of $50,000.

Oddly, there is nothing unique about this strategy. It is essentially the same strategy lawyers use all the time to win custody for women. What is odd is that few lawyers think to advise men the same way. This peculiarity might provide a clue to how you should behave in your conflict: *If you fight like a man, you are going to lose. If you fight like a woman, you will have a fighting chance.*

A variation of the same plan applies under several circumstances: when the crisis is imminent, when the crisis seems distant, and when you and your wife already have an amicable separation.

I. COMMENCING CUSTODY LITIGATION WHEN THE CRISIS IS IMMINENT

If you and your wife are still living together and your marriage has been teetering on the brink for a while, you should take action immediately. Practically speaking, the court will *never* award custody to a father who does not have physical custody of the children at the time of the first hearing. For most, the first hearing will be the *pendente lite* hearing, for some it will be a hearing following the issuance of an *ex parte* civil protective order (see Chapter 14). If a father has the child with him, he has a chance of winning custody. Therefore, you must have physical custody when the first hearing occurs. This means that you have to either:

(1) Persuade your wife to move out of the house and leave the children with you.

(2) Get a civil protective order removing your wife from the house and restraining her from coming near the children. Or:

(3) Take the children and leave.

Each option will be discussed in turn.

(1) PERSUADE YOUR WIFE TO MOVE OUT

If you can persuade your wife to move out, leaving the children with you, then you are well on your way to an amicable divorce. This does not happen too often. But occasionally when a woman wishes to pursue interests other than child-rearing she will agree to such an arrangement. If your wife does agree, you still have to be concerned that she may change her mind later. After she has moved out for an extended period of time, and you have established a pattern of being the primary caretaker, you may wish to draft an "informal" agreement confirming your status as the custodial parent. By informal agreement I mean an agreement that is notarized but not entered as a consent order by a court (see section III below for more on informal agreements.)

(2) GET A CIVIL PROTECTIVE ORDER

If your wife is seriously unstable, or has assaulted you or your children, then you should seek a civil protective order. You must have evidence, witnesses, and if applicable, testimony from the children. If your wife assaults you and you are injured, have the injury photographed, have it treated by a licensed practitioner (doctor, emergency room, etc.), and obtain documentation from the practitioner detailing the cause of and treatment for the injury.

As soon as you can, go to the magistrate for a civil protective order. If you are not seriously injured you should go to the magistrate *before* you have the injury treated. You don't have to be bleeding to seek a protective order. It's enough if your wife threw the dinner plates at you or the children.

Frequently a magistrate will refuse to grant a civil protective order to a man seeking protection from his wife. This is illegal. If it happens to you, get your lawyer to return with you to the magistrate's office and compel the magistrate to obey the law.

At all times, keep your children with you. If that is not possible, leave them with a close relative or friend, where they will be safe from your wife.

(3) TAKE THE CHILDREN AND LEAVE

The last alternative, preemptively moving out and taking the children, is the core strategy. It is also the most likely alternative for a father. It is not an easy or desirable thing to do. If you and your wife have an amicable arrangement, such action may strike you as being horribly duplicitous. It is. But if you hope to win custody, this is your only chance. If you do not take action, *your wife will*. Usually the way these things play out is that the woman forces the crisis. And by firing the first shot, she wins the whole war. Men who have been the victims of these first-strike tactics sit around at support groups railing against the duplicity of women. That could be you. Or, you could win. If you want to win custody, you have to be belligerent.

Recall several of the rules previously established: the court favors the belligerent; the woman is almost always the belligerent; women usually initiate custody disputes; women usually sequester the children prior to the *pendente lite* hearing; judges rule by rote. What happens here is that by reversing the typical roles, you confound the system.

When the mother takes the child and leaves, it is considered normal. If a father does the same thing, it is frequently characterized as "snatching the child." This has no legal meaning, but this is how the mother's lawyer will phrase it, and the judge may see it that way as well. Most lawyers are so used to operating by these unstated rules that while they routinely advise women to take such action, they will advise a father against it. You must find a lawyer who is willing to support you in an "activist" approach.

WARNING: You can only take the children and leave if no one as yet has court-ordered custody. If your wife has already obtained an *ex parte* order for custody, or if you have already been to the *pendente lite* hearing and she has been awarded temporary custody, you cannot do this. You will go to jail. You may even be charged with kidnapping, and be sentenced as a kidnapper, which would mean a lengthy prison sentence.

You *can* take the children under these circumstances:

- If you and your wife are still living together, you can take the children and move out.

- If your wife takes the children and moves out but does not have an order giving her custody, you can "counter-snatch" the children by picking them up at school or daycare; or, if she lets you have visitation, you can take the children to dinner one evening and refuse to bring them back.

- If you have an amicable separation but see your children regularly, you can pick them up one day and refuse to bring them back.

It is not easy to take a child. You have to be prepared to establish daycare, or a school routine for any of your children who are of school age. If your children are of school age you should try, if at all possible, to make your move in the summer so that you can enroll them in a new school district. If you remain in the current school district, you risk having your wife "counter-snatch" the children. You *can* move to another state, but this may not be practical, because the jurisdiction will remain in the state where the children were resident for the last six months (if jurisdictional concerns are important to your case, see Chapter 13 for a full discussion).

The same day you take the children (or the next day the courthouse is open if you take them in the evening or on a weekend), your lawyer should petition for divorce, custody, and child support, and have your wife served notice. You should set a court date as far in the future as possible. Some lawyers, when petitioning for custody on behalf of a father, do not sue for child support. *Be sure* to include child support in your petition. If you do not petition for child support, the judge will be less likely to take you seriously.

Some lawyers feel that when a father moves out with the children, it is a good gesture to contact the wife and her attorney directly to let them know the children are safe. This may help to put a good face on things in court, but it is not essential. In any event, you do not want to tell your wife where you or the children are, and you do not want to tell her what school or daycare facility the children are attending.

Now, you just sit and wait. Your object is to establish for as long as possible the pattern of being the sole caretaker for the children.

Very likely, your wife will now seek an emergency hearing. Because you have already filed petition, you will be notified (that is, given standard advance notice; a week to ten days in most jurisdictions). So, although this is an *ex parte* hearing, your attorney will be present. This, then, will be your *pendente lite* hearing.

Now you must prepare for the *pendente lite* hearing. Since preparation for the *pendente lite* hearing applies in all cases, it is described in a separate section below.

II. COMMENCING CUSTODY LITIGATION WHEN THE CRISIS SEEMS DISTANT

If you are at a stage in your marriage where you and your wife are not getting along and divorce has been mentioned as a consideration, *now* is the time to see a lawyer. If the two of you are seeing a marriage counselor, *now* is the time to see a lawyer. Under these circumstances, you have a distinct advantage over fathers in other situations. You have the time to establish yourself as the primary caretaker (detailed below). One justification courts use for awarding custody to the mother is that they want to maintain the status quo for the children. If the children spend most of their time with the mother, then she is the primary caretaker. If your wife works full time and spends about the same amount of time with the children that you do, this factor can work in your favor.

In the ensuing months, if your marriage continues to degenerate, you should be establishing a pattern of being the children's primary caretaker. Ideally, you want to establish this pattern for at least six months, but if the crisis is growing imminent (for example, if your wife sees a lawyer), do not hesitate to act. Again, you must be the one to force the crisis. When the time is ripe, take the children, move out, and commence litigation as described above.

III. COMMENCING CUSTODY LITIGATION WHEN YOU ALREADY HAVE AN "AMICABLE" SEPARATION

If you and your wife have an "amicable" separation whereby you have already moved out but she lets you see the children regularly, you have given her the strong suit for winning custody. However, if the two of you are still getting along more or less amicably, this arrangement can work positively for you, whether you want to attempt custody or simply wish to legally establish a visitation schedule.

Fathers in the amicable-separation stage tend to believe that things can go on like this forever. You must recognize that you are in an unstable situation. You may have experienced some belligerence from your wife already in the form of her occasionally denying access. Eventually, she may want to remarry and decide that you don't fit in the new family picture; or she may want to move away for a job or school; or she may just decide it's time to cut you loose. If you simply let things go on as they are until your wife decides it's time for a change, it is unlikely that you will be able to obtain your goals.

As long as you are getting along amicably, try to increase the time you spend with your children. Your wife may see this as a big help to her and let you take them more often. If you can increase your time to the point where your children are spending half or more than half of their nights at your place, it will bolster your chances for winning custody. During this time, you should be doing all the things it takes to establish yourself as the primary caretaker (described below), or at least as one of the primary caretakers.

When you feel the time is ripe, then, as in the other situations, you must take the children and petition for custody. If you see signs that your wife is preparing to take action (for example, she tries to get you to sign a unilaterally drafted agreement or begins to sporadically deny access) then you should make your move.

· · ·

Considering the cost and stress of full-blown custody litigation, and the odds against winning, there is good reason to forgo attempting it. Still, the amicable separation can be a good basis for obtaining limited goals. As long as you are getting along amicably, you should try to establish a formal custody-visitation arrangement. After reading the agreement section of this book, consult an attorney and work with him to draft a custody-visitation agreement. You may want to go the straightforward route, with both you and your wife having representation. However, this may trigger a court battle. Another approach is to try to persuade your wife to sign an "informal" agreement. Do not have this agreement typed on your lawyer's stationery. It should have a look of informality, so your wife will believe it is coming from you rather than from an attorney. Plain copy paper will do. If you think it necessary, you might even type it on notebook paper to make it look very informal. This agreement should provide you with at least enough time with your children to establish joint physical custody. (Different states have different minimum requirements for joint physical custody, ranging from a 30 to 41 percent time share. See the detailed discussion of shared custody in Chapter 11.) This agreement must be notarized, that is, signed by you and your wife in the presence of a notary public.

Recall, as noted earlier, that men frequently sign "informal" agreements, believing they are not binding. I use the term "informal" because, though a notarized agreement has the force of law in other civil contracts, it does not necessarily have that effect in custody disputes. Here is the odd thing: If you and your wife sign a notarized agreement giving sole custody to her, the court will regard it as binding. But if you sign a notarized agreement establishing joint custody or sole custody for you (the father), the court is likely to disregard it, if your wife changes her mind. Only a consent order entered by the court will have real validity, and that means going to court.

So why bother with a notarized agreement at all? Admittedly it is a shaky prospect. But, first of all your ex may believe that a notarized agreement is inviolable and for that reason never take you to court. Secondly, such an agreement can serve as evidence of intent in a later court dispute. If the two of you have abided by the agreement for an extended period of time before going to court (say, six months to two years), the court is more likely to regard the agreement seriously. Lastly, you just might get a judge who strictly respects such agreements.

You may be able to establish de facto joint custody without the notarized agreement, by making sure that several witnesses are aware of the regular schedule you have with your children. Since you have already established separate households, when you get to court, you can represent that you and your wife already had a working joint custody arrangement, that joint custody is the status quo; and for the sake of the children it should not be disrupted.

Establishing Yourself as the Primary Caretaker

To establish yourself as the primary caretaker, you should:

- Take the children to the doctor when they need to go.

- Take the children to the dentist.

- Be in contact with your children's teachers.

- Visit the school.

- Be a day parent occasionally if your children's school has parent assistants.

- Be active in after-school activities—piano lessons, soccer, Cub Scouts, Brownies, etc., and make yourself known to the piano teacher or troop leader.

- Take your children to the library often and make sure the librarian knows you and your children by name.

- **Take pictures.** This is important. Ideally at the *pendente lite* hearing you should have a photo album. But if you are rushed, at least be sure to have a handful of pictures. Pictures of you with the child at all stages of life shows continuity. Pictures of you feeding your child as an infant, and pictures of you with the child at the zoo, the puppet show, etc., are good. Pictures of you cooking for your child would be excellent.

- **Keep a diary.** If you take care of your child on a daily basis, make a log. It does not have to be complicated. An entry could look something like this:

> August 15, 1994: 7:00 a.m. Got up with Johnny. Made breakfast. Dropped him off at daycare. Picked Johnny up at 5:30 p.m. Made ravioli for dinner. Read bedtime story. Wife worked late tonight and went to dinner with friends—she did not get home until 8:30 p.m., Johnny was already asleep.

What you are doing here is establishing evidence and witnesses. Be sure family members and friends see you doing a lot of things with your children, especially things like cooking dinner or taking them to the doctor. Have someone go along with you to the doctor or dentist, so you can testify you've been there. It can prove difficult to subpoena a pediatrician. If you have a regular schedule of caring for your children, make sure your family and friends know about it.

On direct examination, your lawyer should ask you questions about the children's schedule, when you took them to school, who picked them up and dropped them off at soccer practice, what you made them for dinner, and so forth.

On cross examination, opposing counsel may attempt to undermine your credibility with numerous detailed questions about the children. "Does your son take any special medication?" "What is your daughter's shoe size?" "What is the name of your son's teacher?" You should know all these things.

THE LANGUAGE OF THE COURT

When you are speaking in court, you have to tell the judge what he wants to hear. It is not that judges have a checklist of things they want to hear. Rather, there are certain buzz words and phrases used often in court to which judges are responsive.

• The best interest of the child

The most important phrase in custody litigation is "the best interest of the child." To appreciate its importance, it helps to know its derivation.

From 1912 until the mid-1970's, the "tender years doctrine," which presumed that the mother was the best parent for young children, dominated custody decisions. "Tender years" definitely meant children five and under; was frequently considered to mean until age 10; and, as it was usually left to the individual judge, could mean until the "age of discretion" (that is, until the age when the child's own desires would be considered), which might be age 12 or 14. The only way a man could win custody was to prove that his wife was unfit.

In 1953, the legal outlook started to change with the California Supreme Court ruling that: "Each [parent] is equally entitled to custody and no showing ... of unfitness is necessary to enable the court to award custody to one or the other in accordance with what, in its sound discretion, is deemed *the best interest of the child*."

By 1980 the "best interest of the child" had become the dominant principle throughout the country. In terms of who gets custody, the change has not been very meaningful. Instead of awarding sole custody to the mother based on "tender years," judges now hear all the evidence, weigh the facts, and award sole custody to the mother because it's "in the best interest of the child." Nonetheless, this phrase can be meaningful if you put it to good use. It appears in the statutes over and over again. Judges are responsive to it. So...

Everything you or your lawyer say must be phrased "in the best interest of the child." You and your lawyer should use this exact phrase from time to time. For example your lawyer might say, "The best interest of these children can only be served by assuring they have continuous and frequent contact with their father." But more important than literal use is that every time you or your lawyer tell the judge what you want, you explain how it will be beneficial to the children. The judge does not care that you love your children and want to spend more time with them. But if you explain that your children love you, that they are used to spending a lot of time with you, and that their lives will be disrupted by a limited visitation schedule, then he may respond. You also cannot simply present evidence and hope the judge will draw a conclusion. For example, it is not enough to have three witnesses and photographs showing that your wife is running around with several men or selling drugs, you must explain to the court that her behavior has an adverse effect on your children. On a tamer level, for example, suppose your wife is caught up in her career and frequently works overtime, while you work 9-to-5 and are always home to care for your children in the evening. You cannot just relate the facts; you have to draw the conclusion. Tell the judge that your wife is too busy with her work and your children need their dad around to look after them.

• Shared parenting vs. joint custody or shared custody

The terms "joint custody" and "shared custody" appear in the codes of most states, but they set off negative bells and whistles in court because they focus on custody (that is, on who controls the child).

"Shared parenting," on the other hand, reminds the court that the child needs time and attention from both parents, and that neither parent can do the job of both. Neither a judge nor opposing counsel can contest the fact that a child needs both mother and father to share the responsibilities of parenting. Again, when it is recognized that the child benefits from such an arrangement, the judge may take notice.

• Look at the judge when you speak

When you are testifying on the witness stand, look at the judge when you speak. For some reason, probably because this is the way it is done on television, people tend to look straight ahead or speak to the attorney who is questioning them. In divorce court, you have an audience of one—the judge. If you speak to the judge, instead of the lawyer or thin air, you may get his attention. Especially when you have an important point to make—like, "My children need an active father, not just a visitor."—be sure to look at the judge. Eye contact at such a moment is crucial.

• Just say "No."

Men tend to attempt excruciating accuracy in recounting the facts of an event. This is not good in court. You can seriously endanger yourself by getting bogged down in detail, especially if false abuse charges are involved.

For example, suppose your wife represents that you were abusive to her, and she testifies that on two occasions, a year and a half ago, you slapped her around. There is no other evidence than her testimony.

You remember the incidents differently. It was at the time when your marital conflict was peaking. She came home one day and started a nasty argument. You tried to be conciliatory but she escalated the argument, then she slapped you, and you shoved her away. In the second incident, a few days later, she again slapped you. This time you slapped her back and some shoving followed.

What do you tell the judge? *You tell the judge that your wife is lying. That nothing ever happened. That you never hit her, ever, in your entire life.*

Now you might have some compunction about "lying." But this is not lying—it is speaking in the language of the court. Trying to describe something in detail in court is a like trying to describe open-heart surgery with smoke signals. You can't do it. The language of the court is simple. Judges do not like detail. Everything must be painted in very broad terms.

Suppose you do like men usually do and recount every little detail: "Well, I remember it was early in the evening. I had just gotten home from work and I was in the kitchen cooking dinner..." You ramble on for five minutes about how your wife came home, started the argument, the argument heated up, etc. Then you wind up the story: "She grabbed my wrist like this. Then I broke her hold and she took a swing at me. I was mad then, and I just shoved her, like that. And she fell against the table, knocking over the sugar bowl."

A man relates a story like this in detail because he thinks the judge will be impressed with his complete honesty, will recognize the triviality of the incident, and realize the wife was really at fault.

This is not what will happen. If you describe the story in detail, you have given the judge something to *think* about. Now, in a world where judges are hypersensitive to women's charges of abuse, the judge has to decide if there was abuse or not. Then he will have to decide if your behavior in this incident is reflective of the way you behave around the children and if there is danger to the children, and whether or not you should have supervised visitation. Of course, he will not think anything about your wife's behavior.

The constant media barrage vilifying men as rapists, wife beaters, and child abusers has made judges reluctant to ignore any abuse charge no matter how trivial or unsubstantiated. It has also made every man feel guilty, so that they feel compelled to explain every minor transgression. The reality, if you have a case like the one above, is that your wife is lying. The question is not whether the two of you exchanged a couple slaps a year and a half ago. The question is, "Are you an abusive person?" And the answer is "No." Two slapping/shoving incidents in a ten year marriage do not make spousal abuse. Your wife is lying by denying that she hit you first, she is lying by representing you as an abusive person, and she is lying for the purpose of winning custody and a bigger property settlement. So don't confuse the judge with irrelevant details. Just say, "No."

- **Don't say anything nice about your wife**

Remarkably, even when a woman has committed adultery, initiated divorce, hidden the children, and brought a false assault charge, a husband might still retain affection for her; or at least a protective attitude. In the 2,000 divorces he has handled, Mr. Dawes has observed: "Women will tell all kinds of lies about their husbands, but men don't want to say anything bad about their wives even when it's true." Worse, men will often get on the stand and say positive things about their wives.

I have witnessed the same phenomenon. I believe men behave this way because for their entire lives they have been inculcated with the idea that they should protect women and children, especially their own wife and their own children. Consequently, testifying into the public record that the mother of his children is an alcoholic, drug abusing tramp goes against a man's entire moral fabric.

If you want to win custody, you have to put aside such compunctions. If your wife has affairs, does drugs, drinks too much, or abuses the children, testify to these facts. Don't make your lawyer beg you.

If you are like many fathers in divorce you probably think your wife is a terrible mother, but not so terrible you would want your children placed in a foster home rather than stay with her. In other words, you think she is at least minimally fit. Nonetheless, *you should never agree that your wife is a fit mother*. All things being equal, if both parents say the other is fit, the mother will get the child.

If the judge or opposing counsel asks you if you think your wife is a fit mother, do not say yes. Express concern about whatever it is she's doing that is detrimental to the children. For example:

> **Wife's Attorney:** Mr. Smith, would you say that your wife is a fit mother?
> **You:** I don't know. She has a lot of different boyfriends. They stay overnight, and I'm concerned about the effect it's having on the children. (Or "I'm concerned about the effect her drinking is having on the children." Whatever it is she does.)

If your wife's attorney presses you for a yes/no answer, as in "Mr. Smith, could you just give me a simple yes or no answer. Is your wife a fit mother?" Say emphatically, *"I don't know.* I'm concerned about that."

Never forget that you are involved in *adversarial* litigation. The court is not a forum for cooperation. Be mean.

The *Pendente Lite* Hearing

The *pendente lite* hearing can take as little as half an hour, or it can be scheduled for three or four hours. If your wife has physical custody of the children at this point, make sure your lawyer schedules a hearing of at least three hours. If you have physical custody, it probably is in your strategical interest to have a short hearing, but this is a judgment you and your lawyer will have to make, based on the merits of your case.

As noted, if you want to win sole custody, you must have physical custody of the children at the time of the *pendente lite* hearing. For joint custody, the same is more or less true.

But it is not only in the matter of custody that the *pendente lite* hearing is important. If you simply want to obtain a decent visitation schedule you must be prepared to forcefully present your case at the *pendente lite* hearing. *This hearing presents your one chance to obtain limited goals and end the conflict quickly.* Ending the conflict at this point can save you a fortune. Your very financial stability is at stake if you have to go through with a full custody trial. Moreover, the longer the conflict goes on, the more likely something terrible will happen (such as false child abuse charges), and the more likely there will be residual animosity after the court battle is over.

Having read the preceding chapters, you are aware that the likely outcome of your case is that your wife will get sole custody, and you will get standard visitation. Moreover, considering the high cost of litigation and the emotional nightmare it will create for your children as well as for your wife and yourself, it is perfectly reasonable to want to simply accept the standard outcome and live with it.

Unfortunately, it is not possible to say, "Look, judge, all I want is visitation every other weekend from Friday evening till Monday morning and six weeks in the summer. If I can get that, there's no need for all this litigation." For one thing your wife's lawyer will absurdly object that that is too much time and it is bad for the children. The motivation here, besides being vindictive, has a practical side. *The court is like an open air market.* Visitation, child support, alimony, and property settlement are

elements in the bargaining. Your wife's attorney will use visitation as
leverage in trying to get a higher monetary concession from you.

As noted elsewhere, the judge will prefer not to make a ruling but to
force the parties into an agreement, which will then be entered as a consent order. Many cases end with such an agreement instead of a direct
ruling from the bench. This relieves the judge of the onus of ruling
against fathers all the time. Instead he can say, "I didn't order that, they
agreed to it." Nonetheless, the outcome is almost entirely driven by the
judge because in the course of the proceedings he will make comments
and "suggestions" that force you into the ruling he wants to make.

Consequently, most lawyers advise that you must sue for custody in
order to get a decent visitation schedule.

Judges have the habit of handing down a miserly visitation schedule at
the *pendente lite* hearing. The judge may omit mid-week visitation (that
is, Wednesday night dinner), and/or give a weekend schedule something
like from Saturday at noon until Sunday at 6:00 p.m. Sometimes the
weekend schedule is absurdly chopped up. Saturday at 9:00 a.m. until
Saturday at 7:00 p.m. and Sunday at 9:00 a.m. until the next morning. The
reason they do this is so that you have something to come back to court
for. Many fathers who have been denied access to their children for
months prior to the *pendente lite* hearing feel they have won something
even when they come out with such a miserly schedule. And if you have
doubts, your lawyer will represent it to you as a victory. "Now," he'll tell
you, "if we can just get them to stretch the weekend, and get some summer
visitation, we're set." But now you have to go on to a full custody hearing
in order simply to get decent visitation.

At the outset of the hearing, some judges will say, "Look if I make the
decision no one is going to be happy, so I want you to try to work it out
between yourselves." Then, frequently the lawyers will go into chambers
with the judge and come out with a decision themselves. Don't let this
happen. Don't let your lawyer out of your sight. The outcome of this
hearing is going to have long-term consequences, so be sure you are
present for all negotiations.

Optimally you want to come out of the *pendente lite* hearing with joint
custody and the access schedule you desire. If you want to have your
children half the time (or more), you've got to say so, emphatically, here
and now. Hold out for the time you want. But if there is a lot of pressure
for you to yield (from the judge, from your wife's attorney), keep in mind
that the judge will probably not pressure you to take less than standard

visitation. Go for "full standard visitation" (i.e., Wednesday nights over-night and alternate weekends from 5:30 Friday evening until the start of school on Monday morning). As a minimum, you should not settle for anything less than Wednesday night dinner (5:30-9:00) and alternate weekends from Friday at 5:30 p.m. until Sunday at 7:00 p.m.

If you are negotiating (rather than having a hearing right away), your wife's attorney may begin the bargaining by arguing for something absurd like visitation for you every other Sunday from 9:00 a.m. to 2:00 p.m. Or worse, he may propose supervised visitation. You might begin by arguing for the same only in reverse. In any event, you should begin the bargaining by demanding at least a 50/50 time split.

If the judge excludes himself from the negotiations, do not waste too much time on negotiating if your wife will not readily agree to a decent visitation schedule. Go back in and have the hearing.

If the judge is present for these negotiations, your lawyer has to use this opportunity to score points with him. He must say plainly that oppos-ing counsel is ignoring the best interest of the children, fomenting conflict, and encouraging the mother to vindictive behavior. He should be saying something to the effect:

> These children are used to seeing their father all the time. Before Mrs. Jones snatched the children, Mr. Jones was the one who got them up in the morning, made their breakfast, got them off to school. He's been active in their school lives. He takes his son to soccer and his daughter to band practice. He cooks dinner half the time, he spends more time with them than she does. These children need continuity. If you cut their father out of their lives, it is going to have a devastating effect on these children.

As the negotiations continue, and your wife's lawyer proposes other minimal weekend arrangements, your lawyer should remind the judge that the children need a father, not a visitor. That an every-other-weekend visit is not parenting. Uncles and aunts see the children that much. The children need a father who is an active part of their lives. Belaboring these points is important.

At a certain point, as negotiations reach a stalemate, the judge will make suggestions. If he suggests a miserly visitation schedule, your law-yer should remind him that the legislators put shared parenting (joint cus-tody) in the statutes because they believe that children are entitled to continue a full life with *both* parents, even after divorce. And again, that a meager visitation schedule will have a devastating effect on the children.

Your lawyer might say, "If you are familiar with the literature, you know that many children of divorce go through mourning, similar to when someone has died, because they have lost their fathers."

If you are ardent, the judge may tilt your way. He said he wanted the two of you to work things out, and he has spent this much time negotiating, so he probably does not want a hearing. If the judge continues "suggesting" a meager schedule, insist on having the hearing. He may be antagonistic to you at this point, but your ardency is important. If you do not get what you want here, you will have an uphill battle to the full hearing. Not all judges, of course, will start by asking you to negotiate.

Another tactic judges use to get their way without making a ruling is to suggest a visitation schedule, then turn to you, the father, and say, "Is that all right with you?" Most fathers, not having previously given clear thought to the schedule they want, and being intimidated by the court, will simply respond, "Yes." You know what your bottom line is. As politely as possible, tell the judge that his suggested schedule will completely disrupt your children's relationship with you and it will have a devastating effect on them. Then tell him that as a bare minimum—so that the children still feel like they have a dad—you must have [whatever schedule it is that you want]. It is important to include mid-week overnights in the schedule, because taking your kids to school in the morning is an essential part of staying in touch with your children's school lives.

If you come out of the *pendente lite* hearing with the minimum standard schedule or better, your custody battle could come to an early close. Your schedule will not improve if you go to a full hearing, and since it is equally unlikely to be reduced, your wife should be willing to have this schedule entered as a consent order. (It will not happen at this hearing, however.)

At this point, you still have a date for a full hearing set, and you will have to return to court anyhow for the presentation of the order. In the intervening weeks, your lawyer and her lawyer will be in contact. You might contact your wife directly and tell her there is no point in the two of you paying more money to lawyers, the case is over, so you should work out summer and holiday visitation and have an order drafted. Then you will have one of your lawyers draft the agreement.

Child support will also be set at the *pendente lite* hearing, usually after visitation is set. There is a problem here, because summer visitation usually is not set at the *pendente lite* hearing, so you cannot get any adjustment of child support for the time the children spend with you. To qualify for the joint custody adjustment, you must have the children a certain minimum percentage of the overnights (see Chapter 11), and you will need the holiday time and six weeks in summer to come up to that percentage. If you bring up this issue at this point, however, it is sure to engender another fight over visitation. The habit of the courts is to ignore the joint-custody support adjustment anyway. But if you want to try to get it, the thing to do is to let the judge set child support at the *pendente lite* hearing without bringing up the joint custody adjustment (but still attempting to get whatever other adjustments you can). Then get the custody-visitation order drawn up separately from the child support order. When you appear in court for the presentation of the orders, have the custody-visitation order entered first. Once it is signed, you have secured joint custody and/or the visitation schedule you want. Then let your lawyer raise the issue about the joint-custody adjustment to the child support order before the support order is entered.

CHAPTER 10

CHILD SUPPORT OR
GENDER EXTORTION?

"Child support" is a misnomer. The monthly payment you will have to make to your ex-wife until your children are 18 or 21 (depending on jurisdiction) is a pure entitlement transfer. Your ex does not have to provide any accounting for how the money is spent. The basic child support figure is not based on an evaluation of how much it costs to support your children in particular, or how much it costs to support children in general.[1] It is determined according to an arbitrary formula that uses your and your wife's combined incomes as a basis.

Examples and instructions on how to calculate your child support obligation are provided in Chapter 11. You may want to skip to that chapter if all you are seeking is practical advice. However, after you have calculated your support—and after you recover from the shock—you may want to return to this section to learn how it got so bad.

Brief History of the Current Guidelines

In 1984, a Child Support Enforcement amendment to the Aid for Families with Dependent Children (AFDC) program was enacted requiring states to create child support guidelines. Oddly, and obviously, this amendment bore no relation to enforcement. The legislation was driven by feminist groups and vested bureaucratic interests[2] under the pretense that it would help get single-mother families off the welfare roles by making absent fathers pay more. No statistical data available then (or since) indicated that such legislation would have the desired effect. Over half the single-mother families living below the poverty level did not (and do not) have valid support orders, so higher child support guidelines could not help them. Secondly, because most unpaid child support is due to unemployment,[3] and because "most noncustodial parents of AFDC children do not earn enough to pay as much child support as their children are already receiving in AFDC benefits,"[4] higher child support guidelines could not help these children.

Although the guidelines were conceived to help children in poverty, they were illogically extended to *all* child support decisions by the Family Support Act of 1988. By 1989, all 54 U.S. jurisdictions had child support guidelines in place.

Promoted as a program that would reduce government spending, the Child Support Enforcement Program has incurred a continuously increasing deficit. In Fiscal Year 1994, the annual loss to the federal government reached almost one billion dollars ($975,880,363 to be exact).[5]

Not surprisingly, the guideline amendment created no measurable improvement in the lives of impoverished single-mother families. But it did create a windfall of income for middle-class and upper-middle-class divorced women. Concomitantly, many middle and lower income fathers have been pauperized by exorbitant payments.

As illustrated in Example A, the inequity of the guidelines is readily apparent. There is no question as to which parent has the preferred situation. The noncustodial parent not only loses the children but pays more taxes, has less income, and has a much lower standard of living throughout the children's minority. No fair-minded arbiter could have fostered the legislation that produced these guidelines. No individual who believed he or she might one day be subjected to this law would support it.

As economist Donald Bieniewicz has observed,[6] under the guidelines children are considered exclusively to be a burden. While children are not property, they do have an "amenity" value, which is why so many people willingly incur the expense of having and raising children. The typical court award of sole custody to one parent and inordinate financial responsibility to the other is akin to resolving a dispute between two co-owners of a car by awarding one party the right to drive the car six days a week, while the other is allowed to drive the car only one day a week but must pay half or more of all gas and maintenance.

Children, of course, are more precious than any material possession. They are one of life's greatest joys. Traditionally, having children has been a major goal in life for men and women alike. Children are a *vital* interest, as dear as life itself. Common sense tells us this. But if it did not, we need only look around at the many childless couples who go to fertility clinics, adopt children from countries thousands of miles away, or take the extreme measures of seeking artificial insemination from an anonymous donor or seeking a surrogate mother. All of these are endeavors that require tremendous investments of time and money. Lastly, the very fact that our courts are jammed with custody disputes, in which both parents endure financial and emotional hardship, is prima facie evidence that chil-

Example A

EFFECT OF CHILD SUPPORT ON PARENTAL INCOME

PRESUMPTIONS: Couple has two children, ages 4 and 8. Each parent earns $40,000 a year. Virginia child support guidelines are applied.

According to the numerical chart the "*basic* child support obligation" at this income level is $1,278/month. Since the parents make equal income, each owes 50 percent of the basic support obligation. In addition to the *basic* child support, the noncustodial parent pays 50 percent of the work-related child care costs (here, $500 per month or $6,000/yr) and 50 percent of the health insurance for the children (here, $50/mo per child). Thus, the noncustodial parent pays the custodial parent $939/mo [50% x (1,278 + 500 + 100) = $939] and it is *presumed* that the custodial parent spends an equal amount on the children.

Custodial Parent		Non-Custodial Parent	
SALARY	**$40,000**		**$40,000**
TAX LIABILITY (STANDARD DEDUCTION HEAD OF HOUSEHOLD 3 EXEMPTIONS)	– 4,181	TAX LIABILITY (STANDARD DEDUCTION SINGLE 1 EXEMPTION)	– 6,823
+ BASIC CHILD SUPPORT (TAX FREE)	+ 7,668*	– BASIC CHILD SUPPORT (AFTER-TAX INCOME)	– 7,668*
– 1/2 CHILD CARE	– 3,000	– 1/2 CHILD CARE	– 3,000
– 1/2 HEALTH INSURANCE	– 600	– 1/2 HEALTH INSURANCE	– 600
Take home pay	**$39,887**	**Take home pay**	**$21,909**

---

* 1/2 x $1,278/month = $639/month. $639 x 12 = $7,668. For a complete explanation of calculating child support, see Chapter 11.

dren are a vital interest without compare.

If legislators and judges are unconvinced by the evidence of their own senses, they should take note that the U.S. Supreme Court has long made clear that a parent's desire for and right to the "companionship, care, custody, and management of his or her children" is an interest that is "far more precious" than any property right.[7]

With the typical court award, the custody dispute becomes a winner-take-all contest. And the woman is almost always the winner.

Not surprisingly then, for many fathers child support has the feeling of extortion. You have to pay to "visit" your own children. The feeling is magnified when the support award overtly exceeds what it costs to care for the children. When a father has fought an expensive custody battle, when the court has made an inordinate property settlement in favor of the mother, when alimony or the mother's attorney's fees have been added to the father's burden, the additional monthly obligation called "child support" has no such meaning in the father's mind. When a mother denies visitation or relocates to a distance that makes visitation impossible, the idea that the father is paying to care for his children is lost.

The cruelest irony is that in most cases it is the mother who seeks the divorce, while fathers more often seek to maintain the marriage. Many fathers who have lost their children through divorce have no hope of compensating that loss by starting a new family because the financial burden imposed by litigation, alimony, and child support forecloses that possibility. It is not an impediment that can be overcome by making more money. Any time the father gets a raise, the mother can return to court to increase the "child support."

One factor makes the quality of extortion transparent. The guidelines give no consideration to the expense the father incurs when the children are with him. In the daily practice of domestic-relations court, fathers are cut out of their children's lives and designated the role of inanimate funding source. The current guidelines are based on a model which presumes that *all* fathers are deserters and that they spend no money on their children, other than what they pay in court-ordered child support.[8]

The discrimination built into this model has been compounded by discriminatory statutes and by the discrimination of the courts. The guidelines are presented as a rebuttable presumption. They are virtually never successfully rebutted.[9] The guidelines were devised as upper limits, the courts regard them as a minimum level.

The universal practice of ignoring the father's contribution for the time he cares for the children defeats the very premises of the guidelines. In Example A, for instance, the guidelines assert that for parents at this income level it costs $1,875/month (basic support + child care + health insurance) to support two children. The father pays half of this, $939/ month to the mother, and it is presumed that the mother spends an equal amount (thus her total monthly child-related expenditure is $1,875). Logically then, when the father has the children for a month in the summer, the mother should pay him $939. Instead—and this is the universal practice— the father must pay $939 to the mother, plus incur the full expense of the children for that month. If the guideline assertions are accurate, then in the month this $40,000-a-year father has his children with him, he incurs child-related expenses of $2,817 ($939 + $1,875).

The guidelines were enacted at the behest of women's groups, for women, with the knowledge that women virtually never pay child support. Consider these factors: Nationwide, between 95 and 97 percent of the support orders are against men. In the rare cases where fathers obtain custody, the mother is usually not ordered to pay any child support. In the rare cases where mothers are ordered to pay child support, the support order will be substantially lower than required by the guidelines, frequently only a token amount. Women owing support have a higher rate of nonpayment than men. And when women don't pay support, Child Support Enforcement Agencies virtually never enforce the orders against them. When all of these factors are taken together, the number of women who actually pay child support, and the amount they pay, become negligible.[10]

CHILD SUPPORT ENFORCEMENT

Child support enforcement against fathers is unquestionably the most punitive form of debt collection in the United States. Fathers who do not pay can have their salaries garnisheed, the unpaid amounts may be withheld from their federal and state tax refunds, liens may be placed on any and all of their property, drivers licenses and professional licenses may be revoked, direct reports may be made on their credit rating, and they might find their names and faces published on a "10 most wanted" list of supposed "dead-beat dads." Moreover, while for all other situations debtor's prison was abolished in the United States 200 years ago, it still exists for non-payment of child support, regardless of one's ability to pay and even when the ex-wife and children are living in affluence.

DEADBEAT DADS

Nowhere is the prejudice against fathers more apparent than in the media myth of the Deadbeat Dad. Before entering this arena, I too believed that there were legions of callous fathers who ran off to live the high life while leaving their ex-wives and children in dire poverty. Since then, I have learned that:

- Between 80 percent and 100 percent of due child support is paid voluntarily by fathers who are fully employed.[11]

- Most failure to pay support is due to unemployment.[12]

- Willingness to pay child support bears a direct relation to a father's access to his children. The 1992 U.S. Census reported that fathers with joint custody pay 90 percent of child support owed, fathers with visitation pay 79 percent, while fathers with neither joint custody nor visitation pay only 45 percent.[13]

- Deadbeat Dad statistics published by the U.S. government include fathers who are only marginally behind in child support, fathers who are paid up on child support but whose ex-wives have falsely reported them as not paying, fathers who have moved back in with the mother and children, and fathers who are literally dead (according to the Government Accounting Office, 14 percent of "Deadbeat Dads".)[14]

The media has created the impression that it is commonplace for men to desert their families. Inexplicably, they explain, this is just something men do.

It is not, and it is ridiculous to think so.

Abandoning one's children is not a "normal" thing to do. It is natural for a father to love his children. For most fathers only extreme circumstances could force the breaking of this bond. Consider too, how difficult it must be to pick up and leave, not only one's children, but one's hometown, family, friends, and job, and how difficult it is to enter an underground cash economy—all to avoid supporting *one's own children*! Someone would literally have to be crazy to do this, unless there were extraordinary pressures to uproot.

For fathers who have gone many rounds with the courts, lost their children, had their property seized, had their wages garnisheed, and spent time in jail, flight becomes a rational alternative. Deadbeat Dads are men who have "voted with their feet." They would more appropriately be called "Refugee Dads" or "Fathers in Exile."

NOTES

[1] Contrary to popular belief, child support guidelines are based not on the cost of caring for children, but on estimated *expenditures*—that is, how much parents at various income levels typically spend on their children. Making expenditures the basis for child support is a poor premise to begin with, because divorced or separated parents have to bear the cost of two homes, while intact families bear only the cost of one.

More problematic still is the way expenditures are estimated. The child support guidelines for 33 states were determined by Robert Williams of Policy Studies, Inc., Denver, Colorado. Mr. Williams uses the Betson-Rothbarth model, which is based on the Rothbarth estimator, an antique formula used to determine the percentage of family expenditures spent on children. Rather than directly measure expenditures on children, the Rothbarth estimator measures expenditures on alcohol, tobacco, and adult clothing; the expenditures on children are inferred on the presumption that people who spend less on alcohol, tobacco, and adult clothing spend more on children! When it was devised in 1943, when there were not a lot of statistics available on consumer spending, the Rothbarth estimator might have had a limited purpose. Today, with the vast databases of the Consumer Pricing Index, there is no justification for using the Rothbarth formula.

See: "Estimates of Expenditures on Children and Child Support Guidelines," submitted by Lewin/ICF to the Office of the Assistant Secretary for Planning and Evaluation, U.S. Department of Health and Human Services, October 1990.

[2] The legislation received support from the NOW Legal Defense Fund, the National Women's Law Center, the American Public Welfare Association, and the National Council of State Child Support Enforcement Administrators.

[3] This, and much of the information for this chapter is derived from:
Gay, Roger, "A Brief History of Prevailing Child Support Doctrine," *Presentations at CRC's Sixth National Conference, March 1992.* Children's Rights Council, Washington, D.C. Regarding the relationship between unpaid child support and unemployment, Gay cites numerous studies:

Young, 1975, Arthur Young & Company, *Detailed Summary of Findings: Absent Parent Child Support: Cost-Benefit Analysis*, Washington, DC: Department of Health, Education and Welfare, Social and Rehabilitation Service, 4-46, 62-64.

Chambers, D., 1979, Making Fathers Pay: *The Enforcement of Child Support*, Chicago, University of Chicago Press.

Wallerstein, J.S., and D.S. Huntington, 1983, *Bread and Roses: Nonfinancial Issues Related to Fathers' Economic Support of their Children Following Divorce*, in J. Cassety (Ed.), The parental child-support obligation, Lexington, MA: Lexington Books.

Pearson, J., and N. Thoennes, 1986, *Will this divorced woman receive child support?*, Minnesota Family Law Journal.

Sonenstein, F.L. and C.A. Calhoun, 1988, *Survey of Absent Parents; Pilot Results*, Paper presented at the Western Economic Association, Los Angeles.

Braver, Sanford, Pamela J. Fitzpatrick, and R. Curtis Bay, 1988, Non-Custodial Parent's Report of Child Support Payments, presented at the Symposium "Adaptation of the Non-Custodial Parent: Patterns Over Time" at the American Psychological Association Convention, Atlanta, GA, August, 1988.

[4] Garfinkel, Irwin, and S. McLanahan, 1986, Single Mothers and Their Children, A New American Dilemma. The Urban Institute Press, Washington, D.C., 1986, p.24-25.

[5] Department of Health and Human Services, Office of Child Support Enforcement *Nineteenth Annual Report To Congress, For the period ending September 30, 1993* (Table 20, p77). See also the *Eighteenth Annual Report* (p48).

[6] Donald Bieniewicz, "Principles for Guiding Court Intercessions in the Parenting of Non-Married, Separated or Divorced Parents." Working paper for presentation at CRC conference, 1991. Mr. Bieniewicz is author of "Child Support Guideline Developed by the Children's Rights Council," published in the Department of Health and Human Services, Office of Child Support Enforcement, *Child Support Guidelines: The Next Generation*, April 1994.

[7] May v. Anderson, 345 U.S. 528, 97 L. Ed. 1221, 73 S. Ct. 840 (1952).

[8] Gay, op cit. page 25.

[9] Ibid.

[10] As discussed in Chapter 1, the data on child support paid by women to men is so scanty that the 1992 U.S. Census report provides *no* information, though it provides copious information on support paid by men to women. Men pay women an estimated $14 *billion* in so-called child support every year.

[11] "Mothers Say Fathers Unable to Pay," *Speak Out for Children*, newsletter of the Children's Rights Council, Washington, D.C. Winter 1992/1993, Vol. 8, No.1.

[12] Ibid.

[13] U.S. Bureau of the Census, "Child Support and Alimony: 1989," Current Population Reports, Series P-60, No. 173 (Washington, D.C.: GPO, 1991)

[14] "Mothers Say Fathers Unable to Pay," *Speak Out for Children*, newsletter of the Children's Rights Council, Washington, D.C. Winter 1992/1993, Vol. 8, No.1.

CHAPTER 11

CALCULATING CHILD SUPPORT

Despite the huge complexity of the child support laws, child support orders are usually determined quickly, arbitrarily, and with no relevance to the needs of the children or to the real capacity of the father to pay the assigned amount.

Throughout the U.S. there are two principal models for calculating child support—the **income-shares model** and the **percentage-of-income model**. The income-shares model is the most prevalent. It is used in some form by 41 of the 54 U.S. jurisdictions.

Below I give sample calculations for each model, using Virginia as the example for the incomes-shares model, and Washington D.C. for the percentage-of-income model. Regardless of the precise model or laws that apply in your state, it is valuable to read this discussion to become familiar with the basic components of child support; the same issues—e.g., gross income, medical insurance, tax consequences—arise everywhere.

Nonetheless, you must also thoroughly verse yourself in the statutes for your jurisdiction. Ask your lawyer for a copy of the statutes, or go to a university law library and look them up yourself. *It is essential that you calculate your child support obligation yourself, before going to court.* Your lawyer may do a proper calculation, but you cannot depend on it. Compare your calculation to your lawyer's. If you come up with a lower figure, show your lawyer why you think you should be paying less. Be sure he is versed in the key arguments regarding the "adjustments" that apply in your case. If you are not completely prepared for your support hearing, the lawyers will do a superficial calculation, or the judge will do a superficial calculation, and it may result in a payment higher than that mandated by the already inflated child support guidelines.

DON'T BE GENEROUS

Like everyone else, fathers coming into court have been deluded by the Deadbeat Dad myth. Fathers naturally want to be generous with their children, and they certainly don't want to be associated with Deadbeat Dads. Also, most people coming into court trust that the child support tables were created with regard to the real costs of raising children. Often, when fathers hear the astronomical amount of "child support" they are required to pay, they believe that there is something wrong with themselves for thinking it is too much. Thus, the wife's attorney, maybe even the father's own attorney, and the judge, can shame a father into *agreeing* to a sum higher than he can afford. (If you agree to an amount, it is much harder to get it changed, ever.) Only after the emotional turmoil of the trial is over does the father realize that he is not paying to support his children, he is merely giving money to his ex-wife. The more money you pay your ex, the less you will be able to care for your children yourself when they are with you, and the less you will be able to help them directly with college and other costs as they get older. You want to keep control of your money as much as you possibly can. You want to be able to be generous to your children directly. Don't be embarrassed to fight for as low a "child support" order as you can get. Later you'll be glad you did.

NEGOTIATING CHILD SUPPORT

Frequently, the support amount is arrived at not by the guidelines but as part of the total settlement package. Like custody-visitation settlements, these negotiations are frequently conducted on the courthouse steps.

Again, preparation is vitally important. You might have two guideline calculations prepared. One, to go before the judge, which should include all the adjustments (adjustments are described below) you think the judge might realistically consider; the second, which should include every applicable adjustment the statute allows, to be used if you are negotiating a settlement. Remember, the court works like an open air market, and there is always the chance that your lawyer is a better negotiator than your wife's. The lower the figure you use to open the bargaining, the more likely you are to keep the support level down. You might also hold out on some element of the property settlement, later conceding it for a lower support amount. Property settlement is one factor that statutes in some states list as a consideration in determining child support. Although judges rarely consider this factor, your wife's attorney may not know that. Your lawyer may be able to use the law to induce your wife's attorney to make a reasonable settlement.

In some jurisdictions, like Washington D.C., this advice is not relevant because before any consent order can be entered, the court must run the guidelines, and the mother must be advised if the agreed amount is less than the guideline amount.

PRIOR AGREEMENTS

Prior agreements that are not court orders are usually ignored. If you and your wife have been separated for a long time and have your own notarized agreement as to child support, the court is required to consider it in making its determination. However, if your agreement requires you to pay less than the guideline amount, the tendency of the court is to ignore your agreement and raise support to conform with the guidelines.

WAGE GARNISHEEING

At one time, only fathers who had fallen in arrears on child support had their wages garnisheed (withheld), and then only if the mother petitioned the court for such action. However, the federal Family Support Act of 1988 required wage withholding in all new child support orders. States were slow to implement this law because of the administrative complexity involved, but by 1994 most states had implemented it. The only way your wages will not be garnisheed is if your ex signs an agreement providing that you pay her directly. To add injury to injury, some employers charge for the cost of garnisheeing your wages. The charge is usually 2 percent of the total amount. So, if your support order is $600 per month, you might have to pay $12 per month, or an additional $144 per year, for the privilege of having your wages withheld.

MODIFICATION OF THE CHILD SUPPORT ORDER

At a later date, if you seek to have the child support amount decreased, you must make a motion to modify support based on a change of circumstances. Your wife would also have to do this if she wants to have the support increased. The change of circumstances must be substantial. Thus, if you simply make a bad deal in the settlement, you cannot go back to court to have the support level changed, unless you can show that your wife lied in representing factors pertaining to the original order. For this reason, it is important to have documentation of her income, child-care costs, and health insurance. Going in for a change of circumstances is always a risky business. Judges are not very inclined to reduce support obligations, and they are inclined to increase them.

In many states, the age of the child is not taken into account as an adjustment factor. However, if you have pre-school children, your costs are usually much higher because you have to pay for child care. You will probably want to go back to court for a change of circumstances after your children start school, because the change in the support level will be substantial.

THE INCOME-SHARES MODEL

While this discussion is based specifically on Virginia statutes, the laws and practices are similar in other jurisdictions using the income-shares model. As noted earlier, 41 of the 54 U.S. jurisdictions use some form of this model.

With the income-shares model, child support is determined with regard to a numerical chart, based on the number of children in the family and the combined monthly income of the parents (see Appendix C). People refer to this numerical chart as "the guidelines." However the guidelines are actually comprised of the numerical chart plus the cost of health insurance for the child, plus the cost of work-related child care *plus* consideration of adjustment factors. Each state will have its own list of adjustment factors; in Virginia there are 17, enumerated at § 20-108.1.B and § 20-107.2 of the Virginia Code (see Appendix C). These factors *should* be used to adjust the amount prescribed by the numerical chart. As a rule, though, the courts almost always ignore most of these factors. Nonetheless, I discuss some of these factors below. There are two kinds of adjustments: adjustments that apply to your gross income (that is, before the presumptive calculation is made); and adjustments that modify the presumptive calculation itself.

Gross Income

The determination of child support begins with ascertaining the *gross* income of each party. "Gross income" means all income from *all* sources, including such things as bonuses, workman's compensation benefits, rental income, unemployment insurance, gifts, and prizes. Every imaginable kind of payment you receive (like compensation for a car accident) can and probably will be considered gross income.

Proof of gross income is usually determined from recent pay stubs, income tax returns, Schedules C, and forms W-2, 1099, and K-1. Asset statements can also be requested. You and your ex can either produce this material voluntarily, or you can require it to be produced through discovery (see Chapter 8).

There is a problem here. While on the face of it this process is fair, in practice it is not. If your ex does not produce the documents that you have subpoenaed, it is not likely that the court will make her do it. You must be prepared to vociferously protest this violation of your rights. Insist on a continuance until your wife produces the subpoenaed documents, and insist on a suspension (or at least a reduction) of any support order until proper evidence is produced. Raise holy hell about her being in contempt of court for failing to respond to the subpoena. If your attorney simply stands there in shock while the judge rules without evidence, you will be stuck with an unfair support order.

ADJUSTMENTS (DEDUCTIONS) FROM GROSS INCOME

There are a few adjustments from gross income that the court will normally respect. But again, you must fight for these. The judge will not automatically factor in these deductions; he will not even ask you about them. Nor can you depend on your lawyer to do so. You must be vigilant in getting every allowable deduction. The adjustments normally taken into consideration are as follows:

(1) If you are self-employed, you may deduct reasonable business expenses (or "income expended to produce revenue") from your gross income.

(2) If you have to pay your wife spousal support (alimony), you will get a deduction for that.

(3) If you have alimony or child support payments from a previous marriage, these will be taken into account.

(4) If you have remarried and have children by the new marriage, the cost of raising your new children *might* be taken into account. This adjustment is not as assured as the three adjustments mentioned above.

ADJUSTMENTS TO CALCULATIONS

Here, and in the examples, I explain the established practice for calculating child support in Virginia. The established practice does not conform with the statute.

The first step is to determine the basic monthly child support according to the numerical chart. To this figure, add the cost of health insurance for the child and the cost of work-related child care. If appropriate, also add in the cost of extraordinary medical or dental bills (that is, more than $100 for one condition not covered by insurance). This figure, commonly referred to as the "guideline amount," is considered the *presumptive* amount. It is, however, a *rebuttable* presumption. If for any reason the court considers the guideline amount to be "unjust or inappropriate," then it may deviate from that amount (up or down) by taking into consideration the 17 factors enumerated in § 20-108.1.B and § 20-107.2. If the judge deviates from the guideline amount, he is required to make a written finding in the record for why he did so.

As discussed, the presumptive amount is usually not successfully rebutted, because few adjustment factors are ever taken into consideration, and most judges are reluctant to make a written finding in the record deviating from the guidelines (unless they deviate upward). There are a few important factors, though, that might be taken into account if you make an issue of them.

(1) If you pay the health insurance for the child(ren) directly, that amount will be deducted from the total child support. This factor will definitely be taken into account if you bring it up.

(2) (§ 20-108.1.B.15) "Tax consequences to the parties regarding claims for dependent children and child care expenses [should be taken into consideration]." The common practice is that, unless specified in your court order, your wife will get the entire tax benefit for the children, though you may be paying a staggering portion of your income to her every month. Your agreement should specify that either you get the tax credit or that it is traded off every year (get a copy of IRS Form 8332); or the tax credit should be calculated according to income shares and deducted from your monthly support obligation.

Another method of getting the tax credit, is simply to take it when you file your tax return; then defend the deduction if the IRS questions it. I have known several fathers who have done this successfully. The tax code provides that the parent who pays the majority of the child's living costs receives the deduction. (See IRS Publication 504, *Divorced or Separated Parents*.) Note, though, if you do this, you should be prepared to face an audit.

(3) (§ 20-108.2.F) In calculating support, only work-related child care can be included, and "Child-care costs shall not exceed the amount required to provide quality care from a licensed source." This is to prevent gouging. Be sure that your wife does not try to include

baby-sitting costs for times when she is out shopping, on a date, or on a vacation. Also, she cannot seek $600/month to have her maid look after the children when a nearby licensed child-care center only charges $400/month.

(4) If you live a distance of more than 100 miles round-trip from your children, you should receive appropriate reductions for travel related to visitation (car for local, airfare for extended distances) and for long-distance telephone calls to keep in touch with your children.

(5) If your ex remarries, her new husband's income *might* be taken into account.

See Examples 1 and 2 for sample calculations using the income-shares model.

THE PERCENTAGE-OF-INCOME MODEL

While this discussion is based specifically on the District of Columbia statutes, the laws and practices are similar in states using the percentage-of-income model. As with the Virginia statute, adjustment factors are given in the D.C. statute that would rebut the presumption, but as a matter of common practice, these factors are not applied. Also, as with the other model, virtually any kind of income imaginable is counted to your gross income.

Although it would seem that "percentage-of-income" would be a simple calculation, child support is difficult to calculate in the District of Columbia. A sample calculation is given here, but for the most part, people do not perform these calculations themselves. At the D.C. Superior Court there is a computer available which performs them. Anyone can go to the courthouse to use it. You just type in the numbers and the computer will perform the calculation and give you a printout.

See Example 3 for a sample calculation using the percentage-of-income model; and see Figure 1, "Sample Calculation from D.C. Superior Court," for an example of the computer printout.

INCOME-SHARES VS. PERCENTAGE-OF-INCOME

Generally speaking, fathers will have a higher child support obligation under the percentage-of-income model than they do under the income-shares model. To give you some idea of the inequity, I've provided a comparison of Virginia and D.C. obligations. To give you some idea of the quirkiness of this system, I've included one situation (no. 2) where the income-shares model yields a higher obligation. This would change, though, as the children grew older.

COMPARISON OF CHILD SUPPORT USING THE INCOME-SHARES MODEL (VA) VS. THE PERCENTAGE-OF-INCOME MODEL (WASHINGTON, DC)

1. 2 children, ages 4 and 12. Father earns $30,000, Mother earns $25,000. Child care costs are $3,000 annually. Health care not factored in.

Income-Shares	Percentage-of-Income
$670	$690

2. 2 children, ages 4 and 8. Each parent earns $40,000 annually. Father has health insurance of $50/mo per child ($100/mo) deducted from his paycheck. Child care is $500/mo or $6,000 annually.

Income-Shares	Percentage-of-Income
$839	$712

3. 2 children, ages 16 and 18. Each parent earns $75,000 annually. Father has health insurance of $50/mo per child ($100/mo) deducted from his paycheck. There is no child care.

Income-Shares	Percentage-of-Income
$926	$1,169

4. 2 children, ages 4 and 12. Father earns $50,000. Mother does not work. Health care not factored in.

Income-Shares	Percentage-of-Income
$892	$1,342

SHARED CUSTODY CALCULATION
(also called Joint Custody or Shared Parenting)

Having a shared custody arrangement is desirable from every point of view. You get to spend more time with your children, you will have more say in their upbringing, and your child support obligation will be reduced to a level you can actually afford.

Example 4 provides a shared-custody support calculation for Virginia. It starts from the basis of the mother-sole-custody calculation in Example 2. You can see the striking difference in the amount you will have to pay if you have shared custody, instead of your ex having sole custody. Comparing Examples 2 and 4, you see that if your ex-wife has sole custody you would have to pay $682/month, whereas if you have shared custody with a 35 percent "custody share," you would only have to pay $305/month.

CAVEAT

This section explains the arithmetic by which increasing your custody share (visitation) decreases child support. Spending more time with your children and paying less extortion to your ex is probably exactly what you want. Before you become euphoric over this concept, however, you should be aware that while what is described here is legally accurate, it is not likely to occur.

It is very rare that a judge will award joint *physical* custody.[1] Joint *legal* custody is awarded with some frequency, but it serves as little more than a salve to the losing parent (the father). After all, what benefit is there in having "joint legal custody" when your ex moves across country and you only see your children at Christmas and for four weeks in the summer?

Moreover, suppose the miraculous came to pass and the court did award joint physical and legal custody. Would the court enforce its own order? In one of the few cases I am aware of, where a court did award joint physical and legal custody, the mother soon after took the children and moved 2,000 miles away. When the father petitioned for redress, the court did nothing.

The judicial reluctance to award joint physical custody stems in part from legislative reluctance. Assailed by women's groups, the legislators are reluctant to cut into the women's free lunch. Thus, the shared custody provisions in many jurisdictions are designed to make sure that it never happens, and that if it does, the woman will still get a lot of money. To take the worst example—in Washington D.C. you have to have your children with you 41 percent of the time in order to get any reduction in child support. If you only care for your children 40 percent of the time, your contribution is worthless. If by some miracle you cross the 40 percent threshold, they then introduce an "adjustment factor," multiplying your obligation one and a half times before giving you the shared custody deduction. What is the logic behind this? Because, they say, it costs more to maintain two households than one. Of course it does, but it always did. A father is paying all the cost of the extra household when he takes care of his children 40 percent, 30 percent, or 25 percent of the time. The "adjustment factor" makes no economic sense. It is there to ensure that women get money.

In reality, when a father gets joint custody it is almost always because his ex agreed to it, and it is usually because the father agreed to pay the full "child support" for the privilege of having joint custody of his children.

Why bother reading this section then? Because the legal tools are in place to obtain joint custody and to reduce your child support accordingly. Just because it has been a rare occurrence in the past does not mean that you cannot make it happen. If enough fathers fight for it in court, it will become a more frequent occurrence.

DESIGNATION

"Joint custody," "shared custody," and "shared parenting" all refer to the same thing. However, the terms "joint custody" and "shared custody" are likely to set off bells and whistles with your wife's attorney and the judge. "Shared parenting" is by far the best phrase to use in court. "Shared custody" is the phrase most used in the statutes, so I will use that here.

In most jurisdictions, to obtain the shared-custody benefit in calculating child support, your custody arrangement must be designated as shared custody—and it must mean specifically shared physical and legal custody. In a few jurisdictions, though, (Maryland is one) you do not need to have any formal designation. If your visitation time exceeds the threshold, you are entitled to the shared-custody reduction.

THRESHOLDS AND "CUSTODY SHARES"

In order to obtain the shared-custody reduction, you have to have your children with you a certain minimum amount of time. This threshold varies from jurisdiction to jurisdiction. Virginia defines it as "more than

110 days" (30 percent of the time). Maryland states it as "keep[ing] the child or children overnight for more than 35 percent of the year" (128 overnights). D.C. states it as "visitation that exceeds 40 percent of the year" (147 days). Maryland is one of the few states which actually specifies that the "time" with your children is measured by overnights. But almost every jurisdiction uses overnights as the standard measure, so that is what I am using here. (Unfortunately, in 1995, this standard ceased to apply in Virginia.[2])

It is important to be sure you get at least the required number of overnights and not one less, because if you fail to meet the minimum you get no credit whatsoever for the expenses you incur when caring for your children yourself.

Ironically, a shared custody situation actually makes it easier for you to care for your children. The most common variation of standard visitation is to allow you to have your children Wednesday nights for dinner and every other weekend from Friday evening until Sunday evening, plus one month in the summer and certain holidays. Under this common arrangement you already have your children for about 78 nights per year.

$$2 \text{ nights x 26 weeks} = 52 \text{ nights}$$
$$30 \text{ nights summer} \quad + \underline{30 \text{ nights}}$$
$$82 \text{ nights}$$

You might subtract 4 nights to avoid double-counting two weekends in summer, but I am presuming that holidays during the school year bring back those 4 nights. Nonetheless, it is also possible that the mother get a period of two to four weeks in the summer for "unfettered" time, during which you will miss your regular visitation for two weekends. So for one reason or the other, you may have to deduct 4 nights.

$$82 \text{ nights} - 4 \text{ nights} = 78 \text{ nights}$$

Then, dividing 78 by 365 shows that, if you have standard visitation, you presently care for your children approximately 21% of the time and get no credit for it.

Now, if you merely had the most generous version of the standard visitation schedule, you would achieve the threshold number in many jurisdictions. If, instead of Wednesday night dinner and every other weekend from Friday evening to Sunday evening, you had a schedule of

Wednesday night overnight, and Friday evening till Monday morning (taking the children to school), you would get:

Wednesday overnight x 52	= 52 nights
3 weekend nights x 26 weeks	= 78 nights
30 nights summer	= 30 nights
	160 nights

If your ex has 30 days in the summer, then you would subtract 4 Wednesday nights and 2 weekends (6 nights). Even so, you still obtain a 41 percent custody share.

$$160 - 10 = 150 \text{ nights} \qquad 150 \div 365 = 41\%$$

As you can see, there are many other variations that can push you over the threshold. For example, having your children for the entire summer would increase your custody share dramatically.

If your state only requires a 30% threshold, and you have the every-other-weekend-plus-one-month-in-summer standard visitation, you could gain the shared-custody benefit simply by being allowed to take your children to school on Monday morning instead of returning them to their mother's on Sunday night (an arrangement that makes more sense anyhow, and which most fathers seek). By this simple change you would increase your "custody share" to 108 days (29.5% of the time). Add three more days in summer and you have the magic 111 days for shared custody.

The calculations here are by no means incontrovertible. Lawyers will try to interpret these things to the best advantage of their clients. As noted, not every judge will accept overnights as the measure, and will entertain arguments about the definition of a day. But what does "day" mean if the child is in school from 8:00 a.m. to 3:30 p.m. and in extended care till 5:00 or 6:00 p.m., five days a week? Make sure your attorney knows what the standard is in your jurisdiction.

Each jurisdiction also has a clause to the effect that the shared-custody reduction "shall not create or reduce a support obligation to an amount which seriously impairs the custodial parent's ability to maintain minimal adequate housing and provide other basic necessities for the child." This is simply an out for judges to award more money to the mother. You must argue forcefully that there can be no gender discrimination and that it costs you just as much as it costs her to take care of the children.

EXAMPLE 1

INCOME-SHARES CHILD SUPPORT CALCULATION

BASIS: *Each parent earns $40,000 annually. Two children, ages 4 and 8. Health care for children is deducted from Mother's paycheck. Virginia guidelines applied. (Note: In most states, including Virginia, age of children is not an adjustment factor. Here it is provided to establish costs for one child in full-time daycare, and one child in after-school care.)*

Step 1: Calculate Monthly Gross Income by dividing annual gross income by 12. ($40,000 ÷ 12 = $3,333).

Step 2: Add parents' incomes together to get combined monthly income ($3,333 + $3,333= $6,666).

Step 3: Look in the numerical chart in the Virginia Code at §20-108.2 to find the monthly basic support for a couple earning $6,666 with 2 children. Note that $6,666 is not in the chart. You must interpolate between $6,650 (with support at $1,277) and $6,700 (with support at $1,283).
You and your ex supply the figures for child-care expenses and health insurance.

Step 4: Add 3 a, b, and c to get the total monthly child support.

Step 5: To determine the percent obligation of each party divide his or her monthly income by the their combined monthly income (here: 3,333 ÷ 6,666 = 0.5 or 50%).

TWO CHILDREN	Mother	Father
1. Monthly Gross Income	3,333.00	3,333.00
2. Combined Monthly Income	6,666.00	
3. a. Monthly basic child support (for 2 children)	1,279.00	
b. Child-care expenses	500.00	
c. Health Insurance for children	100.00	
4. Total monthly child support	1,879.00	
	Mother	Father
5. Percent obligation, each party	50%	50%
6. Monthly support, each party	939.50	**939.50**

Father pays Mother $939 per month.

Step 6: Multiply the percent obligation by the total monthly child support to get each party's actual cost (0.5 x $1,879 = $939.50). The non-custodial parent (father) pays the custodial parent this amount. It is *presumed* that the custodial parent would spend the difference on the children, bringing her total monthly expenditure up to $1,879.

This example shows how the basic child support was calculated for Example A, Effect of Child Support on Parental Income (see page 109).

EXAMPLE 2
INCOME-SHARES CHILD SUPPORT CALCULATION

BASIS: *Mother earns $30,000, Father earns $40,000. One child, 4 years old. Health insurance for child is $50/month, deducted from mother's paycheck. Virginia guidelines applied.*

Step 1: Calculate Monthly Gross Income by dividing annual gross income by 12. ($30,000 ÷ 12 = $2,500; $40,000 ÷ 12 = $3,333).

Step 2: Add parents' incomes together to get combined monthly income ($2,500 + $3,333= $5,833).

Step 3: Look in the numerical chart in the Virginia Code at §20-108.2 to find the monthly basic support for a couple earning $5,833 with 1 child. Note that $5,833 is not in the chart. You must interpolate between $5,800 (with support at $744) and $5,850 (with support at $749).

Step 4: Add 3 a, b, and c to get the total monthly child support.

Step 5: To determine the percent obligation of each party divide his or her monthly income by the their combined monthly income (here: 2,500 ÷ 5,833 = 0.43 or 43%; 3,333 ÷ 5,833 = 0.57 or 57%).

ONE CHILD	Mother	Father
1. Monthly Gross Income	2,500.00	3,333.00
2. Combined Monthly Income	5,833.00	
3. a. Monthly basic child support (for 1 child)	747.00	
b. Child-care expenses	400.00	
c. Health Insurance for children	50.00	
4. Total monthly child support	1,197.00	
	Mother	Father
5. Percent obligation, each party	43%	57%
6. Monthly support, each party	514.00	**682.00**

Father pays Mother $682 per month.

Step 6: Multiply the percent obligation by the total monthly child support to get each party's actual cost (0.43 x $1,197 = $514; 0.57 x $1,197 = $682. The noncustodial parent (father) pays the custodial parent this amount. It is *presumed* the mother spends the difference on the child to bring her total expenditure to $1,197 per month.

See Example 4 to see how much lower the support obligation would be if the parents had a shared custody arrangement.

EXAMPLE 3

PERCENTAGE-OF-INCOME CHILD SUPPORT CALCULATION

BASIS: *Father earns $30,000, Mother earns $25,000. 2 children, ages 4 and 12. Child care costs are $3,000 annually. Health care not factored in. Washington DC guidelines applied.*

Step 1 — Determining the Basic Support
The first step is to take a fixed percentage of the non-custodial parent's (the father's) gross income. As in Virginia, gross income means every kind of income imaginable.

In the D.C. Code, § 16-916.1, there are four charts for determining the percentage of income to take. The charts correspond to the number of children, with Chart 4 being for four or more children.

In this example there are two children, so you would look up Chart 2. The oldest child determines the percentage of income. Since in this example the oldest child is 12, you look under Ages 7–12 of Chart 2. For an annual gross income of $30,000 with 2 children the required percentage is 30.8 percent.

> **Perform this calculation:** .308 x $30,000 = $9,240. $9,240 ÷ 12 = $770/month.

If the mother does not work, there would be no child care. Hence this would be the total calculation for child support.

Step 2—Reduction for Mother's Income
Since in this example the custodial parent (the mother) does work, the noncustodial parent (the father) receives a reduction from the full percentage, according to a formula that takes into account the mother's income, the "threshold amount," and the cost of work-related child care.

The idea of the "threshold amount" is that this amount of the mother's income is disregarded because she is *presumed* to spend this much on her children. The threshold amount is $16,500 for one child plus $2,000 for each additional child.

The reduction formula is:

$$\frac{\text{Mother's income} - \text{threshold amount} - \text{child care}}{\text{Father's income} + (\text{Mother's income} - \text{threshold amount} - \text{child care})}$$

The mother's income is $25,000. Since there are 2 children, the threshold amount here is $16,500 + $2,000 = $18,500. The cost of child care is $3,000 annually.

$$\frac{\$25,000 - \$18,500 - \$3,000}{\$30,000 + (\$25,000 - \$18,500 - \$3,000)} = \frac{\$3,500}{\$33,500} = 10\%$$

Therefore the father's monthly payment (determined in Step 1) will be reduced by 10 percent.

> $770 – (.10 x $770) = $770 – $77 = **$693/month.**
>
> **Father pays mother $693 per month.**

(See the monthly figure in D.C. computer calculation in Figure 1; it is slightly different, $690.)

(continued on next page)

EXAMPLE 3—PERCENTAGE-OF-INCOME CHILD SUPPORT CALCULATION (continued)

Health Insurance Adjustment

If the father pays the health insurance directly, that amount would be deducted from his annual income before the Step 1 calculation was made. For example, if he paid $50/month per child, that would be $100/month or $1,200 annually.

$30,000 – $1,200 = $28,800.   .308 x $28,800 = $8,870.

$8,870 ÷ 12 = <u>$739/month</u>. This figure would then be used in the Step 2 calculations. In this case it would result in an 11% or $81 reduction. So $739 - $81 = <u>$658/month</u>.

Other Adjustments

The D.C. Code at § 16-916.1 (l) 1–8 provides eight factors for adjusting the payment (similar to the 17 factors provided in the Virginia Code). Generally the judge is not going to be interested in them unless it is to *increase* child support.

D.C. also has special provisions for determining child support when the mother has children by several different fathers. This may help to reduce your support payment. In the computer calculation it is the entry for "Multiple Family."

D.C. also has special provisions for determining child support if you (the father) have other children living in your household with you.

FIGURE 1
SAMPLE COMPUTER CALCULATION FROM D.C. SUPERIOR COURT

```
                        NEW CHILD SUPPORT GUIDELINES WORKSHEET
                        (Enter all data *ANNUALIZED* with no commas)


    NON-CUSTODIAL PARENT:      GROSS INCOME:                       $ 30000
                                 OTHER CHILD SUPPORT PAID:         $
                                 HEALTH INS. PAID FOR CHILDR.:     $
    CUSTODIAL PARENT:          GROSS INCOME:                       $25000
                                 CHILD CARE COST                   $ 3000
    CHILDREN:                  NO. CHILDREN SUPPORTED:                2
                                 AGE OF OLDEST CHILD:                12
    (MULTIPLE FAMILY ONLY:  ENTER NO. CHILDREN WITH CUSTODIAL PARENT: )
    ---------------------------------------------------------------------
              GUIDELINE     HIGH      LOW    :  GUIDELINE PERCENTAGE:    .308
                                             :
    YEARLY     $8,275     $9,175    $7,375   :  ADJUSTED INCOME:      $ 30,000
                                             :
    MONTHLY     $690       $765      $615    :  BASIC SUPPORT:        $  9,240
                                             :
    BIWEEKLY    $318       $353      $284    :  OFFSET:               $    965
                                             :
    WEEKLY      $159       $176      $142    :  ADJUSTED SUPPORT:     $  8,275
```

EXAMPLE 4

Income-Shares Child Support Calculation with SHARED CUSTODY ADJUSTMENT
(also called Shared Parenting or Joint Custody)

BASIS: *Mother earns $30,000/year; Father earns $40,000/year. One child, 4 years old. Health insurance for child is deducted from mother's paycheck. Mother's "custody share" is 65%; Father's 35%.*

This shared custody example is based on Example 2. To calculate child support in a shared custody situation, you first perform the standard child support calculation. In Example 2, it was established that the Mother's percent obligation is 43%, and the Father's is 57%.

In shared custody neither parent is considered the custodial parent. So child support is calculated on the premise that each parent owes the other his or her "income share" multiplied by his or her "custody share" (the amount of time each parent cares for the child). The one who owes more pays the other the difference. There is also a "shared custody adjustment factor."

Step 1: Determine the Adjusted Total Monthly Support. Multiply the basic child support by the "shared custody adjustment factor" (in Virginia 1.25). 1.25 x $747 = $934. Add health insurance and childcare expenses to get Adjusted Total Monthly Support. Add cost of child's health insurance and work related child care.

Step 2: Determine each party's income share by multiplying the adjusted total support by each party's percent obligation (mother's is 43%; father's is 57%).
0.43 x $1,384 = $595.
0.57 x $1,384 = $789.

Step 3: Since the father's custody share is 35%, mother owes father 35% of her income-share obligation.
0.35 x $595 = $208.

The mother's custody share is 65%, so father owes mother 65% of his income-share obligation.
0.65 x $789 = $513.

Step 4: The one who owes more pays the other the difference.
$513 – $208 = $305. Father pays mother $305/month.

SHARED CUSTODY ADJUSTMENT		1 child
1. Multiply the basic monthly child support (from Example 2) by the "shared custody adjustment factor."		$747.00
		x 1.25
		$934.00
Health Insurance (from Example 2)		50.00
Child Care (from Example 2)		400.00
Adjusted Total Monthly Support		$1,384.00
	Mother	**Father**
2. Percent obligation (from Example 2)	43%	57%
Monthly support (Income-share obligation)	$595.00	$789.00
3. Multiply each parent's income share by the other parent's custody share.	$595.00	$789.00
	x.35	x.65
	208.00	513.00
4. Income share obligation	$208	$513

$513 – $208 = $305. **Father pays mother $305/month.**

NOTES

[1] Many states now have some kind of presumptive joint custody law: Connecticut, Florida, Idaho, Iowa, Louisiana, Maine, Massachusetts, Michigan, Minnesota, New Hampshire, New Mexico, Oregon, and Utah. However, most of these laws include restrictions such as "if agreed to by both parties." The statutes of other states—Kansas, Mississippi, Missouri, Montana, Oklahoma—express a preference for joint custody.
In 1995, Texas enacted both presumptive joint custody and a 34 percent minimum visitation law. In 1996, Washington D.C. enacted a presumption for joint custody. This legislation definitely marks a turn for the better, but it is yet to be seen what concrete effect these new laws will have on custody decisions and child support orders.

[2] In *Ewing v. Ewing*, 21 Va. App. 34 (1995), the en banc Court of Appeals said that for the support calculation, a "day" is a "continuous 24-hour period." During the 1996 legislative session, fathers' rights groups tried to get the statute amended to define a "day," but were unable to, and the Court of Appeals definition stands. Since most children are in daycare or school for a large portion of any 24-hour period, the definition has proven impossible to decipher and has resulted in erratic rulings.

CHAPTER 12

THE AGREEMENT

A custody agreement resolves three questions—custody, child support, and visitation. A divorce agreement, which often includes the custody/support/visitation issues, will also resolve the questions of alimony and property.

Here we are dealing only with the custody agreement. Sometimes the custody agreement is subdivided into two or three agreements (e.g. one for custody, another for support and visitation). Usually, though, all the issues are included in one agreement. At the end of this chapter is a sample agreement resolving all three issues. Item 17 of the sample agreement contains detailed information about child support enforcement, which is required by law in all jurisdictions. This one is for Virginia; there is similar specific language for other states. Additionally, more and more states are coming into compliance with federal regulations requiring garnishment of the payor's wages in all new child support orders. Such language may be added to your order. It is not included here.

Since other chapters explain how child support and custody decisions are made, this chapter will focus on visitation. In terms of typed pages, the visitation schedule makes up the largest part of the agreement. The visitation schedule is extremely important because, unless you obtain custody, this is the only part of the agreement that defines your rights.

THE VISITATION SCHEDULE

Some lawyers are indifferent and will leave a father with an agreement that simply states that the father will have "liberal" or "reasonable" visitation. Such an agreement is worthless. If you do not have your visitation schedule spelled out, it cannot be enforced. The more conflictual your case, the more specific you should be in defining visitation. When you have days and times spelled out, it makes a specific commitment. In addition, you should be specific as to where the children will be picked up and dropped off, and whether you will be picking up and/or dropping off from your ex, or your ex will be picking up and/or dropping off from you.

If your ex does not let you have your children on a day or time specified in the agreement, she can be found in contempt of court. Unfortunately, the courts are not good about enforcing visitation. However, with a specific agreement you can usually prevail, if you are persistent in going to court. In a few states, such as Ohio and Texas, the statutes include a minimum visitation schedule. This can make it a lot easier for you to get what you want. Ask your attorney if your jurisdiction has such a statute. Maryland, Virginia, and Washington, D.C. do not.

To obtain a favorable agreement, you should take time well in advance of your court date to define the visitation schedule you want. This means that you have to read this chapter, write out the visitation schedule you want in detail, and have it typed up for your lawyer.

All too frequently, the visitation schedule, like the support order, is created "on the courthouse steps"—that is, in negotiations at court on the day of the hearing. You are under too much pressure to think clearly in court.

Preparing a visitation schedule yourself provides the following benefits:

- It will save you a lot of money. Lawyers can waste a lot of time, and generate a lot of fees, haggling over a visitation schedule.

- It ensures that all the days you want are included. If you leave it up to your lawyer to devise your schedule, you may later find that important days when you could have had visitation have been left out.

- It helps to get the schedule read into the record the way you want it. Having a typed draft of the schedule gives it a certain authority. There is a lot of confusion in courtroom negotiations. If you have a typed draft, it is very likely that your lawyer and your wife's lawyer will want to use it as a basis for negotiation (bring extra copies). Modifications will be made to it, so you may want to pad in some extra time for them to cut out.

NOTE: Fathers hate the word "visitation," because along with "custody" it sounds like a prison situation. Here, I have retained the use of "visitation" for the sake of clarity. In the sample agreement I refer to "Father's time" and "Mother's time."

Standard visitation is one evening a week and every other weekend. In what I call a "full standard" schedule, the mid-week visit is overnight instead of just for dinner, and the weekend goes from Friday evening until Monday morning. This way, you have your children overnight for 5 of every 14 days. Detailed below is a "full" standard visitation schedule with possible variations. Pick the parts that best suit your situation. Modify them to fit your specific needs.

I. VISITATION SCHEDULE FOR PARENTS IN CLOSE PROXIMITY

Note: Although in this text I am specific about alternating holidays, your visitation agreement could begin with the clause:

> For all annually alternating holidays, Mother will have the children in odd-numbered years, Father will have the children in even-numbered years, unless noted otherwise. Unless otherwise noted, visitation will begin from close of school until the morning the children are due back at school. Unless otherwise noted, Father will pick up the children from school and deliver them to school. (Day care and summer camp are to be treated the same as "school.")

Also:

- The agreement should include the date the visitation schedule begins.

- The agreement should include an item giving you first choice to have your children overnight when your wife is out-of-town without them.

- The agreement should include a contingency visitation schedule in the event that either parent re-locates. This way you will not have to come back to court again if either of you moves.

1. WEEKEND VISITATION

Father will have the children on alternating weekends, from close of school on Friday until opening of school on Monday. Father will pick children up from school on Friday and take them to school on Monday.

or:

Father will have the children on alternating weekends, from 5:30 p.m. on Friday until opening of school on Monday. Father will pick children up at Mother's house on Friday and take them to school on Monday.

2. MID-WEEK VISITATION

Father will have children every Wednesday night, beginning at close of school until opening of school on the following day. Father will pick children up from school and take them to school the following morning.

Wednesday is the day usually chosen for mid-week visitation, but you can choose another day if it better suits your schedule. Again, you may prefer to pick up the children after work (5:30, 6:00) at their mother's house. Modify the phrase as needed.

3. CHRISTMAS BREAK (OR SEMESTER BREAK) AND EASTER BREAK (OR SPRING BREAK) VISITATION

Parents will alternate Christmas Break (or Semester Break) and Easter Break (or Spring Break) annually. In odd-numbered years, Mother will have the children for Christmas break and father will have children for Spring break. In even-numbered years Father will have children for Christmas break and Mother will have children for Spring break.

or:

Christmas (semester) break and Spring break will be divided equally between the parents every year. *[See Item 12, Religious Holidays.]*

4. SUMMER VISITATION

Father will have the children with him for one month during the summer, from July 1 at 9 a.m. until August 1 at 9 a.m.

So she can take them on a vacation, Mother will have one month of unfettered time with the children during the summer from August 1 at 9 a.m. until September 1 at 9 a.m. Father will not have normal mid-week or weekend visits during that time. The normal visitation schedule will resume on the first mid-week day or weekend after September 1.

or:

Father will have the children with him for the entire summer, from the close of school on the last school day of the year until three weeks before the first day of the next school year.

So she may take the children on a vacation, Mother will have three weeks of unfettered time with the children beginning the day Father's summer visitation ends. During these three weeks Father will not have

normal mid-week or weekend visitation. The normal visitation schedule
will resume on the first mid-week day or weekend on or after the first day
of school.

5. MONDAY FEDERAL HOLIDAYS

If a federal holiday falls on the Monday following Father's regular
weekend, then he will have the children for that day and take them to
school the following day.

6. THANKSGIVING HOLIDAY

From close of school on the day before Thanksgiving until start of
school the following Monday. Parents will alternate annually.

7. JULY 4

From 5:30 p.m. July 3 until 9:00 a.m. July 5. Parents will alternate
annually.

8. HALLOWEEN

Parents will alternate Halloween, or the evening recognized in the
local community as "trick or treat" night, on an annual basis. If on a
school day, from close of school until start of school the next day. On a
weekend, from 4:30 p.m. until 9:00 a.m the next morning.

9. CHILDREN'S BIRTHDAYS

Parents will alternate having the children on their birthdays.

*Or, in a case where you have two or more children, you may want to
split the birthdays up. For example, suppose you have two children, Jenny
and Bill:*

In odd-numbered years Mother will have the children on Jenny's birthday, Father will have the children on Bill's birthday. In even-numbered
years, Father will have the children on Jenny's birthday, Mother will have
the children on Bill's birthday. Father will pick up the children from
school, at the end of the school day, and take them to school the following
morning. Or, if on a weekend or holiday, father will have children from
9:00 a.m. the day of their birthday until 9:00 a.m. the following day.

Note: You will have to develop a special clause if the birthday schedule conflicts with extended visitation periods such as spring break or summer.

10. PARENTS' BIRTHDAYS

Father will have children on his birthday. Mother will have children on her birthday.

11. FATHER'S DAY/MOTHER'S DAY

Father will have children on Father's Day, Mother will have children on Mother's Day. If Father's Day does not fall on Father's regular weekend, he will pick children up at 9:00 a.m. that Sunday morning and take them to school the following morning. If Mother's Day does not fall on Mother's regular weekend, Mother will pick children up from Father at 9:00 a.m. that Sunday morning.

12. RELIGIOUS HOLIDAYS

If both parents celebrate the same religious holidays, and you alternate Christmas and Easter break:

Parents will alternate the Christmas and Easter holidays. Father will have children for Christmas in the years he has the children for Christmas break, and for Easter in the years he has the children for Spring break.

If both parents celebrate the same religious holidays but you split the Christmas and Easter break every year:

Parents will alternate having the children for Christmas and Easter holiday. In even-numbered years, Father's portion of the Christmas break will include Christmas Eve and Christmas Day. In odd-numbered years, Father's portion of the Spring break will include the Good Friday from 9 a.m. until the Monday morning at 9 a.m. following Easter Sunday. Mother will have this access in the opposite years.

If parents are Jewish and Christian:

[Jewish parent] will always have the children on the eve of Rosh Hashanah at 4:30 p.m. until the morning after Rosh Hashanah, the eve of Yom Kippur from 4:30 p.m. until the morning after Yom Kippur, the eve of Purim from 4:30 p.m. until the next morning, the first two nights of

Passover from 4:30 p.m. on the eve of the first night until the morning after the second night, and the first night of Hanukkah from 4:30 p.m. until the next morning.

[Christian parent] will always have children from 9 a.m. December 24 until the morning after Christmas Day, and from 9 a.m. Good Friday until the morning after Easter Day.

The religious holiday schedule takes precedence over the standard visitation and school break schedules. In years where Christmas Eve or Christmas Day coincide with the first night of Hanukkah, Hanukkah will be celebrated on the night of December 26. When Easter weekend coincides with the first or second night of Passover, parents will share the weekend accordingly and/or alternate precedence from occurrence to occurrence.

If you celebrate other holidays, you should include them in the same manner.

13. MAKE-UP TIME

When Mother's time on Thanksgiving Holiday, July 4, Halloween, Children's Birthdays, Parents' Birthdays, Mother's Day, or religious holidays interferes with Father's normal *mid-week or weekend* time with the children, that time will be made up in the following week.

If you have substantially more than standard visitation, you may want to include a clause giving mother some make-up time as well, but only weekend time (since she is losing the time she can spend alone with the children).

If Father's time on Thanksgiving Holiday, July 4, Halloween, Children's Birthdays, Parents' Birthdays, Father's Day, or religious holidays interferes with Mother's normal *weekend* time with the children, that time will be made up to her.

14. WHEN MOTHER IS OUT OF TOWN

You want to be sure that you have the first right of refusal to care for your children when your wife goes on a trip without them.

15. AND 16. AGREEMENT REGARDING RELOCATION

Increasingly, courts are making it easy for mothers to just pick up and move away, taking the children with them. To prevent this, you should get a clause in your order that prohibits it. However, since this might not be included, or if included might not be upheld by the court, you could alternatively, or in addition, include a requirement for a 30 to 60 day relocation notice. Some states require that such a notice be included in a custody or visitation agreement. With notice, you have time to bring a court action and show that the move is not in the best interest of your children—which is probably the only reason the court would block the move.

Also, you should have a visitation schedule like the one described below included in your order, in the event your ex does move away. This way you will avoid having to fight for visitation all over again.

II. VISITATION SCHEDULE FOR PARENTS LIVING AT A DISTANCE THAT MAKES MID-WEEK AND/OR WEEKEND VISITS IMPRACTICAL

Father will have the children with him according to the following schedule:

Thanksgiving Holiday from close of school Wednesday until the following Sunday at 9:00 p.m.

Christmas Break or Semester break from the close of school the day before the Break begins until 9:00 p.m. the night before school resumes for the next semester.

Easter Break or Spring Break from close of school the day before the Break begins until 9:00 p.m. the night before school resumes.

Summer from close of school the day before the summer break begins until 9:00 p.m. on the day that is one week before the new school year starts.

Parents will share the cost for the children's transportation to and from the noncustodial parent's home.

On the following pages, you will find a Sample Consent Order which combines selected visitation elements with custody and child support information in a comprehensive custody agreement. You can use this as a model when developing your own agreement.

There are several things you should note about this order:

(1) While the parties in this case have agreed to joint physical and legal custody, primary residence is still given to the mother. This is by no means essential. I did it this way so that I could also show how a typical access (i.e., visitation) schedule looks. If you can persuade your wife to agree to joint custody with a 50/50 sharing of time, by all means do so.

(2) I use the terms "Father's time" and "Mother's time" rather than "visitation." It is not only psychology more positive, but it also helps to reinforce the fact that you have joint legal and physical custody, rather than joint legal custody with visitation.

(3) The information at the top of the first page—the state, the name of the court, the matter, the litigants, the case number—is called the "style" of the case. There are minor differences from court to court. For example, depending on jurisdiction, the parties may be called petitioner/respondent, complainant/defendant, or plaintiff/defendant. Obtain a motion that has been filed in your jurisdiction to see the precise way to style your case.

In the following Sample Consent Order, the father has the children for Christmas Break and July 4 in even-numbered years and for Thanksgiving and Spring Break in odd-numbered years. That way the children are spending half their holidays with each parent every year.

The names used in the following Sample Consent Order are fictitious.

V I R G I N I A:

IN THE JUVENILE AND DOMESTIC RELATIONS DISTRICT COURT
OF THE COUNTY OF ARLINGTON

IN RE: FRANCINE SUSAN JONES and GREGORY LEE JONES

THOMAS S. JONES	:	
Petitioner	:	
	:	
vs.	:	CASE NO. J-812222x
	:	
NANCY JONES	:	CUSTODY, ACCESS,
Respondent	:	AND SUPPORT ORDER

THIS CAUSE was heard upon the petitions of the parties
for custody of FRANCINE SUSAN JONES and GREGORY LEE JONES
and support for FRANCINE SUSAN JONES and GREGORY LEE
JONES and upon consent of the parties to the terms
hereof, after partial hearing of testimony and upon
consideration whereof, it is

ADJUDGED, ORDERED AND DECREED as follows:

The Respondent, Nancy Jones (hereinafter "Mother"),
and the Petitioner, Thomas Jones (hereinafter "Father"),
will share joint legal and physical custody of their
children, Francine Susan Jones and Gregory Lee Jones. The
primary residence of the children will be at the Mother's
home.

IT IS FURTHER ORDERED that the Father will have time
with the children according to the schedule detailed
below. Interference with this schedule by the Mother will
constitute grounds for a change of primary residence.

- 1 -

1. Weekend Father's Time

Father will have the children on alternating weekends, from close of school on Friday until opening of school on Monday. Father will pick children up from school on Friday and take them to school on Monday. If school is not in session, Father will pick the children up at the Mother's home on Friday at 5:30 p.m. and return them to her home on Monday at 9:00 a.m.

2. Mid-Week Father's Time

Father will have the children on Wednesdays, overnight, beginning at close of school Wednesday until opening of school Thursday. When school is in session, Father will pick children up from school and take them to school the following morning. If school is not in session, Father will pick the children up at the Mother's home on Wednesday at 5:30 p.m. and return them to her home on Monday at 8:30 a.m.

3. Christmas (or Semester) Break and Spring Break

Parents will alternate Christmas Break (or Semester Break) and Spring Break annually. In odd-numbered years, Mother will have the children for Christmas break, and Father will have children for Spring break. In even-numbered years, Father will have children for Christmas break, and Mother will have children for Spring break.

4. Summer Parenting Schedule

Father will have the children with him for one month during the summer, from July 1 at 9 a.m. until August 1 at 9 a.m.

So she can take the children on a vacation, Mother will have two weeks of unfettered time with the children during the summer, from August 1 at 9 a.m. until August 15 at 9 a.m. Father will not have normal mid-week or weekend visits during that time. The normal visitation schedule will resume on the first mid-week day or weekend on or after August 15.

5. Monday Federal Holidays

If a Federal Holiday falls on the Monday following Father's regular weekend, then he will have the children for that day and take them to school the following day.

6. Thanksgiving Holiday

From close of school on the day before Thanksgiving until start of school the following Monday. Parents will alternate annually, with Father having children in odd-numbered years and Mother having children in even-numbered years.

7. July 4

From 5:30 p.m. July 3 until 9:00 a.m. July 5. Parents will alternate annually, with Mother having children in odd-numbered years and Father having children in even-numbered years.

8. Halloween

Parents will alternate Halloween, or the evening recognized in the local community as "trick or treat" night, on an annual basis. If on a school day, from close of school until start of school the next day. On a weekend, from 4:30 p.m. until 9:00 a.m the next morning. Father will have children in even-numbered years, and Mother will have children in odd-numbered years.

9. Children's Birthdays

Parents will alternate having the children on their birthdays. In odd-numbered years, Mother will have the children on Francine's birthday, Father will have the children on Gregory's birthday. In even-numbered years, Father will have the children on Francine's birthday, Mother will have the children on Gregory's birthday. Father will pick up the children from school at close of school and take them to school the following morning. If the birthday falls on a weekend or holiday, Father will have children from 9:00 a.m. the day of the birthday until 9:00 a.m. the following day.

10. Parents' Birthdays

Father will have children on his birthday. Father will pick up the children from school at close of school and take them to school the following morning. If the birthday falls

on a weekend or holiday, Father will have children from
9:00 a.m. the day of the birthday until 9:00 a.m. the
following day.

Mother will have children on her birthday. If her
birthday falls on a weekend or holiday that is normally
Father's time, she will have the children from 9:00 a.m.
on that day until 9:00 a.m. the following day, and she
will return them to Father if Father's time is continuing.

11. Mother's Day/Father's Day

Father will have children on Father's Day, Mother will
have children on Mother's Day. If Father's Day does not
fall on Father's regular weekend, he will pick children
up at 9:00 a.m. that Sunday morning and take them to
school the following morning. If Mother's Day does not
fall on Mother's regular weekend, Mother will pick
children up from Father at 9:00 a.m. that Sunday morning.

12. Religious Holidays

Parents will alternate the Christmas and Easter holidays.
Father will have children for Christmas in the years he has
the children for Christmas (or Semester) break, and for
Easter in the years he has the children for Spring break.

13. Make-Up Time

When Mother's time on Thanksgiving Holiday, July 4,
Halloween, Children's Birthdays, Parents' Birthdays,

Mother's Day, or religious holidays interferes with Father's normal mid-week or weekend time with the children, that time will be made up to him in the following week.

14. When Mother is Out of Town

If Mother goes out of town overnight without the children, the children will stay with their Father until their Mother returns.

The visitation schedule will commence on *[date of the agreement]*, beginning with Father having the first weekend after this date.

For all annually alternating holidays, Mother will have the children in odd-numbered years, Father will have the children in even-numbered years, unless noted otherwise. Unless noted otherwise, visitation will begin from close of school until the morning the child is due back at school. Unless noted otherwise, Father will pick up the children from school and deliver them to school. For the purposes of this agreement, "day care," "summer school," and "summer camp" are to be treated the same as "school."

15. Agreement Regarding Relocation

a. In order to ensure a continuing relationship between the children and their Father, Mother agrees not to relocate to a distance more than 50 miles from her present home without agreement of the Father.

b. In the event Mother or Father relocates to a distance from his or her present home that makes mid-week visitation impracticable for the Father, Father will have the children with him as detailed above, with the following modifications:

Alternating Weekends from close of school on Friday until 9:00 p.m. on Sunday. Father will pick children up at school and return them to Mother's home.

Summer from close of school the day before the summer break begins until 9:00 p.m. on the day that is one week before the new school year starts.

c. In the event Mother or Father relocates to a distance from his or her present home that makes mid-week and weekend visitation impracticable for the Father, Father will have the children with him according to the following schedule:

Thanksgiving Holiday from close of school Wednesday until the Sunday following at 9:00 p.m.

Christmas Break or Semester break from the close of school the day before the Break begins until 9:00 p.m. the night before school resumes for the next semester.

Easter Break or Spring Break from close of school the day before the Break begins until 9:00 p.m. the night before school resumes.

Summer from close of school the day before the summer break begins until 9:00 p.m. on the day that is one week before the new school year starts.

d. In the event of relocation, Mother and Father will evenly share the cost for the children's transportation to and from the noncustodial parent's home.

16. In the event that either parent intends to relocate the children more than 50 miles from their current residence, he or she must give 60 days notice to the court and to the other parent.

17. The amount of periodic child support is set at $_____ per month, payable on the first of each month, effective _____.

18. The following information is furnished pursuant to Section 20-60.3 of the 1950 Code of Virginia as amended:

a. Notice that support payments may be withheld as they become due pursuant to §20-79.1 or 2079.2 of the Code of Virginia from petitioner's earnings as defined in §63.1-250 of the 1950 Code of Virginia, as amended, without further order of this court or having to file an application for services with the Department of Social Services.

b. Support payments may be withheld pursuant to Chapter 13 (§63.1-249 et seq.) of Title 63.1, without further amendments to this Order, upon application for services with the Department of Social Services.

c.   The name and date of birth of the persons to whom a duty of support is now owed by petitioner are as follows: FRANCINE SUSAN JONES, born [_____] and GREGORY LEE JONES, born [_____].

d.   The date of birth of the Mother is [_____], and her social security number is [_____]. The date of birth of the Father is [_____], and his social security number is [_____]. The place of employment of the Father, the person responsible for the support is [*Name of business/Address of employer*] The home address of the Father is [*Street/City/State/Zip*]. The place of employment of the Mother, the person receiving the support, is [*Name of business/Address of employer*]. The home address of the Mother is [*Street/City/State/Zip*].

e. The [*Father/Mother*] shall maintain the children under insurance coverage with [*his/her*] existing (or the equivalent) policy of health, medical, and/or dental insurance for so long as they are eligible under the terms of the coverage.

f. Support arrearages do not exist.

g. Notice is further given that in determination of a support obligation, the support obligation as it becomes due and unpaid creates a judgement by operation by law.

h. There is no provision for child support payments to be paid through the Department of Social Services.

ENTERED: _____
                      [date]

                              _____
                                    [Name of judge], Judge

_____
[NAME OF YOUR LAWYER] ESQUIRE
Counsel for Petitioner
[Name of Law Firm]
[Address of Law Firm]

_____
[NAME OF WIFE'S LAWYER], ESQUIRE
Counsel for Respondent
[Name of Law Firm]
[Address of Law Firm]

_____
[NAME OF GUARDIAN AD LITEM, if any] ESQUIRE
Guardian Ad Litem
[Name of Law Firm]
[Address of Law Firm]

CHAPTER 13

JURISDICTION

"Jurisdiction defines the powers of courts to inquire into facts, apply the law, make decisions, and declare judgment."[1] In practical terms, jurisdiction defines which court has the authority to hear your case. There are 54 U.S. jurisdictions (the 50 states, Washington D.C., Guam, Puerto Rico, and the Virgin Islands). A case might also be found to be under the jurisdiction of a foreign country.

Jurisdiction also defines which court within a state has the power to hear a custody case. In some states, district courts (i.e., special juvenile or family courts) handle these issues. In other states, they are handled by circuit courts.

THE HOME STATE

In a child-custody dispute, the state in which the child has lived for the last six months will usually be considered the "home state," and it will have jurisdiction unless both parties and the child move from the state. If the child is currently residing in a state in which he has not lived for six months, then the last state in which the child lived for six months may be considered the "home state."

WHAT THIS MEANS TO YOU

If you and your wife and child have lived continuously in one state, neither you nor your wife can suddenly take the child, move to another state, and sue for custody. For example, if you live in Virginia and come home one day to find that your wife has taken the child, moved back to New York with her parents, and is now suing for custody in New York, you can file suit in Virginia, and Virginia will have jurisdiction. Obviously, it is better for you to have jurisdiction close to home. You do not want to have to hire a lawyer 200 miles away, and you do not want to have to travel 200 miles to appear at a hearing. However, you may still have to retain counsel in New York and file a motion to dismiss your wife's New York custody suit, if the New York court does not dismiss the action voluntarily.

Once custody and support have been set in one state, all other states must respect that court order in perpetuity. Only if all of the parties have moved out of the state (usually for at least six months) can a new state take jurisdiction. If you remain in the state that originally awarded custody and your wife and child move to another state, the original state still retains jurisdiction. Thus, for example, if the custody and support award was originally entered in State A, and your wife and child move to State B, which has higher child support guidelines, your wife could not go to court in State B to get a higher support award.

But that does not mean she can't try. I have heard of several instances where women have tried this tactic. And even though the law is clear on this point, if your ex tries this tactic, it could cost you a substantial amount in legal fees before the matter is settled.

"Jurisdiction" also means that once your ex has been awarded custody in one state, you cannot take the child on vacation in another state and sue for custody there.

Jurisdiction can be changed if the state holding jurisdiction defers jurisdiction to a state seeking it. But this must be for good cause.

LAWS

The laws governing jurisdiction are the Uniform Child Custody Jurisdiction Act (UCCJA) and the federal Parental Kidnapping Prevention Act of 1980 (PKPA). The UCCJA is a state law. All 50 states have it, and it varies slightly from state to state. While many lawyers and judges rely on the UCCJA, it is irrelevant if contradicted by the PKPA. Because the PKPA is a federal law (written to supersede state law), it has precedence over the UCCJA. Be sure, if you have an interstate dispute, that your lawyer argues exclusively from the PKPA.

According to attorney Richard Crouch,[2] most judges and lawyers are still unfamiliar with the PKPA. From what I have observed, he is correct. Lawyers frequently make erroneous arguments on the subject of jurisdiction, and judges frequently err in their decisions.[3] If you have an interstate dispute, you should become familiar with the PKPA yourself. Relying on lawyers and judges to accurately interpret the law can prove costly.

FORUM SHOPPING

As noted above, women sometimes "forum shop" for the jurisdiction where they can get the highest child support. Similarly, you might shop for a jurisdiction that is most favorable to fathers.

Actually, I have never known a father to do this (probably because, as noted elsewhere in this book, fathers are usually taken by surprise in divorce). But, if you live in a metropolitan area that overlaps several jurisdictions—like the greater New York City area (New York, New Jersey, Connecticut), or the greater Washington D.C. area (D.C., Virginia, Maryland)—forum shopping could be a practical consideration.

Taking the greater D.C. area as an example: Virginia virtually never awards custody to fathers. D.C. occasionally awards custody to fathers, but its exorbitant "child support" guidelines make it a jurisdiction to be avoided if at all possible. Maryland and Virginia have comparable child support guidelines; too high, but substantially lower than those in D.C. In Maryland, you have a slight chance of winning custody, and the "child support" is as good as you'll get. Thus, in this tri-state area, Maryland is the most favorable jurisdiction for fathers.

Therefore, in a situation where there was no custody award, if you and your wife were living in Virginia or D.C. and you sensed your marriage was dissolving, you might consider establishing residence in Maryland. Many couples, when breaking up in an amicable way, agree to a "trial separation." If you had such an arrangement, you could move to Maryland. If during this period, say six months to a year, your child stayed with you several nights a week, you then might have grounds to sue for custody in Maryland.

JURISDICTION AS A CUSTODY STRATEGY

In a situation where a custody award already exists, you might be able to get your children back if all parties move out of the original state.

Suppose the original custody order was in State A, but your wife and child moved to State B and you moved to State C, and you have all been out of State A for more than six months. If your child came to stay with you for an extended period, say two months for summer vacation, you could sue for custody in State C. You would have to have good cause, of course, showing that it is in the best interest of the child for custody to be changed. If your child is a boy, the fact that he is older (i.e., ten, instead of four) and needs to spend more time with his father to have a positive male role model, may be considered good cause. You may even be able to keep your child with you from the time you petitioned to the time the case came to trial, during which time you would be establishing a status quo of being the primary caretaker.

Again, though, going to court is never a promising venture.

NOTES

[1] Black's Law Dictionary, 6th Edition, 1990.

[2] Richard Crouch, "Interstate Custody Litigation Myths and Fallacies: The UCCJA and PKPA," *Virginia Lawyer* January 1990 (37–41).

[3] In fact, Mr. Dawes, the co-author of this book, recently had a case in Arlington, Virginia where he represented a father who already had a court order for custody in Washington, D.C. The Virginia judge simply ignored the D.C. order and awarded custody to the mother. This errant decision made it possible for both parties to file kidnapping charges against each other in their respective jurisdictions.

CHAPTER 14

Ex Parte Complaints for Domestic Violence

Ex parte complaints for domestic violence are also called civil protective orders, civil protection orders, peace bonds, exclusionary orders, orders to vacate, and protection-from-abuse orders (PFAs), depending on jurisdiction. Within this book I use the terms *ex parte* order, protective order, and exclusionary order interchangeably.

With such an order, a wife can have her husband evicted from their home immediately. *Ex parte*, pronounced "ex par-tay," means "on one side only." An *ex parte* hearing is a hearing in which only one party is present. An order issued at such a hearing, at the request of and for one party, is called an *ex parte* order.

In other words, your wife can go to a judge or other official (see Table 1) and obtain such an order without any notice being given to you. You will know she has obtained such an order when the police evict you from your home.

FALSE ALLEGATIONS

The exclusionary order is the most abused statute in the state codes. I first became aware of its widespread use at fathers' support-group meetings, where I would frequently meet men who had been evicted from their homes for allegedly assaulting or threatening their wives. I was amazed. Could all these men, all of whom protested their innocence, really be dangerous threats to their wives? They seemed so normal. They certainly didn't fit any stereotypes of rough and rude characters. These men were accountants, computer programmers, real estate brokers, lawyers. Then too, it seemed a little remarkable that all these men suddenly became "dangerous," just when their wives were seeking divorce and custody.

According to the lawyers I have surveyed, the exclusionary order is used in as many as one-third of divorce-custody disputes, and the vast majority of these orders are obtained under false allegations. Many lawyers abhor the abuse of this code, but a sizable number routinely use the exclusionary order as a tactic to win custody for their female clients.

Divorce-attorney Elaine Epstein, while President of the Massachusetts Bar Association, wrote:

> The facts have become irrelevant. Everyone knows that restraining orders and orders to vacate are granted to virtually all who apply, lest anyone be blamed for an unfortunate result. As one judge patiently told me when I appeared in opposition to the extension of an order to vacate, "You don't understand—I *have* to grant these."
>
> ...
>
> The truth is that it has become impossible to effectively represent a man against whom any allegation of domestic violence has been made. In virtually all cases, no notice, meaningful hearing, or impartial weighing of evidence is to be had. In response to the tidal wave of largely *pro se* restraining order seekers, the courts frequently seem to have taken a rubber stamp approach to dispensing such orders. I have seen restraining orders and orders to vacate granted on the basis of dirty looks, fears—unsupported by past conduct—and virtually anything said in the course of an argument.[1]

THE POLITICS

The original purpose of civil protective orders was to end a domestic quarrel—that is, to protect one spouse from the immediate danger of violence from the other by removing the agitated party from the house for a sufficient period until things cooled down. Thirty days was usually more than enough time.

In the past, protective orders could only be continued for up to 30 days. In recent years, amidst media hype over spousal abuse and "battered-wives," new laws have been enacted that allow protective orders to be continued for six months or a year.

Women's groups promoted these laws under the pretense that they were needed to protect "battered women." These laws cannot possibly serve their pretended purpose, but they do excellently serve the purpose for which they are almost always used—to get the man out of the house when the woman wants a divorce.

These laws cannot really protect truly battered women because, for one thing, if a man is truly so violent that he needs to be restrained from his home for a year, he is not going to pay any attention to a little piece of paper called a court order. Moreover, by the very nature of battered-wife syndrome, a truly battered woman remains for a long time in an abusive situation because of her "learned helplessness."

Any divorce lawyer will tell you that he very rarely sees a truly battered woman. A truly battered woman is extremely reluctant to seek help to begin with. If she does manage to find her way to a lawyer or to a magistrate,[2] she is reluctant to press charges, and even when she does press charges, she is reluctant to testify.

In the vast majority of divorce-custody disputes, no abuse factors are evident. The wife shows no signs of physical abuse, not even bruises; there is no history of violence between the couple; the charges arise only after the woman has consulted a divorce lawyer, and frequently, the woman files a petition for divorce within a day of having her husband evicted.

As noted in Chapter 6, the protective order is a trump card, because in one stroke the woman has created the separation leading to divorce, has effectively won custody, and has obtained possession of the marital home. When a protective order is continued for six months or a year, it ensures that the mother can establish herself as the sole primary caretaker of the children; hence, the father does not have a chance of winning custody. This is the real reason women's groups sought the extended time frame for protective orders, and this is why the protective order is sought so often under false pretenses.

THE PROCEDURE

To obtain a civil protective order, a woman need only go to the proper official (see Table 1) and say that her husband has done her some bodily harm or that she is *afraid he will* do her bodily harm. There need be no physical evidence or testimony from witnesses that he has actually done any such thing. In divorce-custody disputes, the civil protective order is always coupled with an *ex parte* order giving custody to the mother. Once the *ex parte* order is issued, a hearing before a judge, with both parties present, is held within a few days. Below, and in Table 1, I've summarized the procedure in three U.S. jurisdictions. Something similar applies in all states. Consult your lawyer for details.

In Maryland, the protective order stands for seven days unless it is continued by a judge. The hearing is automatic and must be held within five days. At this hearing, the judge decides whether or not the order will be continued, and may continue it for up to one year. At the end of that year, it can be continued for another six months "for good cause shown."

In Virginia, the protective order stands for 30 days unless it is continued by a judge. It can be continued for up to one year. A hearing is required within 15 days from the day of service, but it is not automatic. A father who has been evicted from his home by an *ex parte* exclusionary order, must petition the court for a hearing.

	Maryland	District of Columbia	Virginia
TABLE 1 **PROTECTIVE ORDERS**			
Whom do you go to, to get a protective order?	District Court Commissioner	Corporation Counsel or a Private Attorney who takes it before a judge	Intake Officer (IO) at the courthouse drafts petition and takes it before a judge. In some jurisdictions, a magistrate issues protective orders.
When can you file?	24 hours a day	During business hours	During business hours
When is the hearing for the defendant to present his defense?	Within 5 days of service	Within 14 days of service	Within 15 days of service
How long does the order stand if not continued?	7 days	30 days	30 days
How long can the order be continued for?	1 year + 6 months "for good cause shown"	1 year	1 year

In D.C., the protective order stands for 30 days unless it is continued by a judge. A hearing is required within 15 days. The order can be continued for up to a year.

Because of the current spousal-abuse hysteria, many judges are afraid to do anything but continue a protective order. In some cases, where it is glaringly obvious that the allegations are false, a judge will rationalize that there is a great deal of hostility in this household and continue the order for the mutual safety of the parties. Nonetheless, simply by continuing the order he has favored the mother, who is now assured of winning custody.

Only in rare instances are these cases bound over for criminal trial. When they are, the tendency is for judges to uphold the assault charge, but suspend the sentence. This is further evidence that the judges know that no danger exists, and that the woman's purpose was accomplished when the father was removed from the house.

HOW TO PREVENT YOUR WIFE FROM OBTAINING SUCH AN ORDER

You may get certain indications that your wife is contemplating obtaining a civil protective order. Whether a woman decides to take the children and leave, or to evict her husband via a civil protective order, is determined by her own conscience and the degree to which her attorney provokes her. Some attorneys will make it plain to their female clients that a woman can bring a false assault allegation with impunity.[3] Even so, few women are prepared to do something so overtly unlawful without serious consideration. Obviously, if your wife is the kind of person who could never countenance such an act, she will move out instead. Even those who do eventually seek the order usually try to rationalize it to themselves first. This can produce some very bizarre behavior.

What usually happens in these cases is that after seeing a lawyer, the wife will try to get her husband to sign a unilateral agreement giving her custody, etc. When he refuses to sign it, her thoughts turn to having him evicted.

This is when bizarre behavior sets in. Your wife may start acting very paranoid in your presence, exclaiming things like "Don't touch me! Just stay away from me!" She may call her friends and tell them she is really afraid of you. She may, out of the blue, call the police once or twice, then when they come to the house tell them "It's okay, nothing's wrong." Fathers relating such stories have no idea what is going on. The male response in these circumstances tends to be incredibly dense. The man typically thinks his wife is going crazy, and he wants to know what he can do to help her. She is not going crazy, or if she is, there is method to her madness.

If your wife behaves in this manner, what she is doing is building a chain of evidence, so that when she goes for the exclusionary order she can create the impression that she has a real fear of bodily harm. Her friends will testify that she expressed fear of you for weeks prior to the alleged assault. The police will testify that she called them on two occasions, and though she told them to go away, she seemed very upset. No one has testified that they saw you hit your wife, and your wife has no physical signs of abuse. It is all circumstantial evidence, and, properly speaking, inadequate. Nonetheless, it is usually sufficient to obtain an *ex parte* civil protective order, and very likely will be enough to persuade a judge to continue the order.

If there is any indication that your wife is going to get a protective order, leave the house immediately and contact a lawyer. As long as your wife has not obtained a protective order, you can return to your home. To avoid losing custody or possession of the house, you should return to your house as soon as possible, but only when you have a reliable witness or witnesses (the more the better) with you. If your wife has changed the locks, you can change them back. It is still your home. A good tactic under these circumstances is to return to your house every day for a few hours with some friends (witnesses). You can sit around, play with your children, watch TV, play cards, eat the food. Unless you can get a close relative, preferably your mother or a sister, to stay with you, you should avoid staying overnight.

If Your Wife Attacks You

In extreme cases, your wife may actually assault you.[4] The idea here is to get you to physically defend yourself; then she will go to the magistrate and say you attacked her. One strange phenomenon I have heard related several times is the wife attacking her husband in his sleep. Perhaps the logic behind this is that a man waking to an assault will fight back without thinking. This is only conjecture. In the particular instances mentioned, the men did not strike back.

If your wife attacks you, you should seek a civil protective order. If she injures you, you should have the injuries photographed, have them treated by a doctor or emergency room, and obtain the report showing the cause of and treatment for the injuries. However, as long as you can still walk and talk, you should seek a civil protective order before you do anything else. It is crucial that you get to the magistrate before your wife gets there. Some magistrates refuse to issue civil protective orders for men. This is illegal. If you encounter this problem, get your lawyer to return with you to the magistrate's office and compel him to obey the law.

If You Are Evicted From Your Home

If you are served with a civil protective order, you must move out of your home within the time frame specified by the order. Usually, this will be within hours. Move out; otherwise you will be arrested. Then contact a lawyer.

Have your lawyer schedule a hearing *as soon as possible*. At the hearing, your lawyer must spell out for the judge that this allegation is entirely false; that there is not a shred of evidence that you ever harmed or threatened to harm your wife; and that your wife sought the protective order to gain advantage in your divorce-custody dispute. (If she has not petitioned for divorce yet, you can testify that she has told you she intends to seek divorce and custody.) Your lawyer must tell the judge that this is a gross abuse of the law for personal gain and it cannot be tolerated. If you lose at the first hearing, have your attorney appeal the ruling.

NOTES

[1] Elaine M. Epstein, Esq., President, Massachusetts Bar Association, "Indiscriminate Evictions" *The Liberator*, October 1993 (25).

[2] In many jurisdictions, a court official other than a judge may issue protective orders. Although I use the term magistrate, the titles of these officials vary from jurisdiction to jurisdiction (see Table 1).

[3] Occasionally, when it is shown that a mother has obtained a civil protective order under false allegations, it can work against her and even result in the father getting custody. This depends on the judge's predisposition. Usually a false assault allegation alone would not be enough, but if the mother also brought false child abuse charges, the judge might view her as seriously unstable.

[4] Studies based on reporting *by women* indicate that women initiate domestic violence as often as men. (See Murray A. Straus, "Physical Assaults by Wives: A Major Social Problem," *Current Controversies on Family Violence*. Beverly Hills, CA: Sage Publications, 1993). Here, though, I am speaking of a specific circumstance where a woman who has never assaulted her husband before suddenly becomes violent when the aforementioned elements (divorce, lawyers, agreements) come into play.

CHAPTER 15

False Child Sex Abuse Allegations

False child sex abuse allegations have become rampant in divorce-custody disputes. Fifteen years ago, it was highly unusual for a child sex abuse charge to come up in the context of divorce. Today, according to a study of divorce-custody litigation in 12 U.S. cities,[1] nearly one in thirty divorcing fathers is accused of sexually molesting one of his children. The same study found that 50 percent of these allegations were determined to be unfounded.

As remarkable as this figure is, it is a conservative estimate of the number of false allegations. The study was funded by the National Center for the Prosecution of Child Abuse (NCPCA). This organization, and the people they surveyed—Child Protection Services workers and court-appointed social workers—are groups that have a vested interest in finding that sex abuse charges are valid.

Other studies and expert opinions assert that false allegations run closer to 75 percent.[2] Moreover, these are only the cases that are reported. Allegations are probably made far more often than court studies indicate, because false sex abuse allegations need never reach court. Several lawyers have told me that they have handled cases where sex abuse was alleged, but the allegations were dropped when the father agreed to a higher property/alimony/support settlement.

For some lawyers, the child abuse allegation has become a standard tactic. In an article in *National Review*, Barbara Amiel reports:

> One family law expert stated that in today's witch-hunt atmosphere,
> "a lawyer is coming close to negligence if he does not advise a client
> that in child-custody cases and property disputes, the mere mention
> of a child-abuse allegation is a significant asset." [3]

Similarly, Arlynn Presser, a lawyer and author in Chicago who has written about divorce laws, says that a divorce lawyer once told her that he "would feel like he was committing malpractice if he didn't explain to female clients what the consequences of charging

163

their husbands with child sexual abuse would be." [4]

In the cases I am personally familiar with, false child sex abuse charges nearly always take the form of sex abuse charges against the father when the child or children are female. The practical advantage to bringing this kind of charge is that there is no need for physical evidence. A father need only be accused of inappropriate "touching." The child, usually young, can be easily manipulated by her mother and a therapist to repeat the charge. Or, the therapist can interpret something the child says to be evidence that the child has been abused. The Eric Foretich/Elizabeth Morgan case and the Woody Allen/Mia Farrow case are two prominent examples of this familiar pattern.

The child sex abuse allegation is extremely effective, because a mother need only breathe the words "sex abuse" for a judge to cut off all access between the father and his children. In the months or years that it takes for the court proceedings, the mother's position as the custodial parent becomes firmly entrenched. If a father seeks to fight the charges, such a case—involving lawyers, therapists, guardians *ad litem*, and social workers—can easily cost $80,000.

Even in cases where a mother takes the child to a series of therapists before she finds one who will support her charges, judges tend to favor the mother. Even when the mother has brought prior abuse charges that have been disproven in court, it is common for a judge to require hearings on the new charge.

Frequently, when abuse charges are brought, the judge will terminate all access between the father and his children without any evidentiary hearing. A father is presumed guilty until proven innocent. In custody disputes, the child abuse charge is usually *not* brought as a criminal charge. Thus, most accused fathers do not obtain the civil rights accorded to alleged criminals—that is, the father does not have the opportunity to confront his accusers, he does not have the right to a trial by jury, and his accusers never have to produce any evidence.

Child psychologists confirm what common sense dictates: that the false abuse charge is, in and of itself, a form of child abuse. But even when the abuse charge is successfully disproven, there is usually no punishment imposed on the parent who brought the false charge.

Increasingly, though, judges will recognize false abuse charges as evidence that the person bringing such charges (usually the mother) is an unfit parent.

How to Prevent False Child Abuse Allegations

If no abuse charges have been brought against you, but your wife seeks to have your child examined by a mental health expert, you should make a motion to the court that the therapist must be someone approved by the court, or agreed to by both parents, and that videotaping must be done at all sessions. You and your lawyer may also want to determine the specific credentials of any therapist hired to examine your child. Believe it or not, *anyone* can call himself or herself a therapist. You probably want to specify, for example, that your child can only be taken to a psychiatrist (that is, a person who is a medical doctor) or a psychologist (someone with a doctorate in psychology). At the very least, any therapist you employ should be a licensed clinical social worker (LCSW), but I recommend a psychiatrist or psychologist.

If your wife has already hired her own mental health expert, and you cannot get the court to dismiss that therapist and approve a mutually acceptable one, you must hire your own mental health expert for an independent examination. Again, make a motion to have the sessions with your wife's therapist videotaped.

If You Are Accused

If false child abuse allegations are made against you, you must take action immediately. Have your lawyer make this **standard motion** to the court:

> The minor child(ren) of the parties to this divorce may not be taken to any therapist, psychologist, psychiatrist, social worker, counselor or other mental health professional without: a) prior notice to the court, b) prior notice to all parties to the divorce, c) videotaping of all sessions with such mental health professionals from start to finish, with the non-taking party (the father) paying the cost of such videotaping if necessary.[5]

In any appearance before the court, your lawyer must *emphatically* assert that the allegations are false and are being brought only to gain advantage in the custody dispute. He must tell the court: "The creation of false child abuse allegations is a symptom of Mrs. Smith's own mental illness. False allegations themselves are a form of child abuse and are highly destructive to the child. Any parent who would do such a thing is incapable of seeking the child's best interest. It is a definite reason for transferring custody to the father."

In seeking a psychiatrist or psychologist to examine your child, you should look for one who is familiar with the work of Dr. Richard A. Gardner, Clinical Professor of Child Psychiatry at Columbia University. Dr. Gardner has published many books and articles on false child abuse allegations and his "Sexual Abuse Legitimacy Scale" is widely accepted as a standard for determining whether child abuse charges are true or false.

You should obtain *The Parental Alienation Syndrome and the Differentiation Between Fabricated and Genuine Child Sex Abuse* by Dr. Gardner (Cresskill, NJ: Creative Therapeutics, 1987). It is available through the Children's Rights Council (see Chapter 17). You should read the book yourself and be sure that your child's therapist is familiar with it.

You must not underestimate how dangerous these charges can be. If bound over into a criminal charge, you could very well go to prison.

> There are states in which an adult found guilty of touching (and *only* touching) a little girl's vulva may be given a mandatory jail sentence of 25 years or even life imprisonment.[6]

If you find yourself accused, and your wife has already taken your child to a "validator" (that is, a therapist who readily interprets anything a child says to confirm abuse), you must first attempt to get this therapist dismissed and your child examined by a court-approved therapist, or one that you select. Second, you must be very aggressive in researching the background of the "validator." Subpoena all records he or she keeps on your child, all insurance forms filed in regard to the case, his financial statements, credentials, etc.

For a detailed strategy on how to fight these charges, write to Bruce G. Gould Publications, P.O. Box 1070, Okanogan, WA 98840 for a copy of "Suggestions When Falsely Accused." Also, join your state chapter of Victims Of Child Abuse Laws (VOCAL). If your state does not have a chapter, contact the National Association of VOCAL Organizations (NASVO), or the National Child Abuse Defense and Resource Center, to see who in your area can help you (see Chapter 17 for more on these resources).

• • •

With the child sex abuse hysteria, as with the child support/Deadbeat Dad phenomenon, we again find the federal government reaching into the private lives of individuals and causing far more harm than its intended good. Dr. Gardner has observed that the Child Abuse Prevention and Treatment

Act (Public Law 93-247), sometimes referred to as "The Mondale Act," has played an important role in causing the sex-abuse hysteria we are witnessing today.

While well-meaning, the legislation created a new and ever-growing bureaucracy, ever seeking to sustain itself and related agencies, and ever-prone to abuse by overzealous employees. This, of course, is a problem with every bureaucracy. Here, though, two provisions in the federal law made these new bureaucracies especially dangerous. In order to qualify for federal funding, the states had to pass legislation that:

(1) provided immunity from prosecution for all those reporting child abuse, and

(2) required specific persons (such as health-care professionals, law enforcement officials, teachers, and school administrators) to report suspected child abuse to the appropriate child protection agency. Such mandated reporting, by necessity, had to be backed up by penalties (usually fines and/or prison sentences) for failure to report. In effect, this provision made it a criminal offense for such designated persons not to report suspected abuse.[7]

The result of the "immunity" provision has been that overzealous and incompetent social workers feel uninhibited in bringing any child abuse charge, no matter how frivolous or unfounded. At the same time, the "mandated reporting" provision has resulted in forcing professionals who are knowledgeable about sex abuse to report frivolous accusations that they know are false, because they themselves would face criminal charges if they did not.

Making legislative changes to remove these provisions—first at the federal level, then among the states—will be an important step in reducing the current sex-abuse hysteria.

NOTES

[1] Eric Felten, "Divorce's Atom Bomb: Child Sex Abuse," *Insight,* Nov. 25, 1991, p.10.

[2] Felten, p.10.

Also: In Texas, child protective services report that 70% of alleged sexual abuse cases are false when a claim is made by a divorcing parent. *Transitions* September/October 1992. (Cited in *The Liberator,* January 1993, p.5.)

Also: The epidemic of false child abuse allegations is not limited to divorce custody situations, nor to sex-abuse allegations. The National Center on Child Abuse and Neglect reported approximately 1.9 million false allegations of child abuse in 1994—about 66 percent of all reports. See: Department of Health and Human Services, National Center on Child Abuse and Neglect. *Child Maltreatment 1994: Reports from the States to the National Center on Child Abuse and Neglect* (page ix).

[3] Barbara Amiel, "Feminism Hits Middle Age," *National Review*, Nov. 24, 1989, p.25.

[4] Felten, p.36.

[5] Bruce G. Gould, "If You Are Falsely Accused of Child Abuse...," *The Liberator,* January 1993, p.9+.

[6] Richard A. Gardner, M.D., *Sex Abuse Hysteria: Salem Witch Trials Revisited.* New Jersey: Creative Therapeutics, 1991.
    See also Richard A. Gardner, M.D., *True and False Accusations of Child Sex Abuse.* Cresskill, N.J.: Creative Therapeutics, 1992.

[7] Richard A. Gardner, M.D. "Revising the Child Abuse Prevention and Treatment Act— Our Best Hope for Dealing with Sex-Abuse Hysteria in the United States," *Conference Proceedings Booklet of the Seventh National Conference of the Children's Rights Council, April 28–May 2, 1993.*

CHAPTER 16

Representing Yourself

Someone who represents himself in court is called a *pro se* (pronounced "pro-say") litigant. Representing yourself is a challenge, but it is not necessarily more stressful than having an attorney. It may require a lot of time in the law library. Fathers who are new at representing themselves often waste a lot of time trying to get procedure right. You should not get too hung up on procedure, however, because frequently domestic-relations judges do not require strict procedure from *pro se* litigants. Also, frequently, the judge has already decided whether you are going to win or lose, so it doesn't matter what you do.

I have known a lot of people to represent themselves, and I have done it many times myself. Overall, fathers representing themselves seem to do as well as fathers with attorneys. This does not mean that *pro se* litigants don't sometimes bomb out; they often do. But so do the lawyers. Overall, the results are close to the same, partly because fathers usually lose whether they have a lawyer or not, and partly because it's the luck of the draw. If you get a good judge, you are more likely to get a fair decision.

Most fathers I know who have represented themselves usually did not do so initially. Most had a lawyer through the main custody fight, but in subsequent returns to court—usually, to get their ex-wives to obey the visitation order, or to reduce child support—they represented themselves.

One advantage in going through the first part with a lawyer is that you will build a collection of sample pleadings—motions, requests for subpoenas, and so forth—which you can copy and modify when representing yourself.

If you want to represent yourself, you should definitely be in a fathers' support group, because there will probably be fathers there who have done it themselves and can help you. The very best arrangement is to get a lawyer who will advise you in representing yourself, someone you can consult with when you have a question. It will cost you something, but much less than if the lawyer has to do all the leg work and make the appearance.

The advantage to representing yourself is that you know your case better than anyone. You can give your full effort to what you do and say.

Lawyers often pull punches because they do not want to offend judges, or they want to hurry up to get to another appointment. You don't have to do that. The disadvantage to representing yourself is that if you are up against a lawyer, especially a lawyer who appears often before this judge, the judge isn't likely to let you win no matter how good your case is.

If you are a lawyer, it can be particularly unwise to represent yourself, especially in the initial hearing. First of all, you are crashing the club. Judges are there to make money for lawyers, and you are spoiling it because you are depriving a local lawyer of the opportunity to make money off you. Also as a lawyer, you can readily recognize when the judge is straying from law, as they so often do in divorce-custody cases. So he will want to get you out of there fast.

To some judges, a lawyer-father representing himself appears as an evil ogre using his law skills to terrify the poor little wife who has to hire a lawyer and shell out thousands in legal fees. A lawyer-father I know who represented himself ended up with the largest "abusive litigation" award against him in Virginia history. All he was doing was seeking joint custody.

The Men's Defense Association in Minnesota has produced a number of good pamphlets specifically for fathers representing themselves in divorce-custody matters. The Nolo Press and HALT publish general materials for *pro se* litigants. (See Chapter 17 for details and addresses.)

Remember, in representing yourself, just as when a lawyer represents you, everything you utter must relate to the best interest of the child.

• • •

There are two circumstances in which fathers represent themselves most often. One is enforcing visitation after you have obtained a court order. The second is defending yourself when you have fallen behind in child support.

ENFORCING VISITATION

After the order has been entered assigning custody, visitation, and child support, your ex is legally bound to obey the order and let you see your children at the appointed times (in theory anyhow). I am presuming here that your ex has custody and you have visitation. If your wife does not let you see your children on the days and times specified in the order, you will have to take her back to court to get the order enforced.

In most states, the police cannot enforce a visitation order. They

FIGURE 1

SAMPLE LETTER IN RESPONSE TO VISITATION DENIAL

```
                                    Your address
                                    Your town, State

                                    May 8, 199-

Ms. Jane Doe
Her address
Her town, State

Dear Jane:

    Pursuant to the court order, I came by to pick
up Johnny and Jackie at 5:00 p.m. on Friday, May
7 for weekend visitation.  Contrary to the court
order, you would not let them come with me.

    Pursuant to the court order, I will come by
again on Friday, May 21 at 5:00 p.m. to pick them
up.  I hope you will not interfere with visita-
tion again.  Also, I would like to arrange make-
up time for the missed weekend.  Either the
weekend of May 14 or May 28 would be fine.
Please let me know if you will agree to that.

                                    Sincerely,


                                    John Doe

cc: Court File
```

cannot make your ex give you the children at 5:00 p.m. on Friday, just because you have a court order that says she is supposed to. They will, however, enforce the custody provision of that same order. If you bring your children back an hour late, you could end up in jail.

Here are the things you can do if your wife denies access. First of all, every time she denies access, you can go to court and file a Rule to Show Cause for denial of access. A rule is like an automatic motion. A court date will be set at which you will both appear. You will tell the judge that she denied access on such and such a date, and she will have to "show cause," that is, give a good reason, or she will be found in contempt of court. Unfortunately, it is very easy for women to "show cause." All they have to do is say that little Johnny was sick that day or that he had to do his homework, or some such thing. If she gives a flimsy excuse like this, you have to argue that you are just as capable as she is of taking care of the child when he's sick; or you are just as capable of helping him with his homework, or whatever.

The judge may not believe your wife's excuse for denying access, but he is unlikely to impose any sanction. You'll be lucky if he tells her not to do it any more.

Another strategy is not to go to court every time she denies access, but to let it happen a few times, then file a Rule to Show Cause. If you take this approach, you must document every time she denies access. You should document it two ways: 1) by having a friend go with you to pick up your children on the days you are supposed to have visitation. This way you have a witness. You can go one better, if you have your friend bring a videocamera and tape the whole thing. 2) After your ex denies access, write her a letter like the one shown in Figure 1. After she denies access three times, and you have sent three letters, go into court and file a Rule to Show Cause. Your case will be very strong. If she continues to deny access after a judge has told her to stop, repeat the above procedure and go to court again.

STAYING OUT OF JAIL FOR CHILD SUPPORT

If you fall behind in paying your child support, you can be served with a Rule to Show Cause, and you will have to appear in court to explain why you haven't paid the full amount required by the court order.

Even though the order is probably unfair, and even though anyone can see that the divorce has put you in the poor house, the judge may decide you just do not want to pay the full amount and find you in contempt. He can then send you to jail for being in contempt of court. This is an extortionary tactic they use to force you to beg, borrow, or steal the money any way you can.

As you are probably aware, it is not legal in the United States to send anyone to jail for owing money. Here, the pretense is that they are not sending you to jail for owing money, they are sending you to jail for being in contempt of a court order.

First you must argue that putting you in jail will not be in the best interest of your child, because a) then you will not even be able to pay as much child support as you have been paying; b) you may lose your job, which means it will be a long time before you can pay child support again; c) if you lose your job, you may be evicted from your residence, or have your car repossessed, etc. which means it will be even longer before you get to the point where you can pay any child support, much less the full amount that you allegedly owe; and d) if you are in jail, your children will be unable to visit with you, and that is a terrible deprivation for them.

Second, since you are appearing without an attorney, you should argue that this is a quasi-criminal offense and that you cannot be jailed without an attorney. In *Argersinger v. Hamlin*, the Supreme Court ruled that "Under no circumstances under any court in the land may anyone be imprisoned, however briefly, unless he was represented by or waived his right to counsel." *See* 407 U.S. 25, 32 LEd 2d 530, 92 S.Ct. 2006 (1972). You have to get a copy of this case law to hand up to the judge. Be sure that you do not say that you are waiving your right to counsel. You do not have counsel because you cannot afford it. This may dissuade the judge from jailing you, since he will not want to appoint counsel for you. On the other hand, the judge may just ignore these arguments and send you to jail anyway.

Third, before appearing in court on a contempt charge for child support, you should prepare an appeal and a stay of the order, and have a lawyer or friend ready to file these in the higher court as soon as you are sentenced to jail.

Last, before appearing in court on a contempt charge for child support, you should also prepare a Writ of Habeas Corpus and have a lawyer or friend prepared to file it if you are sent to jail. If you are sentenced to jail, try the appeal first. If that fails, try the writ. The writ is filed in a federal court, while your custody/divorce/support case is in the jurisdiction of a state court. It costs more to file the Writ of Habeas Corpus than to file an appeal.

Habeas Corpus is an ancient common-law writ, issued by a court or judge directing one who holds another in his custody to produce the body of the prisoner or person detained. The purpose of the writ is to prevent unlawful imprisonment, and to transfer jurisdiction from a lower court to a higher court. Theoretically, it tests the legality of the detention or imprisonment, not whether the detained person is guilty or innocent.[1] Consequently, you should argue the constitutional argument that you cannot be imprisoned for debt.

However, since child support is a political hot potato, many judges are reluctant to make any decisions on a constitutional basis. So, in preparing your Writ of Habeas Corpus, also argue your innocence. You should include a financial statement to show the federal judge why you cannot pay child support at the amount set by the lower court. You should also argue that the guidelines were not properly applied (if, for instance, the judge refused to consider any rebuttable factors, like costs incurred for the time your children spend with you, or the tax benefits your wife derives), or that your wife lied about her income and child care expenses, thus driving the support level much higher than it would be, or whatever circumstances apply to your case.

NOTES

[1] Sources: Black's Law Dictionary, 6th Edition, 1990. Encyclopedia Britannica, 1964.

CHAPTER 17

Resources

There are several hundred fathers' groups and related divorce-reform organizations nationwide. For an extensive national list of resources, including children's rights groups, fathers' rights groups, grandparents' rights groups, stepfamily organizations, divorce reformer, and child abuse law reform groups, contact the Children's Rights Council for their *International Directory of Parenting Organizations*. The address is given below. If the kind of group you are looking for has a chapter in your area, the Directory will probably list it.

If you have access to the Internet, you should get on it as soon as possible. To find a fathers' group near you, or to get in touch with individuals who have experience with issues similar to your own case, the Internet is the fastest way to get connected. To start, type "fathers rights" into a netsearch. A host of "hits" will come up, and as you follow these leads, you'll find more and more information pertinent to your case. Some important Internet addresses are given in the following pages.

• • •

To fight your case effectively, whether you are represented by a lawyer, or are representing yourself, you are going to have to make a serious investment of time and money. Fathers are frequently penny-wise and pound-foolish in these matters. I knew a father who was saving up $10,000 to take his ex-wife back to court over custody, but would not spend $25 to join his local fathers support group.

Support and advocacy groups, and the materials they provide, are your best resources. When you compare the $25 to $50 for one year of membership to the $100 to $200 for one *hour* of lawyer's time, the value is remarkable. These groups can provide you with:

- information on lawyers, child psychologists, mediators, and investigators

- assistance in calculating your child support obligation

- updates on laws affecting custody, visitation, and support

- strategic information on fighting for custody, and for fighting false assault charges, false child abuse charges, and false spousal rape charges.

But the greatest benefit you will derive from joining such a group is emotional support. It helps to know other people who are experiencing similar troubles and how they are handling them. Women run to support groups at the first sign of trouble. Fathers tend to avoid them until it's too late. Don't let this happen to you. Get with a support group immediately.

Even the best of these groups is still in the stage of rag-tag army. So don't expect some big official association with fancy offices and professional lobbyists. Nonetheless, they can be a help to you—and you can help them. When you get some distance from your case, you can help these groups to work on changes through the legislature.

GENERAL RESOURCES

Children's Rights Council
Suite 230
220 'I' Street, NE
Washington, DC 20002-4362
(202) 547-6227 or 1-800-787-KIDS (i.e., 787-5437)
Internet website: http://www.vix.com/crc/aboutcrc.htm
Membership $35

The Children's Rights Council (CRC) is the foremost organization working for divorce reform. Its goal is to "demilitarize divorce" by getting divorcing couples out of adversarial litigation and into cooperative mediation. It is a leading advocate of shared parenting (joint custody), constantly reminding legislators that "the best parent is both parents" and that "every child has a right to two parents." Comedian David Brenner is the honorary chairman. Attorney David L. Levy is the president. CRC's annual conference attracts leading scholars and professionals from around the country.

CRC's Catalog of Resources includes legal briefs which you can adapt in writing a brief to support your argument for joint custody. Their excellent book, "The Best Parent is Both Parents," can help broaden your, and your lawyer's, understanding of divorce. It may be helpful to send one to the judge.

CRC currently has chapters in Alabama, Alaska, California, Colorado, Delaware, Florida, Georgia, Indiana, Illinois, Kansas, Kentucky, Maryland, Massachusetts, Michigan, Missouri, Nebraska, New Jersey, New York, Ohio, Pennsylvania, Texas, Virginia, and Vermont, and may have more by the time you read this. Contact CRC's national headquarters to find a chapter near you. If they do not know of a chapter in your area, they will help you start one.

As noted above, CRC also offers an International Directory of Parenting Organizations, which lists most of the children's rights groups and fathers' rights groups in the United States.

Membership includes a subscription to the quarterly newsletter *Speak Out for Children,* which is an excellent chronicle of federal and state legislation affecting custody-related issues.

Fathers' Rights and Equality Exchange (F.R.E.E.)
Anne P. Mitchell, Esq., President
701 Welch Road, No. 323
Palo Alto, California 94304
Phone: (415) 853-6877, Internet: free@vix.com
Membership: $95

On the Internet, F.R.E.E. is the dominant fathers' rights newsgroup, and an excellent resource when seeking advice on specific situations. It can be accessed for free. Other benefits, including books on divorce-custody litigation, come with membership.

The Liberator, *Defender of the Traditional Man*
Men's Defense Association (a.k.a., Men's Rights Association)
17854 Lyons Street
Forest Lake, MN 55025-8854
Fax: (612) 464-7135 • Internet: mensdefens@aol.com
Subscription: $24 (Published monthly)

The Liberator, edited by Richard Doyle, is the flagship newsletter of the legitimate men's rights movement. It is not related to the Robert Bly meet-in-the-woods/beat-the-drum/talking-stick movement.

The Liberator provides a chronicle of the demonization of men in the media and the courts, as well as an ongoing analysis of the political power and government funding of radical feminism. *The Liberator* is also a clearinghouse for a full range of men's rights perspectives, from scholarly articles to the letters of fathers in jail.

It will give you an in-depth perspective of what you are up against. Many fathers' and men's rights groups communicate through *The Liberator,* so it's an excellent way to keep in touch with the developing movement.

National Congress for Fathers and Children (NCFC)
851 Minnesota Avenue
P.O. Box 171675
Kansas City, KS 66117
Phone: (913) 281-9943 • Membership Line: 1-800-733-DADS
Fax: (913) 342-1414 • Media: 1-800-733-0484
Internet: ncfc@primenet.com
NCFC is the largest national organization dedicated specifically to the issues of fathers' and children's rights.

American Fathers Coalition (AFC)
Phone: (202) 835-1000 Ext. 14 • (202) 328-4377
Internet: afc@cap.gwu.edu   Home page: http://www.erols.com/afc/
AFC is the Washington, D.C.-based lobbying arm of the National Congress for Fathers and Children. Stuart Miller is the Senior Legislative Analyst.

American Fathers Alliance (AFA)
Phone: Washington State (206) 272-2152, Washington D.C. (202) 328-4377
This national group is headed by Bill Harrington, one of the Commissioners on the U.S. Commission for Child and Family Welfare.

RESOURCES FOR COMBATTING FALSE ABUSE ALLEGATION

National Child Abuse Defense and Resource Center
Kimberly A. Hart, Executive Director
P.O. Box 638
Holland, OH 43528
Phone: (419) 865-0513 • Fax: (865-0526)
According to my sources, this is the number one organization to contact for help with false abuse allegations.

National Association of State VOCAL Organizations (NASVO)
P.O. Box 1314
Orangevale, CA 95662
(916) 988-9482

Victims of Child Abuse Laws (VOCAL)
Help line: (303) 233-5321

So many parents and children have been terrorized with false child-abuse allegations that VOCAL chapters have sprung up all over the country. For the one nearest you, contact NASVO or the VOCAL help line.

False Memory Syndrome Foundation
Pamela Freyd, Executive Director
3401 Market Street, Suite 130
Philadelphia, PA 19104
Phone: 1-800-568-8882 or (215) 387-1865
Membership: $100

Although fathers in divorce are not frequently accused under the guise of false memory syndrome, it is worth contacting this organization because they have one of the best collections of published materials on false child abuse allegations. Their resources include many case summaries that you or your attorney can use to discredit false allegations.

They also provide a referral list of attorneys and psychologists who are experts in this field. According to my sources, their referral list is more comprehensive but less selective than referrals from the National Child Abuse Defense and Resource Center.

The referral service is for members only. Anyone can obtain the publications though. Bibliographies can be requested and publications ordered from them at cost, without membership.

REPRESENTING YOURSELF
(PRO SE LITIGATION)

HALT (Help Abolish Legal Tyranny)
An Organization of Americans for Legal Reform
1319 F Street, NW • Suite 300
Washington, DC 20004
(202) 347-9600

They publish a number of useful self-help legal books, including a book on filing a no-fault divorce, a book on how to use a lawyer, and a book on how to sue a lawyer for malpractice.

Nolo Press
Self-Help Law Center
Internet: http://nearnet.gnn.com/gnn/bus/nolo
Look for Nolo Press publications at any large bookstore.

OTHER RESOURCES

American Retirees Association
Captain Frank Ault, USN (Ret.), Executive Director
2009 N. 14th Street, Suite 300
Arlington, VA 22201
(703) 527-3065
Membership: $25 per year.

This organization specializes in divorce-related problems as they affect military personnel (both active and retired). They have a useful book entitled, *Divorce and the Military, the Uniform Services Former Spouses Protection Act*. It explains why, if your wife divorces you, she gets half your pension even if she remarries.

Internet News Groups

F.R.E.E. (Fathers Rights and Equality Exchange)

Alt.Dads-Rights

Alt.Child-Support

Fathernet

Computer Bulletin Boards

Liberator	(612) 464-7257
Men's Information Network	(206) 328-0356
Fathers' Express	(814) 362-6546
Fatherboard-North	(302) 737-6041
Canada	(416) 856-4980
National Congress for Men and Children (NCMC)	(602) 840-4752

Afterword

After reading this book, you might have the sense that there is no certain plan of attack to ensure that you will win custody; that even if you concede custody, in the hopes of averting a costly court battle and sparing your children great emotional trauma, there is no certainty that you will avoid such a battle; and, that no matter how fair or generous you are, there is no sure way to avoid being saddled with an outrageous alimony, child support, or property settlement. These impressions are all correct. Any one of the above possibilities could become your reality.

Following the strategies described in this book will greatly improve your chances of winning custody or obtaining a more tolerable custody and support arrangement. However, because our civil justice system has come to work in a way that thwarts quick and reasonable resolutions, the only true, lasting, solution will be to change the laws governing divorce and custody. At present, the courts have the power to take your children away from you at a whim, and to deprive you of your livelihood at a whim. With this power, they create a sense of terror that keeps both parties in litigation while reaping huge benefits for the legal profession, no matter what the outcome of the case.

The first step to resolving this problem is to remove this power from the judges and return it to the parents. This can be done by passing legislation for presumptive joint physical custody for divorced and unwed parents, and to establish as law that no divorced or unwed parent can be deprived of custody of his or her children any more easily than married parents can. In the overwhelming majority of custody disputes, both parties are good and caring parents who could readily get along, if the courts would only promote cooperation instead of conflict.

In reading this book, it may also have occurred to you that what is being described here is unbelievable, and, if true, a violation of constitutional rights on an immense scale. Fathers who have been through the courts often meet with disbelief when they tell people their stories. But these stories are true, and the bottom line is that many men are denied their basic civil rights when they enter a domestic-relations court.

For decades now, men have remained aloof from protecting their own interests in political gender issues, while these issues have grown to dominate public policy. As a result, we have arrived in a strange world. The marriage contract, traditionally one of the most solemn contracts made in society, is still made with state and religious authority, and often before hundreds of witnesses. Yet today, it is totally unenforceable. The divorce contract, on the other hand—at least the man's obligation under a divorce contract—is enforced with the power of a futuristic police state that can hunt you in every corner of this country and abroad.

The problem, in brief, is that the traditional socialization of males has not prepared us to meet this crisis. The characteristics that comprise traditional notions of manhood—inner fortitude, self sacrifice, strong silent stoicism—are counterproductive on the battlefield of gender politics. Men are not supposed to *talk* about their problems. We are supposed to assess a situation, determine what must be done, and do it. From Teddy Roosevelt to Ernest Hemingway to John Wayne and Clint Eastwood, the popular icon of American masculinity is defined by rugged individualism, with brevity of speech as a common corollary.

For many men, joining a group to *complain* that they have been beaten by women, is in itself too humiliating, too emasculating, to endure. In this battle, though—if we properly assess our situation—what needs to be done is for men to *speak* their pain. It is also necessary for us to ask women for help. To win this battle, we will have to turn to our women friends, wives, sisters, and mothers, not to mention women delegates, and ask them to help us preserve our basic liberty interests—the right to enjoy the fruits of our own labor and to be allowed to love our own children.

Right now, reforming the system by political means must be the furthest thing from your mind. But after you have completed the harrowing journey through divorce court, you may realize that you have a lifetime problem, and you will recognize that unless we strive together, politically, nothing will change. One way to effect change is to become active in a fathers' rights, children's rights, or men's rights group.

If your traditional male upbringing prevents you from speaking for your own benefit, then speak up for your children. For, as much as the institutionalized prejudice against men affects our own lives, it has had a disastrous effect on a generation of children. In the United States, 75 percent of juvenile delinquents, 71 percent of pregnant teenagers, and 90 percent of teenage runaways, are children from fatherless homes. Such statistics are endless. Whether the subject is gang involvement, drug abuse, alcoholism, scholastic failure, or teen suicide, the incidence among children from fatherless homes far exceeds the incidence among children from homes where the father is present.[1] Our culture's institutionalized hostility toward men has reached a dimension where it no longer affects only individual families, but is tearing apart the social fabric.

There is no substitute for a father's love and guidance, and not all the "child support" in the world can buy a little boy or girl a new father. Despite the derision that is heaped on fathers by the media, and despite the ridicule you may meet with in court, you should never forget how important you are to your children. Only by fighting together through political unity will we be able to restore some degree of social normalcy. It is not only our right, but also our duty, to remain active fathers to our children.

NOTES

[1] For extensive citations on studies of children from fatherless families, *see* Amneus, op. cit., pages 215-293; and Levy, op. cit., pages 118-120. *See also:*

Barbara Dafoe Whitehead, "Dan Quayle Was Right," *The Atlantic*, April 1993 (p.47-84).

Joseph P. Shapiro, Joannie M. Schrof, Mike Tharp, Dorian Friedman, "Honor Thy Children," *U.S. News & World Report*, February 27, 1995 (p.39-49).

Scott Minerbrook, "Lives Without Father," *U.S. News & World Report*, February 27, 1995 (p.50-55).

Annotated Definitions

access: Most often called "visitation," access refers to the time that the noncustodial parent (usually the father) and the children get to see each other. It is also called "parenting time" or "father's time." "Denial of access" refers to instances when the custodial parent will not let the noncustodial parent and children see each other.

attorney for plaintiff/petitioner: The attorney representing the party who files the suit, petition, or pleading.

attorney for defendant/respondent: The attorney who represents the party defending, or responding to the suit, petition, or pleading.

bailiff: This court official usually goes unnoticed. He or she is in the courtroom, gun in holster to maintain order if necessary. If you are *pro se* (representing yourself in court), you may suddenly become aware of the bailiff. Often bailiffs are unnecessarily rude or harassing to fathers who are *pro se* litigants.

billing event: Any reason whatsoever for your lawyer to charge you money. A phone call may be a billing event. Signing a document may be a billing event.

case file: The file kept at the clerk's office that has a record of every motion filed in your case and every ruling made by the judge.

Child Protective Services (CPS): A governmental agency (usually a part of the Department of Social Services) whose duty is to protect the interests of minors within their jurisdiction. CPS will become involved in any case where child abuse is alleged. Many lawyers and litigants are of the opinion that CPS does more harm than good. Frequently, it is overzealous social workers from CPS who are the driving force behind false child abuse allegations. Occasionally, when a couple is in turmoil, a CPS worker might offer to care for the children "for a week or two." *Never* agree to let CPS take your children. Once they take your children, it will be a long time and cost a lot of money before you see them again.

clerk of the court: The elected or appointed official in charge of accepting court pleadings and scheduling dates.

clerk's office: The office in the court building occupied by the sub-clerks who actually accept the pleadings, issue subpoenas, keep the files, and microfilm the files. If you are representing yourself, you have to go to the clerk's office to file a motion or to see your case file.

codes/statutes: The terms are used synonymously, meaning the laws of the states or of the federal government.

commissioner in chancery: In some states, an official equivalent to a hearing commissioner in other states. (*See* hearing commissioner.)

complainant: *See* plaintiff.

consent order: A court order arrived at by agreement between the parties, rather than by a judge's decision. In other words, it is "consented to." Judges prefer a consent order to making a ruling because it relieves them of any blame for making an egregious error. Consequently, the judge and/ or your lawyer may attempt to browbeat you into signing an agreement. Later, if you object that it is unfair, they will say, "Well, you agreed to it."

court reporter: The person who records all proceedings occurring in the courtroom. In courts of record, there will usually be a court reporter (a few require you to hire your own). In courts not of record, like the many Juvenile and Domestic Relations courts, you must hire a court reporter if you want one to be there. If you want a transcript of all or part of your case, you have to contact the court reporting company and order one. Transcripts usually cost around $3.00 per double-spaced page. Two hours translates into about 80 pages. If you only need a particular testimony, or an extract from a particular testimony, you can ask to have just that part transcribed, but you will be charged for search time.

court: Besides denoting the place where your case is heard, the term "court" is often used synonymously with "judge," as in, "The court ruled in his favor." "Courts" and "judges" are also used synonymously, as in "The courts tend to favor mothers in custody cases."

custody investigator: A custody investigator might be provided by the Department of Social Services, but usually it is an independent contractor hired by one of the parties in a custody dispute. The custody investigator will visit one or both of the parents' homes (if the non-hiring parent agrees to cooperate) and will write a report stating what benefits and drawbacks either home affords to the child. Being at an initial disadvantage, it is often a father who hires a custody investigator. This way, he has a professional witness, and because it is someone who is part of the system, the court respects this person. Many independent custody investigators are former social workers, which reinforces their connection to the court. Many of them are also women. Having a woman who is respected by the court testify on your behalf is good politics.

custodial parent: The parent who receives custody of the children. When one parent has sole custody, she makes all the decisions regarding the child's upbringing, unless otherwise specified in the court order. Almost always, the noncustodial parent must pay child support to the custodial parent.

district court commissioner: The district court commissioner is a lower court official who can perform certain judicial functions when a judge is not available. He can issue arrest warrants for assault, and *ex parte* orders for domestic violence. If children are involved, the *ex parte* order will include an order for *pendente lite* custody. In many jurisdictions, there is a district court commissioner at the courthouse or at a major police substation 24 hours a day.

divorce *a mensa et thoro*: An antiquated term for a "limited" divorce. When the parties have not been separated long enough to get an absolute divorce, a party can still petition the court for certain immediate benefits of divorce such as support, custody, and injunctions. The court may grant the petitions, but the parties will still be legally married until they obtain an absolute divorce. (*See* Chapter 6.)

divorce *a vinculo matrimonii*: an antiquated term for an absolute divorce. Once an absolute divorce is granted, all custody, property, and support issues have been resolved. (*See* Chapter 6.)

ex parte: *Ex parte*, pronounced "ex par-tay," means "on one side only." An *ex parte* hearing is a hearing in which only one party is present. An order issued at such a hearing, at the request of and for one party, is called an *ex parte* order. (*See* Chapter 14.)

grandparents' rights: Some jurisdictions provide statutory rights for grandparents (and other relatives) to obtain visitation with their grandchildren. If your state provides for grandparent's rights, you can have your parents petition for their own, separate, visitation time with your children. This a good way to expand your visitation.

grounds for divorce: *See* Appendix B.

guardian *ad litem*: Often, for no particularly good reason, the judge will appoint a guardian *ad litem* for the child or children in a custody dispute. The guardian is an attorney who, supposedly, will objectively represent the best interests of the children in the dispute. Despite the fact that guardians often have every evidence that one parent is creating trouble to which the other must respond, it is unusual for a guardian *ad litem* to do anything decisive to end a conflict. Hence, within the divorce-custody business, a guardian *ad litem* is often referred to as a "guardian do nothing." Lawyers who accept a lot of "court-appoints" (appointments as guardian *ad litem*), usually do so because they are not particularly good at drumming up business for themselves. Consequently, the role of guardian *ad litem* is sometimes called "Welfare for lawyers." Often the state pays for the guardian *ad litem*, but often too, the court assigns the cost to the parents. The guardian's personal interest is to see that the case lasts as long as possible so he can continue to make $40 to $60 an hour for sitting on his hands.

hearing commissioner: A hearing commissioner is a court official who is not a judge but has the authority to hear certain matters pertaining to divorce and custody. The extent of the hearing commissioner's authority varies from jurisdiction to jurisdiction. In some, the hearing commissioner can hear only support and visitation matters; in others, he can hear all matters.

Generally, if the parties are in agreement about all the issues of the divorce—custody, support, property—the hearing commissioner will read the agreement into the record, and a transcript will be submitted to a judge for signature. If the issues are contested, then the hearing commissioner's role is usually more limited. In some jurisdictions, you will only have a hearing before a hearing commissioner if you consent to it. If you do not consent, then you will automatically have a hearing before a judge.

In other jurisdictions, the hearing commissioner will hear your case and make recommendations to the judge, which the judge may accept even if you oppose them.

joint custody: Both parents share equally, or in large measure, in raising the minor children. Courts may award joint physical and legal custody, but if they award joint custody at all, it is usually joint legal custody. Having joint physical custody means you will see your children often. Supposedly, if you have joint legal custody, you are supposed to have a say in major decisions in the child's life. But if your wife doesn't ask your opinion, who's going to make her? Having joint legal custody, without joint physical custody, usually has little practical meaning. If your wife wants to move the children to another state, having joint legal custody will not necessarily stop her. In some jurisdictions, there is one possible advantage to having joint legal custody; it may help reduce your child support if you eventually obtain more visitation with your children, because then you will meet the criterion for the joint custody calculation.

judge: An elected or appointed official who serves a term of a certain number of years and make decisions and passes orders concerning your case. In Maryland, judges are appointed by the governor for one year, then stand for popular election. In Virginia, judges are elected by the state legislators. Most jurisdictions follow one of these forms for choosing judges. Washington, D.C. is unique. Because it is a federal district, all judges are appointed by the President of United States. All decisions of a commissioner or master must be taken to a judge for final determination.

judgment: A final order of a court.

litigant *pro se*: A party who represents himself in court. (You will also see this term written with the word order reversed— "a *pro se* litigant." The meaning is the same.)

magistrate: In some jurisdictions the term "magistrate" denotes a hearing commissioner (see above); in others, a magistrate is like a district court commissioner (see above) with the power to issue arrest warrants and grant *ex parte* orders.

master: In some jurisdictions, the term "master" denotes a hearing commissioner, as in "Master of Domestic Relations." (*See* hearing commissioner.)

mental health expert: The psychiatrist, psychologist, or licensed clinical social worker (LCSW) assigned by the court, or retained by the plaintiff or the defendant to evaluate the children and/or one or both of the parties. Frequently, the husband and wife will each hire a separate mental health expert.

mental health professional: Same as mental health experts.

motion: A pleading filed with the court requesting the judge to do something in favor of the party making the motion.

no fault divorce: At one time it was necessary for the party seeking a divorce to show that the other party was at fault. Now, under the "no fault" system, the mere allegation of "irreconcilable differences" is a sufficient cause for action. In a no fault divorce, neither party is considered responsible for the divorce, and therefore the court will not take any blame into consideration in making the property settlement, etc. Adultery is the most common allegation in a fault divorce. In practice, it is irrelevant if the woman commits adultery. But if a man commits adultery, many judges are inclined to give the woman a highly favorable property settlement. (*See* Appendix B.)

order: A written ruling signed by a judge settling a particular issue in a case, or all issues in a case.

paternity test: A blood test performed to determine if a certain man is the father of a certain child. Usually, the test is done for the purposes of assigning a child support obligation. There are two kinds of blood tests. The Human Leucocyte Antigens (HLA) test usually costs around $550–$600 (unless it is court ordered and the jurisdiction has an arrangement with a lab for a reduced rate). The HLA test gives a high range of probability, up to 98 percent. The second type of test is the DNA test. It costs about $1,000 and its findings are considered certain.

plaintiff (also called complainant or petitioner): This is the person who initiates the suit by filing a petition. For example, if you initiated the suit by filing a petition for custody, you would be the plaintiff. Your wife could file a cross petition for custody, but you would always remain the plaintiff in the case.

private detective: When a private detective is hired in a divorce-custody dispute, it is usually because one party is trying to prove that the other is committing adultery. It is difficult to establish adultery. To do so, the detective must not only establish that the adulterous couple had the time, place, and opportunity to commit a sexual act, but also that at some time he witnessed them displaying affection. If the couple checks into a hotel, however, it is not necessary to establish the display of affection. A regular pattern of meetings with time, place, and opportunity to commit a sexual act may also preclude the need to establish a display of affection.

In some states, the courts also frown upon a single divorced parent having a lover spend the night when children are present in the house. In Virginia, for example, if you can prove that your ex-wife has her boyfriend spending the night all the time, it could be grounds for a change of custody.

A second major reason to hire a private detective is to research income and assets for determining property settlement and support obligations.

private process server: Person retained by plaintiff or defendant to serve subpoenas or petitions on the opposing party or on a third party.

respondent: *See* defendant.

retainer: The initial fee paid to an attorney for services to be rendered. (*See* Chapter 7.)

service (or, "serving notice"): Sending, or handing, a legal document to the opposing party or to a third party informing them that you are going to ask the court to do something, or that they are required to produce documents or appear somewhere. With the exception of subpoenas, and the initial petition commencing a lawsuit, most service can be done by first class mail. (*See* Chapter 8.)

sheriff (process server): In some jurisdictions you always have to hire a private process server to serve notices, subpoenas, etc., but in other jurisdictions the sheriff's department provides service (you might still want to hire a private process server if you want to be sure that notice is served promptly). An attorney can also serve process on his client's opponent. After the attorneys have entered their appearances, most documents are served on them. Costs for service, whether through a private process server or the sheriff's department vary from jurisdiction to jurisdiction.

subpoena: Court order signed by the clerk of the court or the judge requiring the personal appearance of a party or the production of documents at a particular place.

venue: The most appropriate jurisdiction in which a suit should be filed, as determined by statute and convenience. (*See* Chapter 13.)

verbatim court reporter: same as court reporter. Verbatim means they are recording everything word for word.

shared custody, shared parenting: These terms are synonymous with "joint custody." However, judges generally don't like the sound of "joint custody" with its implication of shared privilege. The term "shared parenting," which carries more of an implication of shared responsibility, works best.

split custody: Sometimes, when more than one child is the subject of a custody dispute, each parent will get custody of one or more of the children.

UIFSA: Uniform Interstate Family Support Act. (For a full explanation, see Appendix D.)

URESA: Uniform Reciprocal Enforcement of Support Act. (For a full explanation, see Appendix D.)

Grounds For Divorce

The specific grounds, or reasons, for which one can obtain a divorce vary from state to state, but the distinctions are generally insignificant. The examples set forth below, from Virginia, Maryland, and Washington, D.C., provide a good sampling of what you'll find across the country. Many states are like Washington, D.C. They are "no-fault" divorce jurisdictions. But even jurisdictions that provide fault grounds for divorce also grant no-fault divorces. A no-fault divorce usually requires a separation period of six months to a year, depending on the requirements of the jurisdiction.

WHY GROUNDS FOR DIVORCE ARE USUALLY UNIMPORTANT

Grounds for divorce are generally inconsequential because:

(1) Most divorces are granted on a no-fault basis. This is true for no other reason than because it is easier to wait a year than to prove fault. Also, in many instances, the hearing date is set so far out that by the time the parties get to court the period of separation has elapsed.

(2) The second reason that grounds are unimportant—at least as far as men are concerned—is because even if you prove fault, it is unlikely to have any effect on the award of custody, child support, alimony, or property settlement. Also, it can be expensive to prove fault. When a father is attempting to prove fault, it usually means he is attempting to prove that his wife committed adultery. Proving adultery usually involves hiring a private detective. Some fathers go to a great deal of expense to prove that their wives committed adultery, and all to no purpose. They may spend a lot of money and fail to meet the burden of proof. Or, they may succeed in proving it, and as noted above, it will have no effect on the judge's ruling.

WHY GROUNDS FOR DIVORCE MAY BE IMPORTANT

Again, we are faced with the double standard. If a woman proves fault against a man, it is very common for judges to use that as an excuse to punish the man with an unfavorable alimony order or property settlement. One thing to be wary of is moving out of the house during separation. Your wife might insist you move out, or you may move out by mutual agreement. Regardless, your wife can turn around and testify that you deserted her. If desertion is a fault ground in your state, the judge can use it as an excuse to punish you.

There is one circumstance in which proving your wife's adultery may be useful—if your wife has a lover spend the night while the children are under the same roof. In some states, this behavior is frowned upon and may lead to a father being awarded custody.

If it appears that the grounds for divorce may be important in your case, ask your lawyer for a copy of the statute, or go to a local law library to obtain one. If there is any reason that your wife may be able to bring a fault divorce against you, discuss this with your lawyer so that you do not get blind-sided.

MARYLAND

There are seven grounds for an absolute divorce in the State of Maryland. For each and every ground for absolute divorce, you must be separate and apart for at least one year, with the exception of adultery. Separate and apart means that the parties may not live under the same roof or engage in sex.

The first ground for divorce is adultery, which does not require any period of separation from your spouse. However, once you find out that your spouse is having intimate relations with someone of the opposite sex, you cannot be intimate with your spouse. If you have sex with your spouse, you are condoning the adultery and cannot use this ground for divorce. Additionally, you cannot procure a sexual partner for your spouse and allege that he or she is committing adultery. In the State of Maryland, adultery is a crime punishable by a $10.00 (yes, ten-dollar) fine.

Desertion is the second ground for divorce. It means that your spouse left for no apparent reason, and you did nothing to cause him or her to leave you. The separation must continue for 12 months before you can file for an absolute divorce, it must be deliberate, and there can be no hope of the parties reconciling.

One-year voluntary separation is the next ground for divorce, and it means that the husband and wife were unable to get along and mutually decided to live separate and apart. In addition, there can be no hope of the parties resuming the marital relationship.

The fourth ground for divorce is a two-year separation. After two years, a divorce will be granted regardless of whether or not the separation was voluntary.

Constructive desertion is the fifth ground for divorce. It means that you left because you would not allow yourself to be abused by your spouse sexually, physically, or mentally.

Next, if your spouse has been convicted of a crime in any state or federal jurisdiction punishable by at least three years in jail and he or she has already served 12 months, you may file for divorce.

Insanity is the last ground for divorce. In most states, if one of the parties has been adjudicated insane, you cannot obtain a divorce because the insane party is not considered competent to go through a court proceeding. However, in Maryland, if your spouse has been confined in a mental facility for at least three years and two psychiatrists will say that the insanity is incurable and there is no hope of recovery, you can obtain a divorce, provided one of the parties has lived in that state for at least two years.

VIRGINIA

The Commonwealth of Virginia has six grounds for divorce. The first ground is adultery, which means that your spouse is having sexual relations with a person of the opposite sex. As in Maryland, this act cannot be with the mutual consent of your spouse, nor must you be separate and apart for any period of time before filing for divorce. However, you cannot have sex with your spouse after you learn about the adultery or you will be condoning the sexual act.

The second ground for divorce is engaging in buggery or sodomy outside the marriage. Therefore, Virginia will grant a divorce based on a homosexual encounter.

If one of the parties is convicted of a felony and is given a sentence of more than one year in jail and no sexual encounter has occurred since the party was confined, you can seek a divorce.

If your spouse deserted and abandoned you without cause, you may file for a divorce after one year.

Fifth, if your spouse constructively deserted you by abusing you sexually, physically, or mentally, you may file for a divorce after a one-year period of continuous separation.

Sixth, you can obtain a divorce if you and your spouse have lived separate and apart continuously for one year without cohabitation. Additionally, if you have no minor children and a written separation agreement, you may seek to dissolve the marriage after a six-month separation period.

Lastly, in Virginia, insanity will not bar a divorce, but the court will appoint a guardian for the insane party to represent his or her interests.

DISTRICT OF COLUMBIA

There are two grounds for divorce in the District of Columbia. They are:

(1) both parties have *voluntarily* lived separate and apart for *six months* prior to the filing of a divorce; or

(2) the parties have lived separate and apart for *one year* prior to seeking a divorce, regardless of whether or not one party opposes the divorce.

The District of Columbia is a no-fault divorce jurisdiction. However, fault becomes an issue when alimony is awarded or property is divided. As a matter of common practice in the District, if a woman commits adultery, there is not considered to be any fault; if a man commits adultery, however, the judge may very likely impose a punitive alimony or property award.

An additional peculiarity of the District is that "living separate and apart" does not mean the parties have to live in separate dwellings. Both parties can remain in the marital home, so long as they refrain from having sex and occupy different rooms in the house or apartment.

Excerpts From the Virginia Code

These excerpts are provided to give you an idea of the laws governing child support. The method used in Virginia—the incomes-shares model—is used in 34 states (and a variation is used in another 7 states). However, the language and details vary from state to state. You must consult the statutes for your own state. (***Virginia residents note:*** *These excerpts are provided for general information purposes only. Be sure to check your law library to ensure you have the most up-to-date version of the Code.*)

§ 20-107.2. Court may decree as to custody and support of minor children. — Upon decreeing the dissolution of a marriage, and also upon decreeing a divorce, whether from the bond of matrimony or from bed and board, and upon decreeing that neither party is entitled to a divorce, the court may make such further decree as it shall deem expedient concerning the custody or visitation and support of the minor children of the parties as provided in Chapter 6.1 (§ 20-124.1 et seq.) of Title 20, including an order that either party provide health care coverage.

§ 20-108.1. Determination of child or spousal support. —
A. In any proceeding on the issue of determining spousal support, the court shall consider all evidence presented relevant to any issues joined in that proceeding. The court's decision shall be rendered based upon the evidence relevant to each individual case.

B. In any proceeding on the issue of determining child support under this title or Title 16.1 or 63.1, the court shall consider all evidence presented relevant to any issues joined in that proceeding. The court's decision in any such proceeding shall be rendered upon the evidence relevant to each individual case. However, there shall be a rebuttable presumption in any judicial or administrative proceeding for child support, including cases involving split custody or shared custody, that the amount of the award which would result from the application of the guidelines set out in § 20-108.2 is the correct amount of child support to be awarded. In order to rebut the presumption, the court shall make written findings in the order, which findings may be incorporated by reference, that the application of such guidelines would be unjust or inappropriate in a particular case. The finding that rebuts the guidelines shall state the amount of support that would have been required under the guidelines, shall give a justification of why the order varies from the guidelines, and shall be determined by relevant evidence pertaining to the following factors affecting the obligation,the ability of each party to provide child support, and the best interests of the child:

1. Actual monetary support for other children, other family members or former family members;

2. Arrangements regarding custody of the children;

3. Imputed income to a party who is voluntarily unemployed or voluntarily under employed; provided that income may not be imputed to the custodial parent when a child is not in school, child care services are not available and the cost of such child care services are not included in the computation;

4. Debts of either party arising during the marriage for the benefit of the child;

5. Debts incurred for production of income;

6. Direct payments ordered by the court for health care coverage, maintaining life insurance coverage pursuant to subsection D, education expenses, or other court-ordered direct payments for the benefit of the child and costs related to the provision of health care coverage pursuant to subdivision 7 of 20-60.3;

7. Extraordinary capital gains such as capital gains resulting from the sale of the marital abode;

8. Age, physical and mental condition of the child or children, including extraordinary medical or dental expenses, and child-care expenses;

9. Independent financial resources, if any, of the child or children;

10. Standard of living for the family established during the marriage;

11. Earning capacity, obligations and needs, and financial resources of each parent;

12. Education and training of the parties and the ability and opportunity of the parties to secure such education and training;

13. Contributions, monetary and nonmonetary, of each party to the well-being of the family;

14. Provisions made with regard to the marital property under 20-107.3;

15. Tax consequences to the parties regarding claims for dependent children and child care expenses;

16. A written agreement between the parties which includes the

amount of child support; and

17. Such other factors, including tax consequences to each party, as are necessary to consider the equities for the parents and children.

C. In any proceeding under this title or Title 16.1 or Title 63.1 on the issue of determining child support, the court shall have the authority to order a party to provide health care coverage, as defined in 63.1-250, for dependent children if reasonable under all the circumstances and health care coverage for a spouse or former spouse.

D. In any proceeding under this title, Title 16.1 or Title 63.1 on the issue of determining child support, the court shall havethe authority to order a party to (i) maintain any existing life insurance policy on the life of either party provided the party soordered has the right to designate a beneficiary and (ii) designate a child or children of the parties as the beneficiary of all ora portion of such life insurance for so long as the party so ordered has a statutory obligation to pay child support for the child or children.

§ 20-108.2. Guideline for determination of child support. —

A. There shall be a rebuttable presumption in any judicial or administrative proceeding for child support under this title or Title 16.1 or 63.1, including cases involving split custody or shared custody, that the amount of the award which would result from the application of the guidelines set forth in this section is the correct amount of child support to be awarded. In order to rebut the presumption, the court shall make written findings in the order as set out in 20-108.1, which findings may be incorporated by reference, that the application of the guidelines would be unjust or inappropriate in a particular case as determined by relevant evidence pertaining to the factors set out in 20-107.2 and 20-108.1. The Department of Social Services shall set child support at the amount resulting from computations using the guidelines set out in this section pursuant to the authority granted to it in Chapter 13 (§ 63.1-249 et seq.) of Title 63.1 and subject to the provisions of § 63.1-264.2.

B. For purposes of application of the guideline, a basic child support obligation shall be computed using the schedule set out below. For combined monthly gross income amounts falling between amounts shown in the schedule, basic child support obligation amounts shall be extrapolated. "Number of children" shall mean the number of children for whom the parents share joint legal responsibility and for whom support is being sought.

SCHEDULE OF
MONTHLY BASIC CHILD SUPPORT OBLIGATIONS

COMBINED MONTHLY GROSS INCOME	ONE CHILD	TWO CHILDREN	THREE CHILDREN	FOUR CHILDREN	FIVE CHILDREN	SIX CHILDREN
0-599	65	65	65	65	65	65
600	110	111	113	114	115	116
650	138	140	142	143	145	146
700	153	169	170	172	174	176
750	160	197	199	202	204	206
800	168	226	228	231	233	236
850	175	254	257	260	263	266
900	182	281	286	289	292	295
950	189	292	315	318	322	325
1000	196	304	344	348	351	355
1050	203	315	373	377	381	385
1100	210	326	402	406	410	415
1150	217	337	422	435	440	445
1200	225	348	436	465	470	475
1250	232	360	451	497	502	507
1300	241	373	467	526	536	542
1350	249	386	483	545	570	576
1400	257	398	499	563	605	611
1450	265	411	515	581	633	645
1500	274	426	533	602	656	680
1550	282	436	547	617	672	714
1600	289	447	560	632	689	737
1650	295	458	573	647	705	754
1700	302	468	587	662	721	772
1750	309	479	600	676	738	789
1800	315	488	612	690	752	805
1850	321	497	623	702	766	819
1900	326	506	634	714	779	834
1950	332	514	645	727	793	848
2000	338	523	655	739	806	862
2050	343	532	666	751	819	877
2100	349	540	677	763	833	891
2150	355	549	688	776	846	905
2200	360	558	699	788	860	920
2250	366	567	710	800	873	934
2300	371	575	721	812	886	948
2350	377	584	732	825	900	963

COMBINED MONTHLY GROSS INCOME	ONE CHILD	TWO CHILDREN	THREE CHILDREN	FOUR CHILDREN	FIVE CHILDREN	SIX CHILDREN
2400	383	593	743	837	913	977
2450	388	601	754	849	927	991
2500	394	610	765	862	940	1006
2550	399	619	776	874	954	1020
2600	405	627	787	886	967	1034
2650	410	635	797	897	979	1048
2700	415	643	806	908	991	1060
2750	420	651	816	919	1003	1073
2800	425	658	826	930	1015	1085
2850	430	667	836	941	1027	1098
2900	435	675	846	953	1039	1112
2950	440	683	856	964	1052	1125
3000	445	691	866	975	1064	1138
3050	450	699	876	987	1076	1152
3100	456	707	886	998	1089	1165
3150	461	715	896	1010	1101	1178
3200	466	723	906	1021	1114	1191
3250	471	732	917	1032	1126	1205
3300	476	740	927	1044	1139	1218
3350	481	748	937	1055	1151	1231
3400	486	756	947	1067	1164	1245
3450	492	764	957	1078	1176	1258
3500	497	772	967	1089	1189	1271
3550	502	780	977	1101	1201	1285
3600	507	788	987	1112	1213	1298
3650	512	797	997	1124	1226	1311
3700	518	806	1009	1137	1240	1326
3750	524	815	1020	1150	1254	1342
3800	530	824	1032	1163	1268	1357
3850	536	834	1043	1176	1283	1372
3900	542	843	1055	1189	1297	1387
3950	547	852	1066	1202	1311	1402
4000	553	861	1078	1214	1325	1417
4050	559	871	1089	1227	1339	1432
4100	565	880	1101	1240	1353	1448
4150	571	889	1112	1253	1367	1463
4200	577	898	1124	1266	1382	1478
4250	583	907	1135	1279	1396	1493
4300	589	917	1147	1292	1410	1508
4350	594	926	1158	1305	1424	1523
4400	600	935	1170	1318	1438	1538

COMBINED MONTHLY GROSS INCOME	ONE CHILD	TWO CHILDREN	THREE CHILDREN	FOUR CHILDREN	FIVE CHILDREN	SIX CHILDREN
4450	606	944	1181	1331	1452	1553
4500	612	954	1193	1344	1467	1569
4550	618	963	1204	1357	1481	1584
4600	624	972	1216	1370	1495	1599
4650	630	981	1227	1383	1509	1614
4700	635	989	1237	1395	1522	1627
4750	641	997	1247	1406	1534	1641
4800	646	1005	1257	1417	1546	1654
4850	651	1013	1267	1428	1558	1667
4900	656	1021	1277	1439	1570	1679
4950	661	1028	1286	1450	1582	1692
5000	666	1036	1295	1460	1593	1704
5050	671	1043	1305	1471	1605	1716
5100	675	1051	1314	1481	1616	1728
5150	680	1058	1323	1492	1628	1741
5200	685	1066	1333	1502	1640	1753
5250	690	1073	1342	1513	1651	1765
5300	695	1081	1351	1524	1663	1778
5350	700	1088	1361	1534	1674	1790
5400	705	1096	1370	1545	1686	1802
5450	710	1103	1379	1555	1697	1815
5500	714	1111	1389	1566	1709	1827
5550	719	1118	1398	1576	1720	1839
5600	724	1126	1407	1587	1732	1851
5650	729	1133	1417	1598	1743	1864
5700	734	1141	1426	1608	1755	1876
5750	739	1148	1435	1619	1766	1888
5800	744	1156	1445	1629	1778	1901
5850	749	1163	1454	1640	1790	1913
5900	753	1171	1463	1650	1801	1925
5950	758	1178	1473	1661	1813	1937
6000	763	1186	1482	1672	1824	1950
6050	768	1193	1491	1682	1836	1962
6100	773	1201	1501	1693	1847	1974
6150	778	1208	1510	1703	1859	1987
6200	783	1216	1519	1714	1870	1999
6250	788	1223	1529	1724	1882	2011
6300	792	1231	1538	1735	1893	2023
6350	797	1238	1547	1745	1905	2036
6400	802	1246	1557	1756	1916	2048

COMBINED MONTHLY GROSS INCOME	ONE CHILD	TWO CHILDREN	THREE CHILDREN	FOUR CHILDREN	FIVE CHILDREN	SIX CHILDREN
6450	807	1253	1566	1767	1928	2060
6500	812	1261	1575	1777	1940	2073
6550	816	1267	1583	1786	1949	2083
6600	820	1272	1590	1794	1957	2092
6650	823	1277	1597	1801	1965	2100
6700	827	1283	1604	1809	1974	2109
6750	830	1288	1610	1817	1982	2118
6800	834	1293	1617	1824	1990	2127
6850	837	1299	1624	1832	1999	2136
6900	841	1304	1631	1839	2007	2145
6950	845	1309	1637	1847	2016	2154
7000	848	1315	1644	1855	2024	2163
7050	852	1320	1651	1862	2032	2172
7100	855	1325	1658	1870	2041	2181
7150	859	1331	1665	1878	2049	2190
7200	862	1336	1671	1885	2057	2199
7250	866	1341	1678	1893	2066	2207
7300	870	1347	1685	1900	2074	2216
7350	873	1352	1692	1908	2082	2225
7400	877	1358	1698	1916	2091	2234
7450	880	1363	1705	1923	2099	2243
7500	884	1368	1712	1931	2108	2252
7550	887	1374	1719	1938	2116	2261
7600	891	1379	1725	1946	2124	2270
7650	895	1384	1732	1954	2133	2279
7700	898	1390	1739	1961	2141	2288
7750	902	1395	1746	1969	2149	2297
7800	905	1400	1753	1977	2158	2305
7850	908	1405	1758	1983	2164	2313
7900	910	1409	1764	1989	2171	2320
7950	913	1414	1770	1995	2178	2328
8000	916	1418	1776	2001	2185	2335
8050	918	1423	1781	2007	2192	2343
8100	921	1428	1787	2014	2198	2350
8150	924	1432	1793	2020	2205	2357
8200	927	1437	1799	2026	2212	2365
8250	929	1441	1804	2032	2219	2372
8300	932	1446	1810	2038	2226	2380
8350	935	1450	1816	2045	2232	2387
8400	937	1455	1822	2051	2239	2395

COMBINED MONTHLY GROSS INCOME	ONE CHILD	TWO CHILDREN	THREE CHILDREN	FOUR CHILDREN	FIVE CHILDREN	SIX CHILDREN
8450	940	1459	1827	2057	2246	2402
8500	943	1464	1833	2063	2253	2410
8550	945	1468	1839	2069	2260	2417
8600	948	1473	1845	2076	2266	2425
8650	951	1478	1850	2082	2273	2432
8700	954	1482	1856	2088	2280	2440
8750	956	1487	1862	2094	2287	2447
8800	959	1491	1868	2100	2294	2455
8850	962	1496	1873	2107	2300	2462
8900	964	1500	1879	2113	2307	2470
8950	967	1505	1885	2119	2314	2477
9000	970	1509	1891	2125	2321	2484
9050	973	1514	1896	2131	2328	2492
9100	975	1517	1901	2137	2334	2498
9150	977	1521	1905	2141	2339	2503
9200	979	1524	1909	2146	2344	2509
9250	982	1527	1914	2151	2349	2514
9300	984	1531	1918	2156	2354	2520
9350	986	1534	1922	2160	2359	2525
9400	988	1537	1926	2165	2365	2531
9450	990	1541	1930	2170	2370	2536
9500	993	1544	1935	2175	2375	2541
9550	995	1547	1939	2179	2380	2547
9600	997	1551	1943	2184	2385	2552
9650	999	1554	1947	2189	2390	2558
9700	1001	1557	1951	2194	2396	2563
9750	1003	1561	1956	2198	2401	2569
9800	1006	1564	1960	2203	2406	2574
9850	1008	1567	1964	2208	2411	2580
9900	1010	1571	1968	2213	2416	2585
9950	1012	1574	1972	2218	2421	2590
10000	1014	1577	1977	2222	2427	2596

For gross monthly income between $10,000 and $20,000, add the amount of child support for $10,000 to the following percentages of gross income above $10,000:

ONE CHILD	TWO CHILDREN	THREE CHILDREN	FOUR CHILDREN	FIVE CHILDREN	SIX CHILDREN
3.1%	5.1%	6.8%	7.8%	8.8%	9.5%

For gross monthly income between $20,000 and $50,000, add the amount of child support for $20,000 to the following percentages of gross income above $20,000:

ONE CHILD	TWO CHILDREN	THREE CHILDREN	FOUR CHILDREN	FIVE CHILDREN	SIX CHILDREN
2%	3.5%	5%	6%	6.9%	7.8%

For gross monthly income over $50,000, add the amount of child support for $50,000 to the following percentages of gross income above $50,000:

ONE CHILD	TWO CHILDREN	THREE CHILDREN	FOUR CHILDREN	FIVE CHILDREN	SIX CHILDREN
1%	2%	3%	4%	5%	6%

C. For purposes of this section, "gross income" shall mean all income from all sources, and shall include, but not be limited to, income from salaries, wages, commissions, royalties, bonuses, dividends, severance pay, pensions, interest, trust income, annuities, capital gains, social security benefits except as listed below, workers' compensation benefits, unemployment insurance benefits, disability insurance benefits, veterans' benefits, spousal support, rental income, gifts, prizes or awards. Gross income shall be subject to deduction of reasonable business expenses for persons with income from self-employment, a partnership, or a closely held business. "Gross income" shall not include benefits from public assistance programs as defined in 63.1-87, federal supplemental security income benefits, or child support received. For purposes of this subsection, spousal support included in gross income shall be limited to spousal support paid pursuant to a pre-existing order or written agreement and spousal support shall be deducted from the gross income of the payor when paid pursuant to a pre-existing order or written agreement between the parties to the present proceeding.

D. Any extraordinary medical and dental expenses for treatment of the child or children shall be added to the basic child support obligation. For purposes of this section, extraordinary medical and dental expenses are uninsured expenses in excess of $100 for a single illness or condition and shall include but not be limited to eyeglasses, prescription medication, prostheses, and mental health services whether provided by a social worker, psychologist, psychiatrist, or counselor.

E. Any costs for health care coverage as defined in 63.1-250, when actually being paid by a parent, to the extent such costs are directly allocable to the child or children, and which are the extra costs of covering the child or children beyond whatever coverage the parent providing the coverage would otherwise have, shall be added to the basic child support obligation.

F. Any child-care costs incurred on behalf of the child or children due to employment of the custodial parent shall be added to the basic child support obligation. Child-care costs shall not exceed the amount required to provide quality care from a licensed source.

G. 1. Except in cases involving split custody or shared custody, a total monthly child support obligation shall be established by adding (i) the monthly basic child support obligation, as determined from the schedule contained in subsection B of this section, (ii) all extraordinary medical expenses, (iii) costs for health care coverage to the extent allowable by subsection E, and (iv) work-related child-care costs and taking into consideration all the factors set forth in subsection B of 20-108.1. The total monthly child support obligation shall be divided between the parents in the same proportion as their monthly gross incomes bear to their monthly combined gross income. The monthly obligation of each parent shall be computed by multiplying each parent's percentage of the parents' monthly combined gross income by the total monthly child support obligation.

However, the monthly obligation of the noncustodial parent shall be reduced by the cost for health care coverage to the extent allowable by subsection E when paid directly by the noncustodial parent.

2. In cases involving split custody, the amount of child support to be paid shall be the difference between the amounts owed by each parent as a noncustodial parent, computed in accordance with subdivision 1 of this subsection, with the noncustodial parent owing the larger amount paying the difference to the other parent.

For the purpose of this section and 20-108.1, split custody shall be limited to those situations where each parent has physicalcustody of a child or children born of the parents, born of either parent and adopted by the other parent or adopted by both parents. For the purposes of calculating a child support obligation where split custody exists, a separate family unit exists for each parent, and child support for that family unit shall be calculated upon the number of children in that family unit who are born of theparents, born of either parent and adopted by the other parent or adopted by both parents. Where split custody exists, a parent isa custodial parent to the children in that parent's family unit and is a noncustodial parent to the children in the other parent's family unit.

3. In cases involving shared custody, the amount of child support to be paid is the difference between the amounts owed by each parent to the other parent, with the parent owing the larger amount paying the difference to the other parent.

To compute the monthly amount to be paid by one parent to the other parent, the following calculations shall be made:

(a) The "basic child support obligation" of each parent shall be the "total shared support" multiplied by the other parent's "custody share." The "total shared support" of both parties equals statutory guideline amount determined pursuant to subsection B for the combined income of the parties and the number of shared children multiplied by 1.25. A parent's "custody share" equals the number of days that parent has physical custody of a shared child per year divided by the number of days in the year.

(b) To each parent's "basic child support obligation" shall be added the other parent's costs of health care coverage, to the extent allowable by subsection E, and the other parent's work-related child care costs to the extent allowable by subsection F.

(c) The obligation of each parent to the other shall be then computed by multiplying each parent's percentage of the parents' monthly combined gross income by the support obligation obtained in subdivision G 3 (b).

The shared custody rules set forth herein apply when each parent has physical custody of a child or children born of the parties, born of either parent and adopted by the other parent, or adopted by both parents, for more than 110 days of the year. Any calculation under this subdivision shall not create or reduce a support obligation to an amount which seriously impairs the custodial parent's ability to maintain minimal adequate housing and provide other basic necessities for the child.

H. The Secretary of Health and Human Resources shall ensure that the guideline set out in this section is reviewed by July 1, 1990, and every four years thereafter, by a panel which includes representatives of the courts, the executive branch, the General Assembly, the bar, custodial and noncustodial parents and child advocates. The panel shall determine the adequacy of the guideline for the determination of appropriate awards for the support of children by considering current research and data on the cost of and expenditures necessary for rearing children, and any other resources it deems relevant to such review. The panel shall report its findings to the General Assembly before it next convenes following such review.

URESA/UIFSA

This is a confusing jurisdictional issue. But if you and your ex live in separate states, it affects you, so you should try to comprehend it.

URESA stands for Uniform Reciprocal Enforcement of Support Act. UIFSA stands for Uniform Interstate Family Support Act. The purpose of these laws is to ensure that if your wife takes the kids and moves to Hawaii, she can still collect child support from you in Alaska, Louisiana, or Ohio without any difficulty.

A uniform law is a model drafted by a national committee, and each state may modify specific sections or interpret the same section differently. Right now we have two uniform laws governing child support, which, for the time being, makes them not uniform.

Until 1992, URESA was the uniform law governing child support in cases where the parents lived in separate states. In 1992, the National Conference of Commissioners on Uniform State Laws approved UIFSA, which now supersedes URESA. As of February 1996, 27 U.S. jurisdictions had enacted UIFSA—Alaska, Arizona, Arkansas, Colorado, Delaware, the District of Columbia, Idaho, Illinois, Kansas, Louisiana, Maine, Massachusetts, Minnesota, Montana, Nebraska, New Mexico, North Carolina, North Dakota, Oklahoma, Oregon, South Carolina, South Dakota, Texas, Virginia, Washington, West Virginia, and Wisconsin.

This means, of course, that the other 27 U.S. jurisdictions are still applying URESA. But this should change, since there is pending federal legislation which would require all states to pass UIFSA by January 1, 1998.[1]

Each state or jurisdiction in the United States has passed some form of URESA or UIFSA, which allows custodial parents to seek child support from noncustodial parents in other states or jurisdictions under the same terms and conditions throughout the United States. Therefore, if the custodial parent (usually the mother) wants to serve process on the noncustodial parent (usually the father) across the country, service of process will be effected in the same way. In addition, the state generally enforces the support obligation without the necessity of the mother having to make a court appearance or retain an attorney in the state where the father lives. The **initiating** state is where the mother lives and the **responding** state is where the father, who has the obligation to pay support, lives. It is generally the responding state that will set the child support obligation, based on the child support guidelines existing in the responding state. This criteria will not apply when the support obligation is based on a pre-existing support order and the obligation is only for child support arrearages.

To give you an idea of the discrimination built into the law, consider that while a father must retain a private attorney to fight a URESA or UIFSA action, the mother can usually file with the initiating state for a nominal fee of $20 and incur no additional costs. Consider also that to obtain visitation when a mother has taken the children out of state, a father must retain a private attorney in the state where the mother lives and incur the costs of transportation to see his children. The father's inability to visit his child across country, or the cost of visitation are rarely considered in setting child support.[2] If a mother denies access, she is unlikely to go to jail for contempt of court. However if a father does not pay support under URESA or UIFSA, he may very likely go to jail.

DIFFERENCES BETWEEN URESA AND UIFSA

Under URESA, spousal and child support are treated the same. But, under UIFSA, spousal support (i.e., alimony) can only be modified by a request to the original state which issued the order. In addition, visitation issues cannot be raised in child support proceedings. Again, there is the belief that time spent with both parents is not as important as the collection of money. In URESA, the responding and initiating states could have different support orders in effect; however, under UIFSA, only one valid support order is supposed to exist. This section of the Act is supposed to prevent an obligor from accumulating arrearages in one state while being in compliance with another. UIFSA also allows administrative agencies, not just courts, to establish support orders. Finally, under UIFSA, out-of-state witnesses may be allowed to testify via a telephone conference.

UIFSA extends the jurisdiction of the court over the potential payor beyond the limits formerly accepted. For instance, if there has been no previous court order regarding support, a tribunal may take jurisdiction over a nonresident if "the individual engaged in sexual intercourse in this State and the child may have been conceived by that act of intercourse." Section 201(6). Not every state has accepted this jurisdictional basis. For example, when Virginia enacted its version of

UIFSA, it deleted this specific paragraph.

As with the Parental Kidnapping Prevention Act (PKPA) of 1980, the state which entered the original child support order has exclusive continuing jurisdiction under UIFSA as long as the party receiving support, the payor, or the child reside in the original state. If all parties leave the state, the court which entered the original order will generally lose jurisdiction to modify child, **not spousal,** support. As mentioned above, the state which first issued an alimony award always retains jurisdiction over spousal support, even if both parties have left the state.

NOTES

[1] U.S. Department of Health and Human Services, Office of Child Support Enforcement. *Child Support Report, Vol XVIII No.2, February 1996.*

[2] This statement is true whether the noncustodial parent or the custodial parent left the home state.

INDEX